The Loyalist Perception and Other Essays

THE LOYALIST PERCEPTION
and Other Essays

By Robert M. Calhoon

in collaboration with
Timothy M. Barnes,
Donald C. Lord,
Janice Potter,
and Robert M. Weir

University of South Carolina Press

Copyright © UNIVERSITY OF SOUTH CAROLINA 1989

Published in Columbia, South Carolina, by the
University of South Carolina Press

Manufactured in the United States of America

Library of Congress Cataloging-in-Publication Data

Calhoon, Robert M. (Robert McCluer)
  The loyalist perception and other essays / by Robert M. Calhoon in
collaboration with Timothy M. Barnes. . . [et al.].

  p.   cm.
  Bibliography: p.
  Includes index.
  ISBN 0-87249-615-5
  1. American loyalists.   2. United States—Politics and government-
-Revolution, 1775–1783.   I. Title.
F277.C84C35   1989   88-35604
973.3'14—dc19   CIP

for
Jack P. Greene

CONTENTS

PREFACE

This volume brings together eleven articles concerning loyalism in the American Revolution originally published between 1965 and 1987. Covering many facets of thought and attitudes of the loyalists and spanning events from the 1760s to the 1780s, they illustrate how scholarship on the loyalists has changed over nearly a quarter century and what it has accomplished during a fruitful time in historical writing and interpretation. Except for the correction of a few errors, citation in the notes of published editions of sources I originally consulted in manuscript, and deletion of repetitious passages, these essays appear here in their original form.

Based on research begun in 1961, when the political content of Revolutionary ideas was a central concern of historians, chapters two through six analyzed the beliefs and experiences of individual loyalists and neutralists. Revised in the mid-1960s when the form and interior structure of Revolutionary ideology had claimed scholarly attention, chapter 1 and—though written a few years later, chapter 7—explored the inner connections, assumptions, and implications of loyalist ideology. Chapters 8 and 9, written in the mid-1970s, reflected the then new interest of historians in warfare and violence during the War for Independence. Finally chapters 10 and 11, written in the 1980s, were part of the wider historical effort to see the Revolutionary era as a whole and to integrate loyalist insights into an overall conceptualization of the period.

Four of the articles reprinted here were co-authored; chapter 3 with Donald C. Lord, chapter 4 with Robert M. Weir, chapter 7 with Janice Potter, and chapter 10 with Timothy M. Barnes, who also worked closely with me in formulating portions of chapter 11 and the bibliographical essay. I appreciate very much their generosity and collegiality. Kelli Logan prepared the index.

Robert S. Lambert and Don Higginbotham made valuable suggestions about the organization and editing of the book. Elizabeth Hunt, Bobbie Carter, and Shirley Roll helped prepare the manuscript. For financial support, I am grateful to Colonial Williamsburg, Inc., the National Society of Colonial Dames of America, and the United States Educational Commission of Great Britain for grants supporting work on chapters 1–6, to the National Endowment for the Humanities and the American Council of Learned Societies for fellowships aiding my work on chapters 7–11, and to the Research Council of the University of North Carolina at Greensboro for sustenance over the past twenty-two years.

Greensboro, July 15, 1988   R.M.C.

INTRODUCTION

The American Revolution was a prolonged and complex event that encompassed several kinds of conflict within the British Empire and American society. Some of these conflicts were central to the attainment of American independence; others were tangential to that process; and still others were part of a pervasive atmosphere of conflict and change throughout the Atlantic world of the eighteenth century. The American colonists who opposed the Revolution, the loyalists, were caught up in all of these changes; characterizing the loyalists' experiences illustrates the complexity of the Revolution and the vitality of loyalist scholarship.

The central conflicts of the Revolutionary era arose from Great Britain's decisions in the 1750s and 1760s to centralize control of the Empire and to secure subordination of the colonies to British authority. Britain's tightening of customs enforcement, imposition of the Stamp Act, and use of Townshend duties revenue as a slush fund to pay the salaries of Crown officials normally paid by the colonial assemblies were the heart of the conflict within the Empire. Those controversies swirled around prominent colonists and future loyalists who held positions as royal governors, lieutenant governors, royal councillors, judges, and attorneys general. They found themselves in the painful position of defending parliamentary statutes that they regarded as harsh and harmful to the well-being of the Empire; they became caught in the middle of clumsy efforts to prosecute patriot activists in the courts or to use British troops to enforce civil order. In these ways, colonists who held Crown offices unwittingly became the point men for a new, tougher royal administration. Underlying those policies were beliefs, ideas, and practices to which Crown supporters in America had to accommodate themselves. These included the doctrine of Parliamentary supremacy, familial rhetoric about Empire as a Mother Country and her colonial children, and a rising level of prosperity fed by British credit and colonial debt. Loyalists did not usually regard Parliament as supreme, but they view the British legislature as the embodiment of the political will of the British nation and a dynamic constitutional force within the Empire. They too could take offense at the notion of the colonists as permanent children of the British parent, but they were also aware that acts of adolescent willfulness only postponed British recognition of colonial maturity. Aware of the fragility of commercial prosperity within the Empire, they fretted about the dangers and hazards of foregoing British military protection and commercial support. The loyalists therefore sought to forestall ideological collision between the regime-oriented values of Parliament and the Crown and the growing libertarianism of colonial politics. When the collision finally occurred in 1774 with the enactment of the Coercive Acts punishing Boston and Massachusetts for the destruction of taxed tea the preceding December, the loyalists produced several imaginative plans for reforming the British Empire; they pointed with alarm to the growing polarization in colonial-imperial relations; and in a few instances they affirmed conservative principles of hierarchy and submission of social inferiors to their superiors in human affairs.

The Revolution did not occur in a vacuum nor was its impact restricted to the British institutions in America that it overthrew or to the new republican ones it created. The Revolution spilled into areas of American life only tangentially connected to the question of Empire vs. independence. The Revolution occurred within a tri-racial society of European immigrants and their descendants, native American Indians, and Afro-American slaves and free blacks. When Lord Dunmore, royal governor of Virginia, called on slaves of rebellious planters to win their liberty by taking up arms in behalf of the King in November 1775, eight hundred slaves responded and made their way to the British base at Norfolk. Slave owners throughout Virginia and Maryland justifiably feared that thousands of others were poised to follow had a favorable opportunity arisen. In South Carolina, a free black ship pilot named Thomas Jeremiah was overheard in 1775 telling another black man that "there is a great war coming" which would "help the poor Negroes." South Carolina patriot leaders brutally executed Jeremiah as an example to other blacks who might share his vision of racial justice and his estimate of the division between British officials and Carolina whites. Ever since the 1740s, the British had cultivated North American Indian tribes as allies against the French. Britain also discovered that through diplomacy, colonial governments could obtain Indian lands needed for the expansion of the white population. The Revolution presented tribes with close ties to the British government—notably the Mohawks in New York and the Creeks,

Introduction

Cherokees, and Seminoles along the southern frontier—with the ambiguous and dangerous choice of being British allies and virtual British subjects in the American Revolutionary war or remaining neutral. Those tribes which chose to fight for the Crown then faced the still more dangerous choice of subordinating themselves to British military commanders or operating as an independent fighting force protecting Indian interests. For agents of the British Superintendents of Indian Affairs and other frontier loyalists, the Indians' presence became a military asset while their ambiguous relationship to the Crown a source of white loyalist insecurity.

Racial minorities were not the only groups of relatively powerless, victimized people which looked to the British Crown for protection during the War for Independence. A variety of ethnic minorities and other marginal groups in American society resisted being coerced into supporting the patriot cause. These included highland Scots settlers in North Carolina; Quakers and German pietist groups in Pennsylvania, North Carolina, and Connecticut; and poor white yeoman farmers—often caught up in Methodist revivals—in places like the Delmarva Peninsula of Maryland, Delaware, and Virginia. The lines separating outright loyalists from politically indifferent and apolitical people were thin and indistinct. Often, the militarization of American life after 1775 exacerbated local feuds. Such antagonisms erupted in northern New Jersey in 1776 and in Georgia and the Carolinas in 1779–1781 as the British military occupied those regions. Racial, ethnic, and social instability—the by-products of the expansionism and exploitive energies of colonial society and the pluralism of its humbler immigrants—seriously jeopardized the Revolutionary cause and created whole new categories of lower-class and marginal loyalists.

In addition to reconstructing what the loyalists did to oppose the Revolution and which groups deliberately joined—or were drawn into—the anti-Revolutionary movement, certain conditions of life in America retarded opposition to British rule, just as others accelerated it. For example, colonial society during the second and third quarters of the eighteenth century became increasingly Anglicized as British styles, products, and national hubris infiltrated American life. People who benefited from this development tended to celebrate British dominance and often became loyalists during the Revolution. These people often felt that disorderly colonial growth needed the stabilizing hand of British regulation. Anglican clergymen who resented the discourtesy and seeming crudeness of Protestant dissenter sects, critics of land speculation who detested the political power of the landed aristocracy, and ethnic minorities fearful of being swallowed up by the English-stock majority all looked to British authority as necessary discipline of colonial society. As family life became less restrictive after mid-century—amid prosperity and social expansion—young men struck off on their own at an earlier age rather than waiting to inherit their fathers' estates. This development prompted some to decry the decline in the authority of fathers over their children just as it inspired others to regard the autonomy of young men as a healthy kind of individualism. Growing generational tension occurred at the very time British officials on both sides of the Atlantic employed familial rhetoric to characterize the colonies themselves as children of the parent, or mother, country and as opposition politicians in the colonies to denounce the oppression of the colonies by British authorities as unbefitting a loving, protective parent.

The most pervasive reality in late colonial life was the colonists' sense of their own provincialism: their dependence on, and remoteness from, the metropolitan center of British life. Provincialism made some colonists hypersensitive to indications that decay and corruption in British life were eating away at the vitals of imperial institutions and values. It underscored their feeling of helpless dependence on the economic power of the British nation and their feeling of excessive dependence on British credit. British opposition figures like the notorious John Wilkes—libertarian, rake, and political rabble rouser—acquired sensational followings in the colonies. The centralizing policies of the British ministry and bureaucracy, especially the Treasury, suggested that the British constitution and the "rights of Englishmen" were in danger of being replaced or subverted. People who looked to Parliament and the Crown to expand the power of the Empire, and thereby control disturbances within colonial culture, were predisposed to support Britain when the Revolution erupted.

The same provincialism that impelled some colonists to desire a new order, centered on American rather than British values, drove others to yearn for an imperial solution to the problems of life on the periphery of the Empire. They looked to Parliament and the Crown to expand the power, wealth, and even boundaries of the empire and to bring back the halcyon days of the Seven Years' War when British dynamism and determination linked people throughout the King's dominions in a common cause. "Seagirt Britannia! mistress of the isles!" rhapsodized one Maryland loyalist in the early 1770s:

> Where Faith, and Liberty, united reign;
> Around whose fertile shores glad Nature smiles,
> And Ceres crowns with gifts the industrious swain! . . .
>
> And, when again our colours are unfurl'd,
> May Britons nobly join one common cause!
> With rapid conquests strike the wondering world,
> In firm support of Liberty and Laws.[1]

Introduction

That vision of a world made whole and coherent and vibrant by British institutions and imperial expansion was also an antidote to disequilibrium in the colonies and an inspiration to thousands of loyalists who rallied to the royal standard during the War for Independence.

Historical understanding of the conflicts inherent in the American Revolution owes much to research and writing on the loyalists during the past quarter century. The essays reprinted in this book played a modest part in the loyalist leavening of the texture of Revolutionary scholarship. Published over more than two decades, they sought to map the terrain between the private, inner, subjective awareness of the loyalists and the public, external, objective dilemmas imposed on them by the Revolution. The title essay "The Loyalist Perception,"[2] explores that terrain and locates three ideal types of pre-Revolutionary opposition to colonial resistance: Principle, Accommodation, and Doctrine. "The Loyalist Perception" seeks to capture the ideas which were the essence of these three positions, to establish the interrelations between them, and to date their demise after 1776.

The next five chapters explore various opposition against, and criticism of, the pre-Revolutionary movement. Chapter 2, " 'The constitution Ought to Bend': William Smith Jr.'s Alternative to the American Revolution,"[3] interpreted a treatise on the nature of the British Empire written by a knowledgeable New York politician and historian, William Smith, Jr., during the midst of the pre-Revolutionary controversy. Smith's criticisms of the imperial constitution were more radical than those of most colonial whigs, and his sense of political equanimity and survival hinged on the capacity of statesmen on both sides of the Atlantic to reconstruct imperial administration in light of growing American power and maturity.

I gained a still closer view of the legal and political—as well as psychological—bonds holding the Empire together when I studied, in collaboration with Donald C. Lord, the controversy over "The Removal of the Massachusetts General Court from Boston, 1769–1772."[4] In that article, we examined the minute and subtle contemporary analysis of the Royal Instructions governing the conduct of royal governors in America. One of those instructions directed Governor Francis Bernard and then his successor, Thomas Hutchinson, to assemble the Massachusetts Assembly in Cambridge rather than Boston as a gesture of disapproval of the assembly's actions. Who was bound by those instructions—the governor or the whole provincial government—and the room an instructed governor had for maneuver in such a situation became central issues in the dispute. The chilling effect of government by instruction on colonial exercise of political liberty and responsibility became the highly charged atmosphere in which the removal controversy occurred. Before a face-saving compromise could be affected, questions of the nature of representative government and the duty of public officials to respect the "public good" tested the integrity of both colonial democracy and imperial rectitude.

The moral issues defined clinically in the removal controversy in Massachusetts spilled into a messier political conflict in South Carolina when Egerton Leigh, notorious plural officeholder, became embroiled in disputes over customs enforcement and legislative control of the purse. Initially a friend, kinsman, and close associate of Henry Laurens, Leigh demonstrated a kind of moral obtuseness in his conduct as judge, husband, and imperial operator that epitomized for the native South Carolina elite the corrupt nature of British rule. In " 'The Scandalous History of Sir Egerton Leigh,' "[5] Robert Weir and I examined this uproarious case study of the redefinition of public ethics in the pre-Revolutionary debate.

Smith, Hutchinson, and Leigh each achieved a measure of prestige in colonial politics by mastering the rules of the political game; each was victimized by a failure to sense how rapidly those rules were changing during the late 1760s and early 1770s. Joseph Galloway, ally of Benjamin Franklin and Speaker of the Pennsylvania Assembly, misjudged this situation still more grievously. " 'I Have Deduced Your Rights': Joseph Galloway's Concept of his Role, 1774–1775"[6] examines his famous, though not fully understood, Plans of Union for the British Empire against the background of his ambition and immense appetite for behind-the-scenes maneuver.

The misperception of political reality and the abruptly clogged channels of political communication in the late pre-Revolutionary debate apparent in Chapters 1 through 4 prepared me to understand the writings of a wholly apolitical critic of colonial resistance, Robert Beverley of Virginia. In " 'Unhinging Former Intimacies': Robert Beverley's Perception of the Pre-Revolutionary Controversy, 1761–1775"[7] I explored the coming of the Revolution from the vantage point of a man innocent of any thirst for power or appreciation for political ideas. Beverley's flatfooted efforts to defend his political neutrality and to condemn political activism provide a kind of mirror image of Revolutionary mobilization in Virginia. Immobilized by the actions of others, Beverley saw at close range the character and intensity of patriot resistance.

Ideas have unpredictable consequences, and no one foresaw in 1775–1776 the extraordinary military and psychological struggles which the War for Independence unleashed. As loyalists, during the war, continued to think their plight and their need for continued British rule, the concrete tasks of supporting military campaigns and undermining the morale and cohesion of the patriot regime made loyalism into a program of *action*. Newspapers were a critical battlefield. "The Character and Coherence of the Loyalist Press,"[8]

Introduction

co-authored with Janice Potter, surveys loyalist polemical journalism during both the pre-Revolutionary period and the War for Independence. Using the remark of Daniel Leonard that the Continental Congress was a repository of "disaffection, petulance, ingratitude, and disloyalty," we show how these four concepts were comprised by the intellectual and ethical universe within which loyalist polemicists lived. Influenced by Janice Potter's mastery of the New York and Massachusetts loyalist sources, I modified my earlier sharp distinction between pre-Revolutionary and Revolutionary loyalist ideology and found new levels of meaning in loyalist discussion of what Leonard called "petulance" and "rebellion." The loyalist press, however, confirmed my expectation that warfare raised the intellectual stakes, revealing that, by the time garrison town newspapers in South Carolina and Georgia began publishing significant political analysis in 1780–1782, loyalists there had attained a new level of sophistication and controlled moral outrage.

The notion that the War for Independence was the most radical and politically charged phase of the Revolution, argued forcefully by Don Higginbotham and John Shy, suggested the value of studying loyalists' understanding of the War. "Civil, Revolutionary, or Partisan? the Loyalists and the Nature of the War for Independence"[9] and "The Floridas, the Western Frontier, and Vermont: Thoughts on the Hinterland Loyalists"[10] trace two intertwined themes. The first was the dangerous and radical gamble run by the British in using loyalist forces and Indians in the southern campaign and in upstate New York; the second—already introduced in the closing pages of chapter 7—was the loyalists' own fascination with a war of retribution and moral vengeance. The ideological finale of this militarization of loyalist thought appeared in the desperate attempts by East Florida loyalists in 1783–1784 to block cession of the Floridas to Spain and secure for themselves justice from a monarch they had served faithfully.

As the patriots tried to deal with their own internal opponents and the loyalists reacted to their own victimization, the ideas and actions of both sides evolved into *practices* shaped by the needs and interests of both sides. Timothy M. Barnes, a specialist on the loyalist press who had generously assisted me in my research for chapter 7, joined me in probing an episode involving the patriot leader, John Witherspoon, and two loyalist printers, Benjamin Towne and James Rivington. Unraveling Witherspoon's role in the denunciation of these men, as well as their culpability in British administration of the garrison towns of Philadelphia and New York, provided us with new insight into what Gordon S. Wood calls "moral republicanism." Witherspoon saw the loyalists as object lessons in the moral vulnerability of republican societies. In chapter 10 and in the subsection of chapter 11,

Introduction

"Moral Republicanism,"[11] we examine the phase of the Revolution during which the patriots sought to create an ethical community in advance of achieving military security, economic stability, or political competence.

For a conference in 1985 at The Johns Hopkins University on "The Unfinished Agenda" of the American Revolution in the mid-1780s, I wrote "The Reintegration of the Loyalists and the Disaffected."[12] Covering events from 1774 to 1787, it synthesizes a large body of scholarly writing on the Revolutionary social order and identifies five distinct steps in the process of loyalist reintegration. These steps coincide with five of the most important recent scholarly discoveries: (1) "A Revolutionary Infrastructure," 1774–1775, paralleling David Ammerman's study of Revolutionary committees; (2) "Moral Republicanism," 1776–1778, amplifying ideas of Gordon S. Wood's about the religious and ethical content of ideology; (3) "Volitional Allegiance," 1779–1780, enunciated in James H. Ketner's pathbreaking study of American citizenship; (4) "Military Triangularity," 1781–1782, exploiting John Shy's study of the War for Independence as a social process; and (5) "Cosmopolitans and Localists," 1783–1787, informed by Jackson Turner Main's work on legislative voting patterns. Although the conference title hypothesized the existence of unfinished tasks in the mid-1780s, the study of loyalist reintegration suggested that this job was substantially completed by that time and that patriots and loyalists had, for their own reasons, invested considerable effort prior to 1783 in lodging the opponents of the Revolution securely in the new American social order.

1. William Eddis, *Letters from America,* Aubrey C. Land, ed. (Cambridge, 1969), pp. 71–72.
2. "The Loyalist Perception," *Acadiensis,* 3 (Spring 1973): 3–14.
3. "William Smith Jr.'s Alternative to the American Revolution," *William and Mary Quarterly,* 22 (Jan. 1965): 105–18.
4. "The Removal of the Massachusetts General Court from Boston, 1769–1972," *Journal of American History,* 55 (Mar. 1969): 735–55.
5. " 'The Scandalous History of Sir Egerton Leigh,' " *William and Mary Quarterly,* 26 (Jan. 1969): 47–74.
6. " 'I have Deduced Your Rights': Joseph Galloway's Concept of his Role," *Pennsylvania History,* 35 (Oct. 1968): 356–78.
7. " 'Unhinging Former Intimacies': Robert Beverley's Perception of the Pre-Revolutionary Controversy, 1761–1775," *South Atlantic Quarterly,* 68 (Spring 1969): 246–61.
8. "The Character and Coherence of the Loyalist Press," in Bernard Bailyn and John B. Hench, eds., *The Press and the American Revolution* (Worcester, 1980), pp. 229–72.
9. "Civil, Revolutionary, or Partisan: The Loyalists and the Nature of the War for Independence," in *Military History of the Revolution* (Washington, 1976), pp. 94–108.

Introduction

10. "The Floridas, the Western Frontier, and Vermont: Thoughts on the Hinterland Loyalists," in Samuel Proctor, ed., *Eighteenth-Century Florida: Life on the Frontier* (Gainesville, 1976), pp. 1–15.
11. "Moral Allegiance: John Witherspoon and Loyalist Recantation," *American Presbyterians: The Journal of Presbyterian History,* 63 (Fall 1985): 273–84.
12. "The Reintegration of the Loyalists and the Disaffected," in Jack P. Greene, ed., *The American Revolution: Its Character and Limits* (New York, 1987), pp. 51–74.

The Loyalist Perception and Other Essays

Part I

IDEAS

1

THE LOYALIST PERCEPTION

The nature of loyalism in the American Revolution is an intractable historical problem, in part, because the loyalists appeared in several distinct social and political settings: pre-Revolutionary colonial society, rebellious American states, the various parts of the British Empire to which they fled, and the post-Revolutionary republic where still more reemerged as respectable citizens. In each of these contexts the loyalists revealed different facets of the values, attitudes, and characteristics which accounted for their adherence to the Crown. While it is dangerous to read back into the loyalists' Revolutionary experience things they said in retrospect, it is also misleading to assume that the loyalists revealed everything they had to say about themselves under the intense pressures of specific crises in the pre-Revolutionary controversy or later during the Revolution itself.

While a perceptive kind of comparative history will be needed to bring together the pieces of the loyalist puzzle, it is also important to explore as analytically as possible the loyalists' perception of reality, the structure of their values, and the pattern of their rational and emotional responses within each of the historical contexts from which they operated. Historians dealing with the loyalists have, for the most part, asked questions about the location and condition of identifiable groups of loyalists, the thrust of loyalist rebuttals to specific tenets of whig belief, and the political and social conditions which made some colonists unusually dependent on British authority for their security and identity. Another kind of question should probe the loyalists' view of themselves and focus on their own statements of self-consciousness and self-awareness. Pre-Revolutionary critics and victims of

3

Part I: Ideas

colonial resistance felt conscious of certain political and social *roles* which they tried to play as the imperial controversy progressed; they wrestled with the *dilemma* of adapting, improving, relaxing, or intensifying their performance of those roles as the pre-Revolutionary movement made those roles increasingly awkward; as each individual realized that he was not going to regain his former authority, influence, or equanimity, he communed within himself and gave some expression to the *anguish* he felt. The loyalists' understanding and presentation of their roles, dilemmas, and anguish in letters, pamphlets, oratory, state papers, and in the way they dealt with public issues and devised strategies for defending themselves revealed a coherent view of external events and their own character in time of crisis.

A useful tool in the examination of this kind of loyalist testimony is the concept of *perception*, the process of giving structure to thought and sensations. Perception seeks explanations and patterns in the random data the senses detect in a social situation: it uses language "to determine or at least to influence what one notices around him": it is a process which creates categories and "category-systems" in the mind. Perception deals with a man's self-image, emotional and intellectual dexterity and stamina, the imperatives govern his conduct in times of crisis and the predispositions which operate in periods of routine. By treating pre-Revolutionary opponents of colonial resistance as verbalizing, category building, reflective, self-conscious figures, one can gain access to the interior of their political thought.[1] As the pre-Revolutionary critics and opponents of colonial resistance responded to the crises of that period, they constructed three reasonably distinct models of political reality. One was the enunciation of principle, the repeated statement of legal, historical, and constitutional rules which bound the Empire together and necessarily circumscribed colonial liberty. A second was the search for accommodation, the belief that grounds for compromise existed and could be discovered and exploited through the use of good sense and prudence. A third was the appeal to doctrine, the sometimes shrill, uncompromising insistence that all colonial resistance and remonstrance was morally wrong and aesthetically abhorrent.

Thomas Hutchinson was, of course, the preeminent loyalist enunciator of principle, combining a sure grasp of fundamentals with a sensitivity for intricacies. "I have but one set of principles upon government in general and the constitution of this province in particular. There must be one supreme legislature in every state." He admitted, however, that "it is a very difficult matter to determine any certain proportion of freedom necessary to the happiness of a subordinate state."[2] He devoted a lifetime to the search for that "certain proportion of freedom" and we know a great deal about the depth and nature of that commitment from Edmund S. Morgan's analysis of Hutchinson in the Stamp Act crisis. Malcolm Freiberg's dissection of his

The Loyalist Perception

ambition and his self-doubts, Clifford K. Shipton's defense of his rectitude, and Bailyn's discovery of his constitutional acumen.[3] What this fragmented, somewhat static, portrait lacks is an appreciation of Hutchinson's emotionality—the passions which integrated his roles and aspirations and aggravated his suffering. One way to fill this void is to focus, not only on his manifest principles, ambitions, and skills, but also on the strange paradoxes and polarities of his political character.[4]

The strongest of those polarities was his belief that he was primarily a defender of colonial liberty and that prudent submission to British authority was a subtle strategy for preserving that liberty. As Edmund Morgan showed in 1948, Hutchinson privately came close to denying the legitimacy of the entire Grenville program and stated categorically that it did infringe on inherent colonial rights; yet in 1770 he privately proposed a horrifying set of coercive measures for Britain to impose on Massachusetts. Hutchinson was never conscious of any contradiction. The coercion he sadly recommended was intended to have a stunning, sobering effect on the shortsighted and excited men and inaugurate a stabilizing period and thereby strengthen Massachusetts' capacity to resist British encroachments.[5] Hutchinson's tremendous personal reserve created the very suspicions which kept his political life in upheaval; against his aloofness, however, tugged his ambition to provide decisive public leadership. He candidly spoke of this tension in his character during his dispute with the General Court over the Boston Resolves in 1773:

> If I am wrong in my principles of government or in the inferences I have drawn from them, I wish to be convinced of my error. I have laid before you the principles of your constitution. If you do not agree with me I wish to know your objections. They may be convincing to me or I may be able to satisfy you of the insufficiency of them. In either case, I hope, we shall be able to put an end to those irregularities which shall ever be the portion of a government where the supreme authority is controverted.[6]

In 1773, that was exactly the kind of dialogue Hutchinson sought to have with his contemporaries—a healing exchange in which he prescribed the premises of the discussion. He could emerge just that far, but no further, from his private contemplation of the issues of liberty and authority.

Hutchinson struggled intelligently with these conflicting impulses toward withdrawal and involvement. He resisted the temptation to dismiss whig argument with superficial rebuttals; he regarded the complexity of the pre-Revolutionary debate with great seriousness; this polarity pitted his dismay against his intellect and curiosity. It enabled him to be at once withdrawn and self-conscious and also capable of seeing himself in a larger context. When he became fully engaged in the task of understanding a tenet of whig belief, Hutchinson brought to his work the full force of his highly controlled

Part I: Ideas

emotionality. During the protracted dispute from 1769 to 1772, over the removal of the General Court from Boston, he tried to breathe life and vitality into the notion that the royal instructions to colonial governors were a positive benefit to the political life of the province. As he elaborated his explanation, the Crown's prerogative became an intimate, all-embracing, pervasive, organic influence which transmuted mobility and finesse to otherwise static executive authority. In turn the governor's receptiveness, discretion, and intelligence in responding to imperial directives determined their effectiveness. Hutchinson constructed an idealized minuet between Crown and governor which was almost poetic and sensuous in its structure and intricacy.[7] Hutchinson, significantly conceived of British power as a throbbing, expansive force which could permeate and activate his own behavior as governor. Colonial leaders conceived of British power in exactly the same fashion; as Bernard Bailyn observes, they were transfixed by the "essential...aggressiveness" of political power and by its "endlessly propulsive tendency to expand itself beyond legitimate boundaries."[8] Confident that he could serve as a channel and instrument of British authority without damaging the liberty of his province, Hutchinson only succeeded in confirming his enemies' deepest fears about the capacity of the Crown to insinuate itself into the political life of the province.

Hutchinson's insistence on principle and his calculated style of debate and exposition distinguished him from William Smith, Jr. and other moderate critics of colonial resistance who shunned dispute over principle and sought practical, improvised accommodation with Britain. In 1767, Smith devised a constitution for the British Empire which he believed should be a malleable instrument which could accommodate the growing political maturity of the colonies.[9]

His ability as a constitutional theorist and diagnostician complemented a different set of Smith's predispositions during the pre-Revolutionary period: his fondness for the intricate strategies which his fellow councillors employed in competing for the ear and trust of successive royal governors, especially William Tryon who arrived in 1771. After one protracted struggle Smith believed he had won Tryon's confidence and made him suspicious of the rival Delancey faction. "I shall feed that spirit," he exulted in a moment of revelation, "to disentangle him from a fear of Council and Assembly." During the Tea crisis in December 1773 he tried to use the same methods to guide Tryon's hand during a hazardous period. He besieged Tryon with suggestions on how to avoid violence if the tea was landed or how to prevent its unloading if violence was unavoidable. The destruction of the tea in Boston took the decision out of Tryon's hands and launched a new period of greater crisis for royal officials. "It must mortify Tryon who had spoken so vauntingly and assured the government of the landing" of the tea, Smith

The Loyalist Perception

noted with customary care. But he was much more aware that his own attempts to guide Tryon's hand had been of little practical value to the governor. "Tryon will think I animated him to render him unpopular," he lamented; "how dangerous it is to give private advice."[10]

Smith appeared in 1774–1775 simply to be a conservative gravitating to the right of his former allies in the Livingston faction; in reality he was wholly engrossed in working out the implications of his chosen roles as constitutional analyst and behind-the-scenes manipulator of government and party policy. He wrote and circulated numerous essays on the constitutional and tactical problems facing colonial leaders and propounded an almost clinical set of negotiating tactics, which included "feeling the pulse of the ministry," proceeding "without a word about rights," and exercising exquisite tact and timing. When all this came to naught he responded by writing his longest and most moving exposition of the issues of the Revolution, one which juxtaposed a scathing indictment of British policy and defense of colonial liberty with an absolute refusal to sanction armed rebellion. The conflict between the two commitments reduced him to an abject state of intellectual immobility long before his apparently opportunistic conversion to the British cause. "I persuade myself," he told an inquisitive committee of safety on July 4, 1776, "that Great Britain will discern the propriety of negotiating for a pacification." He could not relinquish the hope that the elusive search for accommodation would transfix the lives of other men as completely as it had his own.[11]

The enunciation of principle often reflected a concern with law and the details of imperial administration while the search for accommodation expressed an awareness of the subtleties of colonial politics. In contrast, the appeal to doctrine came from men on the periphery of political life and imperial government. Eschewing legal and practical objections to colonial resistance, they focused directly on the immorality and ugliness of discontent. The high Anglican polemicists were, of course, the quintessential doctrinaire loyalists and Bailyn has most effectively shown that their writings struck with jugular accuracy at the most significant tenets of whig theory. In Samuel Seabury's vivid denunciation of violence and intimidation, Jonathan Boucher's taut authoritarian logic, and Thomas Bradbury Chandler's breathtaking endorsement of subordination, Bailyn found "wrathful epitaphs" to an "ancient, honorable, moribund philosophy" of order and obedience.[12]

Seabury's fame as a polemicist rests on his colorful and pugnacious denunciation of whig tactics for enforcing the Continental Association boycott on trade with Britain in late 1774 and early 1775. But his vivid language has distracted attention away from the systematic argument which formed the core of the *Letters of a Westchester Farmer*—the nature of perception itself.

Part I: Ideas

Seabury was fascinated with the way in which the mind handles sense impressions and organizes them into concepts. He beseeched his readers to practice enough sophistication to subject each new impression of rebellion to careful and critical scrutiny. Unless men assessed the future implications of their actions and appreciated the power and destructiveness of mass contagion, they could not prudently restrain their enthusiasms nor calm the passions of their fellow men. The root of the problem was the finite capacity of the mind and the limitless appeal of false political ideas. "At present politics seems to engross almost every body," he complained in 1769, "and leaves no room for more serious and important reflection." The result by 1774 was a "sullen, sulky obstinacy" which "takes possession of us. . . . Preposterous pride! . . . It degrades instead of exalting our characters" and was the product of "all the *insidious arts* that evilminded and *designing* men can possibly make use of." Only by assuming a posture of aloof, watchful skepticism could a man avoid contamination from glib, appealing, but unsupportable patriot contensions. In the midst of a long series of obtuse propositions—one, for example, resurrected virtual representation in terms which no politically knowledgeable loyalist would have defended—Seabury abruptly related the discussion to his central concern. "That you will perceive the force of this reasoning," he told his polemical rival, Alexander Hamilton, "I cannot pretend to say. A person. . .with jaundice sees no color but yellow. Party heat, the fever of liberty, may vitiate the mind as much as jaundice does the eyes."[13]

Hutchinson, Smith, and Seabury only suggest the distinctiveness of the ideas, beliefs, sensibilities, and patterns of response exhibited by men who enunciated principle, searched for accommodations, or appealed to doctrine during the pre-Revolutionary controversy. Although principle, accommodation, and doctrine were not mutually exclusive categories into which men can be placed, the leading prominent opponents of colonial resistance and the most widely circulated anti-whig ideas of the pre-Revolutionary period almost all adhere to one of these three modes of thought and feeling. Principle, accommodation, and doctrine were orientations and assumptions which gave direction and focus to men's thinking and conduct. In some cases individuals shared more than one of these orientations. John Wentworth of New Hampshire was preeminently a man of accommodation with his warm association with the Rockingham Whigs, thorough contempt for the policies and style of officials like Hillsborough, and primary concern for the interests of his province. He gracefully adapted to a substantial reduction in his family's power in New Hampshire during his governorship. He had a rare degree of serenity which enabled him—without a trace of ambivalence—to contemplate the use of military force to uphold British authority and accept without apparent bitterness his own exile from America.

The Loyalist Perception

No other loyalist embodied so fully as Wentworth a congenial attachment to both principle and accommodation.[14]

In most cases, a man who partook of more than one of these orientations was dominated by one particular view of political reality and borrowed incidentally from the others. Joseph Galloway desperately wanted to engineer single-handedly an imperial compromise in 1774. The structure of his ideas about the preservation of liberty and the scope of his ambition to heal the Empire in one brilliant stroke dictated that he pronounce rigid principles about the nature of the Empire and that he insist on the complete acquiescence of other colonial leaders to his leadership. When men did not listen to his explanations of principle and liberty and ignored his pretentions to leadership, they created an unexpectedly severe dilemma: they shattered his image of himself as a master of political theory and public persuasion. Galloway then replaced this shattered self-image with one still more magnificent and yet also consistent with his initial posture as an advocate of accommodation and enunciator of principle: "I have deduced your rights and explained your duties. I have laid before you the constitutional extent of parliamentary jurisdiction. I have pointed to the mode which you ought to pursue for a restoration of those rights." His concept of role and the dilemma in which it placed him compelled Galloway to locate all of the wisdom necessary to a solution of the imperial impasse in his own mind. At each stage his perception undermined his advocacy of accommodation and intensified his insistence on principle.[15]

Orientations toward principle, accommodation, or doctrine not only overlapped, they also cut across without completely severing other intellectual alignments during the pre-Revolutionary controversy. Alan Heimert has associated rationalist theology with loyalism or with lukewarm, insensitive support of the whig movement.[16] In direct conflict with the Calvinist whigs, the rationalist clergy did not believe that British policy sprang from utter human depravity nor believe that confession and repentance was an integral preliminary stage in the defense of American liberty. To the rationalist clergy sin afflicted the thoughtless and unreflective. In political terms the sins which needed confessing and forgiving in 1774–1775 were "turbulent desires, secret views of fostering party spirit, lust for unjust dominion, and impatience with lawful government."[17] In elaboration of Heimert's thesis it must also be pointed out that rationalists were subdivided into accommodating and doctrinaire loyalist positions. The accommodating rationalists included Anglicans like William Smith and Jacob Duche and Congregationalists like Gad Hitchcock and Daniel Shute. They endorsed just enough remonstrance to bring colonial discontent to British attention but not so much as to exacerbate the conflict. The doctrinaire rationalist clergy led by Boucher, Chandler, Cooper, and Seabury eschewed this search

Part I: Ideas

for a moderate position: political opposition was not an instrument which men might employ responsibly; its "bitterness and wrath and anger and clamour and evil speaking...bitter ungodly spirit toward those who differ ...in things civil or religious" were intrinsically evil, explained the Rev. Samuel Andrews of Connecticut in 1775. The "confidence" and sense of "girding" for righteous conflict which he saw all around him—which the accommodating rationalists wanted to dignify, channel, and moderate— blinded men, in Andrews' view, to the truth that political change was the prerogative of God and not of men.[18]

Just as Andrews felt compelled to look squarely at the moral earnestness of his whig contemporaries, most pre-Revolutionary loyalists felt driven to discover and articulate a single quintessential insight into the causes of the Revolution and of their own plight. The reconstruction of their perception leads directly to each man's discovery of some central truth about himself and the Revolution. For Egerton Leigh, it came when he discovered that he could relate every step in South Carolina's political and constitutional development to some stage in his own humiliation and downfall. Once he sensed that unity and coherence in South Carolina history, he could at the same time write a trenchant account of the province's political development and also establish his own identity by accentuating the very presumptions about himself which most outraged Charlestown's planter-merchant elite and made him a pariah.[19] Jonathan Sewall's withering contempt for the whig protest in Massachusetts reflected a conflict he had felt throughout his adult life: tension between his intellectual distinction and courage on one hand and his insecurity about his social and political preeminence on the other. He developed an ironic, slightly cynical, and sometimes bemused dismay over any exuberant human enterprise. These defenses protected him from the kind of volcanic eruptions of rage which racked his cohort, Peter Oliver, and enabled him to locate the source of disorder in Massachusetts, which "is, I say, so truly astonishing, so entirely out of the course of nature, so re-pugnant to the known principles which most forceably actuate the human mind that we must search deeper for the grand and hidden spring....This is an enthusiasm in politics like that which religious notions inspire, that drives men on with an unnatural impetuosity [and] baffles and confounds all calculation grounded upon rational principles."[20]

The loyalist perception of the coming of the American Revolution con-sisted of brilliantly incisive but partially formed and almost stillborn politi-cal fears, apprehensions, uncertainties, impulses toward obstruction, and sensations of ambivalence, immobility, and helplessness. This fragmenta-tion and lack of coalescence in pre-Revolutionary loyalist ideology testified to the fragility of elaborate political ideas in eighteenth-century America and the rapid mortality rate of particular formulations of thought as public

The Loyalist Perception

men struggled continually to revamp slightly out-of-date intellectual postures. In a political culture which took ideas very seriously, this instability cast marginal political figures like the critics and victims of pre-Revolutionary protest into an excrutiating position. This unstable, fluid political culture not only dominated the eighteenth century—as Jack P. Greene's two articles on colonial pessimism and anxiety dramatically emphasized—but elements of this malady continued well into the nineteenth century and provided much of the distraught energy expended by James M. Banner's Federalists and Fred Somkin's Fourth of July orators.[21]

With the commencement of hostilities in 1775 and the Declaration of Independence in 1776, these discrete categories of conservatism and defense of the established order tended to dissolve. War and the creation of new state governments widened the scope of the conflict and caught thousands of previously obscure men in the machinery of internal security. The people that Nelson calls the "Tory Rank and File" were clusters of "cultural minorities" scattered throughout the geographical and social periphery of American life: religious pacifists, pro-British Indian traders, backcountry southern farmers, unassimilated ethnic minorities, as well as isolated individuals everywhere impelled by custom, instinct, greed, accident, resentment, or bad luck to oppose independence.[22] They expressed their opposition to the Revolution in more elemental ways than did their counterparts in the pre-Revolutionary controversy. As the War for Independence created loyalist communities in occupied New York, Charlestown, and Philadelphia and as communities of exiles formed in England and Canada, a new sense of loyalist identity emerged: the loyalists' ironic discovery that they were victims of both American aggression and British incompetence. That understandable, if somewhat irrational paranoia, became a positive force in shaping post-Revolutionary loyalist behavior. It engendered a tough, realistic, and implacable determination to surmount the difficulties of rebuilding their lives and constructing a new political and social order in British North America. The pre-Revolutionary loyalist perception was only one ingredient in this long and fascinating process. But if this interpretation of the stages of loyalist thought is a valid preliminary diagnosis of the historical problem, then the riches of the *Loyalist Papers Project* may well fuel a far-reaching inquiry into the comparative intellectual history of colonial America, Revolutionary America and England, and post-Revolutionary Canada.[23]

AUTHOR'S NOTE (1988): By the time I wrote this essay, the correct name of the organization mentioned in the last sentence was the *Program for Loyalist Studies and Publications,* Robert A. East and James E. Mooney, Executive and Associate Directors. While the complete photocopying of loyalist manu-

Part I: Ideas

scripts, envisioned by the project, was not feasible because of funding limitations, the project did compile and publish *A Bibliography of Loyalist Source Material in the United States, Canada, and Great Britain*, Gregory Palmer, ed. (Westport: Meckler Publishing, 1982).

1. This paragraph is based on a variety of writings in social psychology and phenomenology. Jerome S. Bruner, "Social Psychology and Perception," in E. E. Maccoby et al., eds., *Readings in Social Psychology* (New York, 1958), pp. 85–94 and Roger Brown, *Social Psychology* (New York, 1965), chapter 12 both discuss the major recent writings in the field and quotations are from the Bruner article. See also Frank P. Chambers, *Perception, Understanding, and Society* (London, 1961), p. 51; Maurice Merleau-Ponty, *The Primary of Perception* (Evanston, Ill., 1964), p. 25; Zevedi Barbu, *Problems in Historical Psychology* (New York, 1960), pp. 20–22; the extensive discussion of work on motivation in Robert F. Berkhofer, *A Behavior Approach to Historical Analysis* (New York, 1969), pp. 55–67. This scholarship meshes closely with several recent historiographical articles: Samuel H. Beer, "Casual Explanation and Imaginative Re-enactment," and Bruce Kuklick, "The Mind of the Historian," both in *History and Theory*, 3 (1963): 6–29 and 8 (1969): 313–31, and John Dunn, "The Identify of the History of Ideas," *Philosophy*, 43 (April, 1968): 85–104.
2. Hutchinson to Rev. Eli Forbes, 16 October 1773, and to John Hely Hutchinson, 14 February 1772, Hutchinson Letterbooks, vol. 27, pp. 556–57, 296–300, Massachusetts Archives, State House, Boston (available in typescript at the Massachusetts Historical Society, Boston).
3. Morgan. "Thomas Hutchinson and the Stamp Act," *New England Quarterly*, 21 (1942): 459–92; Freiberg, "How to Become a Colonial Governor," *Review of Politics*, 21 (October, 1951: 646–56; Shipton, *Sibley's Harvard Graduates* (Cambridge and Boston, 1933–), vol. 7, pp. 383–13; B. Bailyn, *Ideological Origins of the American Revolution* (Cambridge, Mass., 1967), pp. 121–23.
4. John A. Garraty, ed., *Interpretating American History: Conversations with Historians* (New York, 1970), vol. 1, p. 74.
5. Morgan, "Thomas Hutchinson and the Stamp Act," pp. 487–92: Donald C. Lord and Robert M. Calhoon. "The Removal of the Massachusetts General Court from Boston, 1769–1772," *Journal of American History*, 55 (1969): 728, n. 9, see below, chapter 3.
6. Hutchinson, *Speeches of... Governor Hutchinson to the General Assembly...* (Boston, 1773), pp. 13–14; see also his "Dialogue between a European and an American [Englishman]," Hutchinson Papers, vol. 28, p. 102, Mass. Arch.
7. Lord and Calhoon, "The Removal of the General Court," pp. 747–48, 753–54.
8. Bailyn, *Ideological Origins*, p. 56.
9. Robert M. Calhoon, ed., "William Smith's Alternative to the American Revolution," *William and Mary Quarterly*, third series, 22 (1965): 105–18, see below, chapter 2.
10. W. H. W. Sabine, ed., *Historical Memoirs from... 1763 to... 1776 of William Smith* (New York, 1956), pp. 118, 156–64.
11. *Ibid.*, pp. 224–28c, 271–77, 279.
12. Bailyn, *Ideological Origins*, p. 312; a highly original but gingerly examination of

13

The Loyalist Perception

high tory ideology is Michael D. Clark, "Jonathan Boucher: The Mirror of Reaction," *Huntington Library Quarterly*, 33 (1969): 19–32.

13. Seabury to Rev. Daniel Burton, 17 December 1769 and 29 March 1770, Society for the Propagation of the Gospel Papers, Fulham Palace, London; ms. sermon, Lambeth Palace, London; Clarence Vance, ed., *Letters of a Westchester Farmer* (White Plains, N.Y., 1930), pp. 152, 72–75, 104, 111–12, 116.

14. Wentworth to Dr. Belham, 9 August 1768, Wentworth Letterbooks, New Hampshire Department of Records and Archives, Concord, N.H., quoted extensively in L. S. Mayo, *John Wentworth*...(Cambridge, 1921), pp. 122–24.

15. Robert M. Calhoon, " 'I have deduced your rights': Joseph Galloway's Concept of his Role, 1774–1775," *Pennsylvania History*, 25 (1968): 356–78, see below, chapter 5.

16. Alan Heimert, *Religion and the American Mind: From the Greater Awakening to the Revolution* (Cambridge, Mass., 1966).

17. William Smith, *The Works of William Smith, D.D.* (Philadelphia, 1803), vol. 2, p. 123.

18. Samuel Andrews, *A Discourse Showing the Necessity of Joining Internal Repentance with the External Profession of It*...(New Haven, Conn., 1775), pp. 15–18.

19. Robert M. Calhoon and Robert M. Weir, " 'The Scandalous History of Sir Egerton Leigh,' " *William and Mary Quarterly*, third series, 26 (1969): 47–74, see below, chapter 4.

20. Sewall to General Frederick Haldimand, 30 May 1775, quoted in Jack P. Greene, eds., *Colonies to Nation, 1763–1776* (New York, 1967), pp. 266–68.

21. Jack P. Greene, "Search for Identity: An Interpretation of the Meaning of Selected Patterns of Social Response in Eighteenth-Century America," *Journal of Social History*, 3 (1970); 189–220 and "Political Mimesis: A Consideration of the British Colonies in the Eighteenth-Century," *American Historical Review*, 75 (1969): 337–67; James M. Banner, *To the Hartford Convention: The Federalists and the Origins of Party Politics in Massachusetts, 1789–1815* (New York, 1970) and Fred Somkin, *Unquiet Eagle: Memory and Desire in the Idea of American Freedom, 1815–1860* (Ithaca, N.Y., 1967).

22. See W. H. Nelson, *The American Tory* (Oxford, 1961), chapter 5.

23. On these patterns see Wallace Brown, *The Good Americans: The Loyalists in the American Revolution* (New York, 1969), chapter 6; David V. J. Bell, "Nation and Non-Nation: A New Analysis of the Loyalists and the American Revolution" (unpublished Ph.D. dissertation, Harvard University, 1969); and Mary Beth Norton, *The British-Americans: The Loyalist Exiles in England, 1774–1789* (Boston, 1972).

2

"THE CONSTITUTION OUGHT TO BEND":

William Smith Jr.'s Alternative to the American Revolution

During the mid-eighteenth century various men proposed improvements in the administration of the colonies. Martin Bladen, Sir William Keith, Benjamin Franklin, James Abercromby, Henry McCulloh, Thomas Pownall, and Francis Bernard were only the more prominent advocates of reform.[1] Most of these writers sought either to streamline colonial administration or to provide mechanisms by which the colonies might better contribute to the defense of the Empire. Franklin, Pownall, and Bernard seemed to sense that more extensive reforms might be needed to bridge the growing gap between colonial practice and imperial theory; but even their proposals did not pay sufficient attention to changes in colonial politics and the new aspirations of American leaders. Just how drastic a change was necessary in imperial institutions and in the assumptions of British officials about colonial politics was suggested by William Smith, Jr., a New York lawyer, historian, and councillor,[2] in his "Thoughts upon the Dispute between Great Britain and her Colonies," printed here below.

Composed between 1765 and 1767 during the Stamp Act crisis and its aftermath, Smith's "Thoughts" drew upon two decades of study and activity in New York politics.[3] He had long been aware of the implications of the rise of the lower houses of provincial assemblies, which, he reasoned, was at the heart of most problems between the colonies and the Mother Country. New York assemblymen, he noted in 1756, were "tenacious in the Opinion that the Inhabitants of this Colony are entitled to all the Privileges of *Englishmen*" and "have a Right to participate in the legislative Power." Royal governors operated on the contrary assumption that the assembly existed

14

William Smith Jr.'s Alternative

only by the sufferance of the Crown. "It is easy to conceive," he predicted, "that Contentions most naturally attend such a Contradiction of Sentiments." These two opposing conceptions of the status of the lower houses persisted, Smith explained, because no one saw the problem as a whole. Colonial officials would not take the claims of the assembly seriously, and colonial representatives were preoccupied with mundane problems like "the Regulation of Highways, the Destruction of Wolves, . . . and the Advancement of the other little Interests of the particular Counties which they . . . represent."[4]

The furor in New York over the Grenville program confirmed Smith's fears. First the Sugar Act, then a long dispute between Lieutenant Governor Cadwallader Colden and the New York legal profession over an appeal to the Privy Council, and finally the Stamp Act dangerously antagonized the province. The ostensible cause of the crisis, as Smith and others noted, was the fear that British taxation would enable Parliament to "take away all we have."[5] But Smith believed that the root of the problem lay much deeper, and his peculiar contribution was to demonstrate how the structure of the Empire contributed to conflicting assumptions of British and colonial leaders about colonial rights and obligations.

Smith therefore based his "Thoughts" on the premise that the colonies' contribution in the Seven Years' War and their growing maturity entitled them to a generous redefinition of their place in the Empire. To have supposed that such a readjustment could be accomplished by commercial restrictions or Parliamentary taxation was, in Smith's judgment, "palpable Blundering." As colonial opposition to the Grenville program mounted, Smith noted how both sides appealed to their respective interpretations of the British constitution. The colonists invoked the rights of Englishmen, and the British replied that the virtual representation of the colonies in Parliament amply protected those rights. Such appeals to constitutional precedent, he contended, were futile: "the Truth is, that the Empire, long after the Constitution was formed, acquired a *new, adventitious State.* . . . The Question therefore is not, what the Constitution was, or is, but what, present Circumstances considered, it ought to be." In the place of fruitless contention about constitutional rights, both sides should seek common ground in the mutual advantages provided by the wealth of the Empire. In order for the colonies to survive and flourish and Britain to maintain its power, "the Constitution (be it what it will) ought to bend, and *sooner or later* will bend." Because Smith remained detached from any particular interpretation of the constitution, he conceived of it as a malleable, flexible set of doctrines which men should adapt to meet changing circumstances.[6]

The recognition by all parties that the constitution of the Empire should remain flexible was, in Smith's view, only a first step. He also wanted boldly

16

Part I: Ideas

to reconstruct imperial institutions. Reiterating the view that the provincial preoccupations of assemblymen precluded the broad vision needed to govern America, he suggested the creation of a continental parliament to supplement the assemblies, drawing members from all of the mainland colonies including Quebec, Nova Scotia, and the Floridas. He also envisioned an American council appointed by the Crown and a Lord Lieutenant modeled on that post in Ireland.

Smith's "Thoughts" assumed that only tangible, workable changes in the structure of the Empire could create a more stable political atmosphere. The constitutional debate revealed to him an unnatural state of anxiety, growing out of the colonists' fears about their political rights and British concern for the security of its economic stake in the colonies. The chief virtue of his approach, he believed, lay in his recognition of that insecurity and his desire to alleviate it effectively. Smith's "Thoughts" therefore aimed all of its proposals toward the object of rebuilding confidence. His immediate purpose was to abolish the necessity for Parliamentary taxation of the colonies by transferring that authority to the new American parliament. He proposed that the Crown should present the American legislature with an annual requisition. The new legislature would then apportion the sum among the various colonies, leaving the raising of the revenue to the provincial assemblies. Significantly, the American parliament would deal in these fiscal matters, not with the Parliament at Westminster, but directly with the Crown. Having secured an exemption from Parliamentary taxation in return for this annual contribution, the colonies would then acknowledge Parliamentary authority over them in all other fields.

The problems of taxation and imperial defense were secondary to Smith's main purpose. He was chiefly interested in analyzing the sources of distrust within the Empire. He attributed the lack of confidence between British and colonial leaders in large part to the proliferation of colonial assemblies. They could neither function effectively nor command British respect because they attracted inferior men, were subject to provincial pressures, and could not cope with problems affecting the colonies as a whole. If, however, colonial institutions were inadequate, taxation by Parliament was no solution. The advocates of virtual representation, Smith observed, were motivated by ignorance and an "overweaning Attachment to their own Interest." To prevent imperial disintegration, politicians on both sides had to visualize the Empire as a whole, anticipate its future development, and then create institutions capable of meeting present and future needs. The expansion of the colonies across the continent had only begun, he noted, while British power had probably reached its zenith. This sense of the future motivated his belief in constitutional reform. British self-interest required a durable link with the colonies, and America could exploit the

William Smith Jr.'s Alternative

resources of the continent most effectively if it could exchange raw materials for British goods. Therefore, he concluded, while both sides needed the Empire, the British probably had a greater interest in preserving it than did the colonies. The authors of "The American Whig, No. V,"—probably Smith and William Livingston—carried this analysis a step further by defining the seaboard colonies and inland territories as an "indispensible substratum of empire" which required for its "foundation...a *regular American Constitution.*"[7] This declaration of nascent manifest destiny in Smith's "Thoughts" and "The American Whig" added a new dimension to the discussion of colonial rights by turning the prospect of American expansion into a compelling argument for constitutional reform.

The subsequent career of Smith's "Thoughts" was less interesting than the content of the document itself. Appointed to the Council in New York in 1767, Smith found himself increasingly concerned with provincial affairs, particularly with a protracted struggle within the Council over the distribution of certain disputed lands situated between New York and New Hampshire. He did attempt to have provisions of his plan incorporated in a petition to the House of Lords in December 1768, but the assembly deleted it.[8] His interest in it revived, however, when General Frederick Haldimand expressed interest in the proposal in 1775 as the imperial crisis moved to its climax. Smith sent the General a copy of his "Thoughts" and Haldimand forwarded it without comment to Lord Dartmouth, Secretary of State for the Colonies.[9] In August 1775 the plan received further attention when a published letter—written in 1769 by Thomas Hutchinson to Hillsborough, Dartmouth's predecessor as Colonial Secretary—spoke of "an Expectation of an American Parliament" by someone in New York. Hutchinson ridiculed the idea because it compromised the supremacy of Parliament. Smith presumed that Hutchinson had not seen his manuscript, but he did recall mentioning its contents to Hutchinson's friend, Andrew Oliver.[10] A few days after he saw the newspaper account of Hutchinson's letter about his plan, Smith heard a rumor that Lord Mansfield had prepared proposals for reconciling the colonies. Smith immediately assumed that his plan was "the Ground work" of Mansfield's recommendations, and he further assumed that Hutchinson's garbled version of the "Thoughts" or Haldimand's complete text had received serious consideration in London.[11]

Though Smith's "Thoughts" in fact received little if any attention from British officials, he remained convinced that inadequate mechanisms of Empire were at the bottom of the imperial crisis. His "Thoughts as a rule for my own Conduct, at this melancholy Hour of approaching Distress," written a few weeks before independence, was a painstaking résumé of the failure of the institutions of the Empire to accommodate both British and colonial aspirations. As in his earlier "Thoughts," he here located the crux

Part I: Ideas

of the problem in a structural flaw of the Empire. "As no Provision was made for constituting an Impartial Judge between [the colonies and the Mother Country]," he lamented, "their Controversies are therefore to be decided by Negotiation and Treaty, or on an Appeal to the Lord of Hosts by Battle."[12]

Few contemporaries read Smith's "Thoughts," and even Haldimand and Dartmouth did not appear to appreciate its importance.[13] But it is an instructive source on the coming of the Revolution. It shows that Smith—an informed, reflective eighteenth-century American—was capable of looking at the constitution, not as a doctrine to obey nor a reality to accept, but as a tool to adapt, improve, and "bend." Because Smith believed that individuals had the ability to perceive and the duty to correct flaws in the constitution, his memorandum minimizes the importance of impersonal, historical forces and enhances the role of individual initiative in colonial politics. Smith might well have agreed with Charles H. McIlwain's well-known view that the American Revolution resulted from "a collision of two mutually incompatible interpretations of the British constitution"[14] or at least the constitution of the British Empire. But unlike the legalistic writers upon whom McIlwain depended, Smith's analysis attributed the constitutional impasse more to the intellectual rigidity among leaders on both sides than to a contradiction of principles.[15]

Two copies of the "Thoughts," one in Smith's handwriting, are preserved among the Dartmouth Papers in the William Salt Library, Stafford, England.[16]

Thoughts upon the Dispute between
Great Britain and her Colonies.

They who speak of the Union between these Countries, barely as of Importance, and even of *vast* Importance, do not express themselves properly. He who knows, that *one third* Part of the Commerce of Britain, depends upon her Colonies; and that if this is lost, she is ruined, will talk of the Union, as essential to the very Existence of the Empire.

What then are we to think of the present Quarrel? It is a Disseuse that affects Life. And as it spreads fast, the Remedy must be speedily administered. A solid Dominion must be founded in Love and Interest. The affection of three Millions of Subjects, situated as we are, if once lost, will scarce ever be regained.

The last War was a glorious one. To *Individuals* it has been profitable; and if our Successes are wisely improved, it will be so to the *Nation,* the vast Increase of the Public Debt notwithstanding.

William Smith Jr.'s Alternative

By the Conquest of Canada, Great Britain was supposed to acquire the Dominion of all North America; and thenceforth to be in a Condition, to seize the West India Islands at Pleasure, humble France and Spain and secure the Tranquility of Europe.[17] But is the Rescue of the Continent from France, the ensuring of it to Great Britain? Surely something more was to be done after the War ceased. The Colonies when delivered from the Enemy, were to be secured to their Protectors.

It was palpable Blundering, to imagine that this could be effected by unusual, exceptionable Taxations, and an embarrassed, partial Commerce. The Minister fell into this Error, in a Fright at the Amount of the national Debt, and for want of Knowledge concerning the Nature and State of our Trade.

He presumed that the Colonies were now out of their Infancy, able to stand upon their Legs, and to give Aid to the Mother Country.

The vast Wealth acquired from us in the Circuits of Commerce were not considered. What respected our Defense from the Enemy abroad, and the Savages at Home, and the internal support of Government, ing[r]ossed all his Attention.

It is agreed that if the Colonies enjoy a free Trade, it will bear Impositions, that may vastly relieve the Charges of the Empire.

A direct Tax was devised in 1764, but not without some Diffidence. A Year's Notice was given, before the burden was actually imposed.

This is the Origin of the controversy. Much has been written upon the Subject. Both Countries fly to the Constitution, for Arguments in Support of Tenets, *diametrically* opposite to each other. On the Part of America, there is a Claim to all the Rights of Englishmen; whence it is inferred, that no Tax can be laid upon them without the Consent of their Assemblies: Great Britain on the other Hand, attempts to justify her Measures, by admitting the Principle, but denying the Consequence; for She contends, that the Americans are *virtually* represented, by the Commons of Great Britain.

It is not proposed to enter into this Controversy here. Let it suffice to observe, that the Litigants on both Sides, seem to be insensible, that the constitutional Principles they appeal to, were established before the Colonies were discovered, and that some of them argue, as if we were in the same Predicament, with a *County* of the Old Realm of England; whereas the Truth is, that the Empire, long after the Constitution was formed, acquired a *new, adventitious State.* And the Question therefore is not, what the Constitution was, or is, but what, present Circumstances considered, it ought to be.

Britain having made a vast Accession to her Dominion, by Discovery, by Conquest and by Cession, the Disputants, instead of spending their Time, in collecting Arguments, all chargeable with a Non Sequitur, should have

Part I: Ideas

pointed to Measures conducive to the common Weal of both Countries; because to that [end][18] the Constitution (be it what it will) ought to bend, and *sooner* or *later* will bend; unless it is the Design of Heaven to infatuate and destroy us as a Nation.

The Colonies became seperate, and with respect to each other independant Societies, by *Accident;* neither the Crown nor the Nation, had any Design in Splitting the Dominions into so many different, petty Governments. Thro' *Necessity* each acquired *Legislative* Powers, in a Mode somewhat similar to the grand Pattern in the Parent Country. There seems to be no Reason to doubt, but that if the whole Continent of North America, had been antiently asked for by one Company; suppose for Instance the Virginia Company in 1606, the Grant would have passed; and *one* Assembly been constituted, to make Laws for this immense Region.

The Case is however otherwise, the Continent consists of Sixteen or Seventeen Colonies and Provinces, under the immediate Government, of almost as many little Parliaments made up of a Governor and a Council differently appointed, and an Assembly of Delegates, chosen by the People.

None can deny, that the Colonies ought to bear some Part of the Public Burdens. If the Royal Requisitions for Aids are to be made to each, the Objections are obvious and unanswerable,

1st The Empire will become too complex, popular and unwieldy;

2ly Persons utterly incompetent for its Affairs, will participate in its Councils; and,

3ly The Empire will be perpetually distracted, and in Danger of a Dissolution, from a want of *Uniformity in Design.*

The Advocates for the British Supremacy, had these Consequences in full View. The Prospect filled them with Terror. We ought to ascribe the fictitious, virtual Representation they talk of, to their Consternation, and *not to Malice.* But their Scheme is manifestly defective; because it does not provide for the Safety of the Colonies; It discovers an overweaning Attachment to their own Interest; and being partial, tends to work the Disunion we all dread, as ruinous to the whole Empire.

America supplicates for Relief; and if she desires no more, than the Parliament's ceasing to act, upon the Principle of unbounded Sovereignty, and that the Crown may again recur, to the old Course of Requisitions to each Colony, the guilt of partiality will be our's.

Let any Man well consider the three Objections, to such a Form of Government above mentioned, and he must be convinced, that it cannot give Stability to so vast an Empire.[19]

If our Experience has not yet furnished Arguments from *Facts,* against such a Distribution of Power, tis because we were formerly too feeble and

William Smith Jr.'s Alternative

exposed, to give the Assistance that will *soon* be justly due, and certainly expected.

The present Contentions are the *first,* in the Train of tragical Consequences, inevitably flowing, from *too manifold a Partition,* of the *Legislative* Authority of the Empire.

It is of Necessity then, that a Constitution be devised, friendly to every Branch of the great Whole, and linking Great Britain and her Colonies together, by the most indesoluble Ties.

As the Contest arose, from a Foresight of the Inconveniences, attending a Resort to so many *seperate* Assemblies, the most obvious Remedy seems to be, a Consolidation of all these little, continental Parliaments into *one.*

It is not proposed to annihilate the Assemblies, but that there be a Lord Lieutenant as in Ireland, and a Council of at least Twenty four Members, appointed by the Crown, with a House of Commons, consisting of Deputies chosen by their respective *Assemblies,* to meet at the central Province of New York, as the Parliament of North America.

A Parliament is no Novelty; and therefore we shall not be perplexed in settling its Powers, and the Privileges of the several Branches. Let it be in general understood, that to this Body the Royal Requisitions for Aids are to be made, and that they are to have Authority, to grant for all, and to settle the Quotas of each; leaving the Ways and Means to their separate Consideration, unless in Cases of Default.

The Number of the Council may depend upon the Royal Pleasure; but to preserve their Independency, they ought to be Men of Fortune, and hold their Places for Life; with some honorable Distinctions to their Fanmilies, as a Lure to prevent the Office from falling into Contempt.

The Number of the Delegates, will naturally be proportioned to the comparative Weight and Abilities, of the Colonies they represent. The two Floridas, Rode Island, Nova Scotia and Georgia ought each to have five. New Hampshire, Marriland, North Carolina and Quebec seven. South Carolina and New Jersey eleven. New York, Pensilvania and Connecticut twelve and Massachusets Bay and Virginia fifteen.[20]

The whole House will thus consist of one hundred and forty one Members. A small Number, considering the Importance of their Trust. Besides Accident, Business and Disease will Occasion the Absence of many. They may be afterwards increased, when the Colonies are become more populous and desire it. The Crown to retain its antient Negative, and the British Parliament its Legislative Supremacy, in *all Cases* relative to *Life Liberty and Property,* except in the Matter of Taxations for *general Aids,* or the immediate, internal Support of the American Government.[21]

This Project is manifestly free from all the Objections, that lay either

Part I: Ideas

against that, which subjects American Property to the British Disposition; or the other, which asks that each Colony, should participate *so largely* in the Councils of the Empire, as to have the Power of refusing Aids; tho' thought necessary for the common Safety, by the *united Voice* of Great Britain and all the Rest of her extensive Dominions.

It may be said of every one of the Colonies, that our Assemblies are unequal to the Task, of entering into the Views of so wise, and so great a Nation as Great Britain is, and from which we are so far removed. Indeed it is not to be expected from an Infant Country, many of those Assemblymen represent little obscure Counties, and are themselves at Streights for a bare Livelyhood. Besides, the scant Districts of the respective Provinces, bring the several Branches of the Legislature into too great a Familiarity, for the Purposes of good Government; and open the Door to frequent Bickerings and Discords, in which the common Interest will be too often sacrificed, to private Piques or partial Aims, and the Royal Voice drowned in the Dinn of Faction, or the Clamours against an obnoxious Governor.

But in a Parliament, chosen *not by the Counties,* but by the *Representatives* of the Colonies, we shall collect the Wisdom of the whole Continent, and find the Members acting upon Principles, doubly refined from popular Lees, and with a Liberality unbiassed by the partial Prejudices, prevalent in the little Districts by which they were sent.

Unspeakable Advantages will also flow, from the Introduction of a *dignified* Government, into a Country long neglected, and where, on Account of its being little known to Great Britain, and the diversity of their Colony Constitutions, many Disorders have crept in, in some Instances dangerous and detrimental to the Colonies, and their British Creditors, and derogative of the just Rights, and many Prerogatives of the Crown, most friendly to Peace and good Order.

But the Capital Advantages of this Scheme, will be the Recovery of the Colonies, to a firm Confidence in the *Justice* and *Affection* of the Parent State. And by opening to her the Conduits of sure, full and constant Information, enabling her so to regulate and improve this vast, dependant, growing Territory, as to unite every Branch of the Empire, by the Cords of Love and Interest, and give Peace, Health and Vigor to the whole.

There are several Reasons, why this Measure should be *speedily* attended to.

I The Colonies are universally agitated, by Suspicion, Fear and Disgust; and doubling by their own Growth in less than thirty Years, will in *Fifty,* equall the Inhabitants of Great Britain and Ireland. Unforeseen Events in Europe, may accelerate this momentous Increase[.]

II By the dissentions in the Mother Country, her rapid Advance in Luxury,

William Smith Jr.'s Alternative

the American Attention to Manufactures, the Alarming Extent of the National Debt, the democratical Assendancy of the Commons, and many other Causes, Great Britain seems to have passed the Zenith of Her Glory, without some great Change in the system of her Affairs.

III If these [*sic*] is a Recourse to the Establishment of a Dominion, founded *only in Fear,* it can last no longer, than till the controuling Power, is destressed by a general War; and the Revisal of the Contest for Liberty at such a Crisis; must be tragical indeed. Members to a Parliament in Europe, the Americans never will send; and every other Scheme, but one as agreeable to them as that now recommended, would soon prove to be but a temporary Palliative and meer Quack Medicine.

IV The Colonies will never be less assuming than at present. If the Disgusts now raised, should continue, we may become a Nest for the disaffected and designing, even in Great Britain and Ireland; Now we demand only an Exemption from *Parliamentary Taxations* as a Right, recognizing at the same Time, the Supremacy of Great Birtain, in *every other Instance* and particularly her Sovereignty in Commerce.[22] It is therefore her Interest to lay a solid Foundation for her Dominion by a voluntary and durable Compact. What we ask as a Favor at present, may be after a few Years offered and refused.[23]

I am sensible that a Jealousy of the Power, which a Union of our Councils would create, may prevent Great Britain from concurring in the Erection of a *third Parliament,* for the Government of the Empire. But this very Jealousy, is Part of the National Disease, and will if it continues, be the Ruin of us all.

If she Means to oppress her Colonies, their common Danger, will in Spite of all Opposition unite them together. The late offensive Laws are a Proof of it, and all History verifies the Position. But if she abandons her partiality, and generously consults the common Weal, What Ground can there be for Jealousy. When once secured in our Property, our Affection will revive; and ten Thousand Cords may be contrived, to tie us together by the Knot of Interest. Prosperity may indeed make us wanton; but Provinces rarely rebell, till the Yoke of Oppression galls, and a deaf Ear to their Complaints, has begot a sullen Abhorrence of their Masters.

It has been apprehended by some, that some extensive Colonies, like an overgrown Child, will exhaust the Parent. The Cases of the antient Phoenicians, and modern Spaniards, have been mentioned on this Occasion. But all that read History, are not able to apply it, and make the proper Distinctions.

If Great Britain is to be ruined as these Speculatists suppose by the Flight of her Inhabitants to America, 'tis high Time to set the new House in Order, for their comfortable Accommodation, and welcome Reception. The

Part I: Ideas

Colonies are growing up, with many distinguishing Peculiarities; and tho' they may be now easily drawn into an harmonious Uniformity, yet by a little longer Negligence, their Prejudices will grow obstinate and humoursome.

If any unforeseen Catastrophe in Europe, should render their favorite Islands, no longer tenable in that Quarter, they may retreat to America; and the Present, is the most Advantageous Season, for laying a solid Foundation, for the speedy Re-establishment of a Dominion, which no Power upon Earth will be able to annoy.

But tho' the Wars in Asia, drove the feeble and defenceless Phoenecians to Carthage, and the Mines of Mexico and Peru depopulated Spain, Yet Great Britain by a wise Conduct, may improve her Colonies, even for the Increase of her own Population, as well as the Aggrandizement of her Power.

Every Body knows, that the Number of her Inhabitants is vastly inhanced since the Discovery of the New World; and can any Man be ignorant, that this is owing to the Augmentation thereby given to her Commerce?

The same Causes will produce the same Effects. The Spanish Emigrations drained the old State, chiefly, because they sent her *Money* instead of *Merchandise.* Spain was converted into a Castle of Indolence; She acquired *Silver* and *Gold* from her colonies, but not *real Wealth.*

If Great Britain is attentive to her own, and the Trade of her Colonies, she may dismiss all Fears of our Increase. Nay it will be then her Interest, to incourage our Increase.

One cannot take the State, Nature, Climates and prodigious Extent of the American Continent into Contemplation, without high Prospects in favor of the Power, to which it belongs. It is sufficient to be the *Granary* of all the Rest of the British Dominions. Fed by our Plough, Britain might attend more to the Cultivation of Sheep. By that Staple, and the Collection of raw Materials *from* us and *by* us, she may convert her own Island, as it were, into one great Town of Manufacturers, undersell every other Nation in Europe, and maintain and exalt her Supremacy, until Heaven blots out all the Empires of the World.

AUTHOR'S NOTE: (1988): Smith's plan received more attention than I realized when I wrote this article. For citations to discussion of his ideas, see Robert M. Calhoon, *The Loyalists in Revolutionary America, 1760–1781* (New York, 1973), p. 520. The historian William Gordon had access to a draft of the plan sometime before 1776 and transcribed it; Gordon's transcription mysteriously found its way into the papers of John Adams, prompting Adam's modern editors to attribute it to Gordon, see Robert J. Taylor, ed., *Papers of John Adams* (Cambridge, Mass., 1977), Vol. 2, pp. 419–28. At the

William Smith Jr.'s Alternative

request of the editor of the *William and Mary Quarterly,* I shortened the title of this article by deleting the quoted words; here the original title is restored.

1. On proposals to rationalize the institutions of the Empire see, in general, Charles M. Andrews, *The Colonial Period of American History,* 4 (New Haven, Conn., 1938): 412–13; on Bladen, see Jack P. Greene, "Martin Bladen's Blueprint for a Colonial Union," *William and Mary Quarterly,* 3d Ser., 17 (1960): 516–30; on Keith, see Roy N. Lokken, "Sir William Keith's Theory of the British Empire," *The Historian,* 25 (1963): 403–18; on Franklin, see Gerald Stourzh, *Benjamin Franklin and American Foreign Policy* (Chicago, 1954), pp. 48–82; on Abercromby, see Andrews, *Colonial Period of American History,* vol. 4, pp. 409–11; on McCulloh, see [Henry McCulloh], *Proposals for Uniting the English Colonies on the Continent of America;* ... (London, 1757) and Jack P. Greene, " 'A Dress of Horror': Henry McCulloh's Objections to the Stamp Act," *Huntington Library Quarterly,* 26 (1962–63): 253–62; on Pownall, see John A. Schutz, *Thomas Pownall*...(Glendale, 1951), pp. 181–214, and Caroline Robbins, *The Eighteenth-Century Commonwealthmen* (Cambridge, Mass., 1959), pp. 311–19; on Bernard, see Edmund S. and Helen Morgan, *The Stamp Act Crisis: Prologue to Revolution* (Chapel Hill, N.C., 1953), pp. 7–20. See also Richard Koebner, *Empire* (Cambridge, Eng., 1961), pp. 86–90, 105–13, 130–41, 147–48 and in general chaps. 3 and 4. Stourzh's study of Franklin and Koebner's posthumously published study have done more than any other works to identify the structure and purposes of empires as categories of eighteenth-century thought.
2. In 1963 I consulted Dorothy Rita Dillon, *The New York Triumvirate*...(New York, 1949); William H. W. Sabine's introduction to the *Historical Memoirs from 16 March 1763 to 9 July 1776 of William Smith* (New York, 1956), pp. vii–xii, I–II; Milton M. Klein's introduction to *The Independent Reflector*...(Cambridge, Mass., 1963), pp. 14–17; and L. F. S. Upton's introduction to *The Diary and Selected Papers of Chief Justice William Smith, 1784–1793* (The Champlain Society, *Publications,* XLI [Toronto, 1963]), vol. 1, pp. xxvi–xxxiii.
3. The composition of the proposed continental government is summarized in "Memoir of the Honourable William Smith, Written by His Son ["William Smith of Canada"]," in William Smith, *The History of the Late Province of New-York, from Its Discovery, to the Appointment of Governor Colden, in 1762,* vol. 1 (New York, 1829), pp. xi–xxiii. The manuscript bears the notation, "written in 1767," but was probably composed in 1765. Many of its ideas appeared in Smith's letter to the Rev. George Whitefield, Dec. 6, 1765, Dartmouth Papers, I ii, 820, William Salt Library, Stafford, England. An unnamed English visitor to New York reported in early November 1765 that he found Smith hard at work on a critique of colonial administration and policy in the light of the Stamp Act crisis. See Rockingham Papers, Wentworth-Woodhouse Muniments, R 24/34, Sheffield City Library, Sheffield, Eng. The fullest discussion of Smith's proposals is in Professor Upton's introduction to Smith's *Diary,* I, *xxvi–xxxiii.*
4. "The Political State" [in ca. 1756], in William Smith, *The History of the Province of New York from the First Discovery to the Year 1732,* Appendix, chap. 5 (London, 1757), pp. 241–43.

Part I: Ideas

5. Smith to Whitefield, Dec. 6, 1765, Dartmouth Papers, I ii, 820. See also Milton M. Klein, "Prelude to Revolution in New York: Jury Trials and Judicial Tenure," *Wm. and Mary Qtly.*, 3d Ser., 17 (1960): 439–62.

6. A remarkably similar analysis of the economic potential and political needs of the Empire, gleaned from *The Wealth of Nations,* appears in E. A. Benians, "Adam Smith's Project of an Empire," *Cambridge Historical Journal,* I (1923–25): 249–83.

7. "The American Whig, No. V," *New-York Gazette, or Weekly Post-Boy,* Apr. II, 1768. The "American Whig," a series of polemics against Thomas Bradbury Chandler's demands for an American bishop, was edited and largely written by Smith's close friend and political ally, William Livingston. "No. V" contained this striking digression on the structure of the Empire, and has been attributed to Livingston in Carl Bridenbaugh, *Mitre and Sceptre*...(New York, 1962), pp. 306–07; however, Smith and Livingston probably collaborated on this number since its arguments and style dovetail so closely with those of Smith's "Thoughts." Chandler himself suspected Smith of sharing authorship of previous issues of the "American Whig." See Chandler to Samuel Johnson, Apr. 7, 1768, in Herbert and Carol Schneider, eds., *Samuel Johnson, President of King's College: His Career and Writings* (New York, 1929), vol. 1, pp. 436–38, and, particularly, Koebner's perceptive discussion of this issue of the "American Whig" in *Empire,* pp. 171–72.

8. Dec. 13, 1768, in Smith, *Historical Memoirs, 1763–1776,* pp. 49–50.

9. Smith to Haldimand, July 4, 1775, Dartmouth Papers, II, 1353.

10. Smith, *Historical Memoirs, 1763–1776,* pp. 235–36; *Pennsylvania Journal* (Philadelphia), Aug. 9, 1775.

11. Smith's information about Mansfield was incorrect. Mansfield made no recorded recommendations about reconciling the colonies in 1775, but he had advocated important conciliatory features of the Quebec Act of 1774, and Smith probably confused the two activities. See Reginald Coupland, *The Quebec Act: A Study in Statesmanship* (Oxford, 1925), pp. 10, 32, 49–50, 100.

12. Smith, *Historical Memoirs, 1763–1776,* pp. 271–77. On Smith's elaborate analysis of the Revolutionary crisis from 1774 to 1776 see William H. W. Sabine, "William Smith and His Imperial 'Compact,'" *Manuscripts,* 8 (1956): 315–18; William H. Nelson, *The American Tory* (Oxford, 1961), pp. 123–25; Upton, ed., *Diary,* pp. xxxi–xxxiii; and Smith, *Historical Memoirs, 1763–1776,* pp. 188–90, 209, 224–25, 228–28c, 235–37, 239–41, 242–51, 257–59, 261–63, 265–66, 271–77, 279–83.

13. It is not clear how a London merchant, Brook Watson, came to possess an unsigned, abbreviated version of Smith's "Thoughts" which he sent to Dartmouth in January 1775. Historical Manuscripts Commission, *Fourteenth Report,* Appendix, Part 10 (London, 1895), p. 262.

14. *The American Revolution: A Constitutional Interpretation* (New York, 1923), p. 5.

15. On Smith's later constitutional ideas see Oscar Zeichner, "William Smith's 'Observations on America,'" *New York History,* 23 (1942): 328–40; Hilda Neatby, "Chief Justice William Smith: An Eighteenth-Century Whig Imperialist," *Canadian Historical Review,* 28 (1947): 44–67; and Upton, ed., *Diary,* pp. xxxiii–xl.

16. Dartmouth Papers, II, 1353, 1354.

17. I have been informed that the Value of the West India Product imported into France in 1754, was near ten Millions Sterling. How immense the Profits on the European Sales! She holds these Sources of Wealth at the Mercy of Great Britain. By Expeditions from the Continent of America, any of these Islands may be easily overwhelmed and reduced. [Smith's Note.]

William Smith Jr.'s Alternative

18. One or more words were apparently omitted inadvertently; the bracketed word has been supplied by conjecture.
19. Its affairs are now directed by more than Twenty Parliaments. What a Multitude of Souls to one Body! [Smith's Note.]
20. From separate Requisitions to the Island Colonies, we have no Inconveniences to apprehend. It is easy to command their Wealth by a commercial Police. They are besides absolutely dependant upon Great Britain and the Continent of America. They owe their Safety to the Protection of the one, and the Supplies of the other, and must of Necessity belong to the Power that rules both. They can never revolt while the present Union subsists. [Smith's Note.]
21. No other than such a *limited Sovereignty* is exercised over Ireland, tho' a conquered Country. [Smith's Note.]
22. This will be consistent with our Exemption from Her Taxations, if the Duties go into the Province Treasuries, or are passed to our Credit, on the Royal Requisitions. [Smith's Note.]
23. These considerations were staples in the discussion of the nature of the Empire. Smith probably drew these ideas from Franklin's essay, "Observations concerning the Increase of Mankind, Peopling of Countries, &c." See Leonard W. Labaree and Whitfield J. Bell, Jr., eds., *The Papers of Benjamin Franklin,* 4 (New Haven, Conn., 1961): 227–34. Both men agreed that colonial population would double within every generation, and that this increase compelled Britain to reform the political system of the Empire. Both feared that concentrations of urban population would encourage the decline of public virtue as was already evident in Britain. See especially [Smith], "A brief Consideration of New-York...," Jan. 18, 1753, in Klein, ed., *The Independent Reflector,* pp. 103–8. Another loyalist who proposed imperial union as a means of averting the American Revolution, Joseph Galloway, also defended this policy on the grounds that colonial population would increase by tenfold within the coming century. Galloway to Richard Jackson, Aug. 10, 1775, Dartmouth Papers, II, 1031.

3

THE REMOVAL OF THE MASSACHUSETTS GENERAL COURT FROM BOSTON, 1769–1772

On June 14, 1769, Governor Francis Bernard ordered the Massachusetts General court to leave its traditional seat in Boston and to reassemble in Cambridge for the remainder of its session. When Lieutenant Governor Thomas Hutchinson, on March 8, 1770, summoned the Court to meet in Cambridge, he provoked a constitutional crisis in Massachusetts and instigated a controversy which lasted for more than two years.[1] Hutchinson claimed that his royal instructions required him to remove the Court from Boston's turbulent influences. The Court, in turn, challenged the power of the Crown to interfere in the provincial matter of calling, proroguing, and dissolving the assembly. It further questioned whether Hutchinson was actually bound by an explicit instruction and suspected him of harassing the Court out of whimsy. In the process of demanding the Court's return to Boston, the house of representatives and council ennunciated Lockean doctrine and alleged that the continued removal from Boston jeopardized the liberty of the province and violated the compact between Massachusetts and the crown.

The struggle forced Hutchinson to justify the Crown's authority to dictate the location of the Court and to explain the obligations which a Massachusetts royal governor owed to the Crown and to the province. He knew that the removal of the Court was a risky step—one which would provide his enemies with a dramatic grievance. At the same time, he was so disturbed by the erosion of royal authority in the province that he was determined to preserve one of the Crown's prerogatives from further deterioration. Thus, until he could coax from the Court a tacit acknowledgment of the validity of

28

The Removal of the Court from Boston

the Crown's prerogative to instruct the governor on the use of his powers, Hutchinson was determined to resist all efforts to compel him to return the Court to Boston. When he finally did return the Court to its traditional seat in June 1772, it was by no means clear whether the Court had won a victory or the governor had secured a qualified, moral triumph by upholding the prerogative for two years. The question of victory became a moot point, however, when fresh controversies in 1773 and 1774 overshadowed the more restrained argument created by the removal of the Court. The inconclusive end of the dispute, the short distance from Boston to Cambridge, and the sometimes tedious semantic haggling over terms like "inconvenience" tended to obscure the significance of the struggle. The controversy provoked both Hutchinson and the Court to conduct a particularly acute inquiry into the sources and disposition of power in Massachusetts politics.

The contest originated with a royal instruction to Bernard, drafted in July 1768, which stated that because a "licentious and unrestrained Mob" dominated Boston, the governor could assemble the Court in Salem or Cambridge for its next session. Such "lenient and persuasive Methods," it continued, might discredit Massachusetts' radical leaders in the eyes of the province's inhabitants. Bernard doubted whether the removal would have any practical effect and considered this rebuke to Boston a necessary gesture. After weighing the problem, he assembled the Court in Boston in June 1769; and he did not remove it to Cambridge until it persisted in denouncing the presence of British troops in Boston. In Cambridge, the house completed its resolutions condemning Bernard's administration and included a brief complaint about the removal from Boston.[2]

When Bernard left for England later in the summer of 1769, Hutchinson was uncertain whether he should continue to assemble the Court in Cambridge. Bernard's proclamation on July 15, 1769, proroguing the Court until early 1770, mentioned neither Boston nor Cambridge as the place of its next meeting. An instruction to Hutchinson, dated December 9, 1769, directed him to call the Court to Cambridge unless he thought there were contrary reasons "of such a nature to outweigh these considerations." Distressed by the uncertainty, he wrote to Thomas Gage that, if left to his own discretion, he would not remove the Court from Boston.[3] In London, Bernard had discussed Massachusetts affairs with Lord Hillsborough and had participated in drafting the December 9 instruction. He sent Hutchinson a candid explanation of its meaning:

> You will... receive Directions for calling the Assembly at Cambridge, but not so peremptory as to oblige you to do it if you should think it best to have it at Boston.... I recommended a peremptory Order that you might be more able to apologise for it. But it was answered that this amounted to a peremptory Order, if your Opinion did not direct you to counteract it, in which Case you

Part I: Ideas

was left at Liberty to do what you thought for the best. But if you thought it best to obey it, you might quote it as a positive Order.[4]

Although subsequent instructions specifically forbade Hutchinson from returning the Court to Boston,[5] he probably assumed that he still possessed discretionary authority to do so as soon as the Court ceased to challenge the prerogative of the Crown to instruct a governor on the location of an assembly. An instruction dated July 3, 1771, reiterated that discretion; and Hutchinson's hands were probably not completely tied at any time during the controversy.[6] In 1775 he explained cryptically and probably accurately that "I never said I had a positive instruction" to keep the court in Cambridge "but that I had such instruction as made it necessary."[7] Fortunately for Hutchinson, his discretion was effectively hidden by a circular letter of 1768 to all royal governors which prohibited them from showing any part of an instruction to an assembly or council. Bernard, in December 1769, pointedly reminded Hutchinson of that restriction and added that it would prevent the Court from learning of "the discretionary Power given to you."[8]

However Hutchinson may have interpreted his instructions concerning the location of the Court, he realized that the removal from Boston was only a temporary and partial expedient. Pessimism about the feasibility of restoring tranquility to Massachusetts politics by any conventional methods pervaded his thinking during the controversy. In March 1770 he offered to resign in order to make way for a new governor with greater stature and more sweeping powers. He recommended to the Crown that Parliament should discipline Massachusetts by outlawing combinations which resisted enforcement of British law, by imposing oaths to support British authority on all colonial legislatiors and councillors, and then by appointing only British noblemen as royal governors for periods of not more than three years. "Nothing but a sharp external force," he concluded, "will bring Boston to a state of due subordination."[9]

Protests against the removal of the Court confirmed his analysis of unrest in the province. The controversy, he later wrote in his *History of the Colony and Province of Massachusetts-Bay*, tended "to alienate the people from their connexion with the parent state, and to reconcile them to an independency both of crown and parliament." His letters at the time used much the same language; and he described the controversy as a "determined design to wrest from the Crown every power which the people do not think convenient," "confirming...our principles of independence." In one sense, Hutchinson's apparent foresight is misleading, for by *independence* he meant only the autonomy which the Court was seeking in 1770. However, he did understand clearly how explosive the presumptions of the court could become if the Crown challenged them directly. "I think it must puzzle the wisest

The Removal of the Court from Boston

heads in the Kingdom to restore America to a State of Government and Order," he wrote at the close of a letter on the removal of the Court. "In general I can say that the wound may be skinned over but can never be healed until it be laid open to the bone. Parliament must give up its claim of Supreme Authority... or the Colonies must cease from asserting a Supreme Legislative power within themselves." Ever skeptical of his ability to make any lasting contribution, Hutchinson saw the removal of the Court as one way of "skinning over" the wound of disobedience in Massachusetts.[10]

Hutchinson's concern was justified. When the house assembled in the "new chapel" and the council met in the library of Harvard College in Cambridge on March 15, 1770, the messages of both chambers revealed a well-stocked arsenal of constitutional and practical objections to the Court's removal from Boston. Though mild in comparison with its later views, the house's initial arguments indicated the road which lay ahead. Arguing that the removal was an infraction of the representatives' essential rights as "Men and Citizens" as well as those "derived to us by the British Constitution and the Charter of this Colony," the house presented a plea for the return of the Court to Boston. The message further complained that the removal was inconvenient both for the members of the Court and for Harvard College.[11] These problems could be remedied, the house argued, if the lieutenant governor would use the power which he "alone" possessed to restore the Court to its "ancient Place, the State House at Boston." Hutchinson protested that he alone did not have the power to return the Court to Boston because he was bound by the King's instructions. The house retorted that while the power to call the Court had once belonged to the Crown, it had been given as a "Grant in Favor" to the governor. The house regarded the governor's sole exercise of this power, free from any Crown supervision, as a protection of the province's liberty. Hutchinson's removal of the Court, therefore, at the behest of a "Ministerial Mandate," eroded one of the province's basic rights. Lest Hutchinson believe that the house stood alone in its conflict with him, the council announced that while it was concerned with the "preservation of the Royal Prerogative," it was also anxious about the good of the people. The Court itself, the council declared, could advise the governor on the proper place to hold the assembly. The house then asked to see Hutchinson's alleged instructions. He replied that he was forbidden to reveal their contents.[12]

By refusing to show his instructions to the house, Hutchinson forced his opponents to adopt a new line of attack. A committee informed the governor that even if he had instructions, these ought not "to be deemed of sufficient Force to invalidate the Law." The House of Commons in 1749 and 1751 had given weight to this argument by refusing to endow royal instructions with the force of law. Even more important, the committee argued,

Part I: Ideas

was an act of 1698 which established the form of the writ used for summoning the General Court; the writ specifically designated Boston as the seat of the Court. Hutchinson quickly observed that the words "The Town of Boston" in the writ, like the words "William the Third," were understood to be mere matter of form. Just as quickly, the house resolved that all the words in the writ, like "William the Third," which by their nature were changeable, were form; those words that were not changeable by their nature, like "a certain Place," were "fix'd and perpetual."[13]

Each side had stated its basic position, but the house faced a circumstance that could weaken its position—the necessity of doing legislative work. If the house refused to consider constituents' petitions which had accumulated, it might lose public support and strengthen Hutchinson's hand. "*Only from absolute Necessity*" the house turned to its business, and it denied that any precedent had been established which acquiesced in the removal from Boston.[14] Practical necessity forced the house to alter its tactics but not to abandon its principles. On April 7, 1770, Hutchinson had asked for laws to strengthen the executive courts because of disturbances in Gloucester. The house replied that the continued presence of British troops in Boston—dispatched there because of rioting against customs officials in June 1768—and the removal of the Court from its "ancient and legal Seat" were bald attempts to intimidate the province and infringe upon its liberty. The house was, therefore, "employed in Matters which concern the very Being of the Constitution" and had no time for questions of executive jurisdiction. In this intransigent mood the assembly was dissolved the following day for annual spring elections. The newly elected house gave little promise of accomodation; Boston, in particular, showed its defiance by returning Thomas Cushing, Samuel Adams, and John Hancock—all outspoken opponents of Hutchinson's removal of the Court.[15]

The "Boston Instructions," adopted unanimously shortly after the election as a guide for the town's representatives, further demonstrated Boston's determination to resist Hutchinson's actions. The instructions warned of alarming signs of a "deep-laid and desperate plan of imperial despotism" which would destroy the "BRITISH CONSTITUTION" and protested against the removal of the Court in violation of "ancient usage and established law." A section of the instructions, drafted by Josiah Quincy, presented a legal argument against Hutchinson's use of the oral instructions; Quincy cut through the ambiguity surrounding the term "prerogative" and directly debated against that concept. Ever since Englishmen had repudiated the "mystical jargon" about divine-right rule, Quincy asserted, the prerogative had ceased to be a subject "too delicate" for public discussion. Only laws passed by Parliament or by a colonial assembly could compel a subject's obedience, he argued. The King's prerogative was therefore only

The Removal of the Court from Boston

binding when it did not exceed or conflict with the law, and indeed it was hedged about with statutes specifically limiting its use. By tradition, moreover, the prerogative could never be used in any way harmful to the interests of the subject. William Blackstone's definition of prerogative, Quincy declared, encompassed these restrictions; the prerogative was " 'the discretionary power of acting for the public good, where the positive laws are silent, [and] if...abused to the publick detriment,...is...unconstitutional.' " Drawing upon these doctrines, Quincy drove his argument to its conclusion: if the removal of the Court did not violate "the principles of crown law" or provincial laws which designated Boston as "the seat of government," not even a "Crown lawyer" could prove that the removal served in any way the interests of the people.

The Boston Instructions were a formidable attempt to construct a legal formula for attacking the royal instructions. First English usage, then parliamentary and provincial laws, and finally the public good stood as limits to the prerogative. If an encroachment slipped by one line of defense, it was sure to collide with the next barrier against arbitrary rule. Implicit in the formula was another tenacious safeguard—the assumption that the Crown bore the burden of evidence to show that an action did not violate the public good, or law, or tradition.[16]

"The doctrine advanced in this piece of rant," Hutchinson wrote of the Boston Instructions, "may as well be advanced against the King's assent to our laws or his appointing a Governor as against the removal of the Court from Boston by His Majesty's order." Determined not to be baited into rash action, he concluded that only the "artful management" of the house by the Boston members could account for its message of April 23. Thus he sought to convince other members of the Court of the integrity of his position. Even before the Boston Instructions, for example, he tried to convince the council that he had not summoned the Court to Cambridge on his own volition nor did he "have reason to think that the [Crown's] motives for ordering it to be done now cease." While he denied personal responsibility for the Court's removal, he insisted in the same breath that he alone could decide when the crown's attitude on the question might change. It was a delicate position that could be sustained, he wrote Bernard, only so long as the Court did "not know that I had any discretion left in the matter." He pleaded, therefore, that his letters to the ministry be kept secret.[17]

When the new Court assembled on May 31, 1770, the conflict was renewed. Speaking for the house, Hancock presented the lieutenant governor with a message that challenged the precedents Hutchinson had sought to establish for the removal of the Court to Cambridge. In addition to a meeting in 1747 when the court had met at Cambridge following the burning of the Boston Town House, Hutchinson had discovered and publicized two other

Part I: Ideas

precedents for his action—one in 1721 and another in 1729. In both cases the court had met at Salem. But the house countered that the Court had met in Salem in 1721 because a smallpox epidemic plagued Boston. The removal, therefore, was for the public good! The 1729 removal was dismissed as an illegal step to which the house had never acquiesced. In neither case would the house grant precedents. Hutchinson's summons was still considered an illegal attempt to make instructions supersede the law.[18]

Hutchinson was not so easily cornered. He uncovered another precedent: the Court had met in Salisbury in 1737. Unfortunately for his case, the council later proved that the Court had met willingly at Salisbury to settle a boundary dispute with New Hampshire. Hutchinson still insisted that his actions were legal. Neither he nor the Crown, he told the Court, intended to make instructions supersede the law. He conceded that the prerogative was not to be used for injury, and he could see none in the removal of the Court. It was preposterous to believe, he stated, that the King had no power to control the government through instructions.[19] Significantly, before Hutchinson could defend the prerogative, he had admitted that it was to be used for the public good and that instructions did not supersede the law—two constitutional concepts dear to the leaders of the Court. Since Hutchinson still refused to show his instructions to the Court, the house resolved by a vote of ninety-six to six that the removal from Boston was an injury to the province and necessitated the Court's continued refusal to do business. The house further resolved that all future election writs contain the words "TOWN-HOUSE AT BOSTON."[20]

Admitting his chagrin at the size of the vote, Hutchinson tried to explain that he had acted as an obedient servant of the Crown. He reminded his opponents that, as speaker of the house in 1747, he had cast the deciding vote on a bill to rebuild the Town House in Boston after fire had destroyed the old structure. Then he had acted for his constituents, now he acted for his king. The house pounced on this boast and cited it as evidence that the lieutenant governor himself had once considered Boston the most convenient location of the Court. The house's new statement of reasons for refusing to do business further argued that, regardless of circumstances in 1747, the present attack on the liberty of the province made the Court's return to Boston imperative. The representatives had no guarantee that Hutchinson would not move them from one remote part of the province to another "till he shall have worried them into a Compliance with some arbitrary Mandate." Moreover, the province's records, located in Boston, were necessary tools for the Court's work.[21]

Frequent complaints about the inconvenience of meeting outside Boston encouraged Hutchinson to believe that the house was "giving up the claim of Right and urging only the Inconvenience" of the removal, "that they are

The Removal of the Court from Boston

silenced as to the illegality" of the meeting in Cambridge.[22] The house's messages in June, however, drew no such distinction. Instead, the representatives mounted a more systematic attack on the foundations of the royal prerogative. Hutchinson's actions, they declared, were admittedly the exercise of a discretionary power; "Such is the Imperfection of human Nature, as to render discretionary Power, however necessary, always...dangerous." They insisted that the "commons," or popularly elected branch of the legislature, ought to be as free as any other part of the government, for the "democratical Branch is at least as important to the People and the Constitution as the monarchical and the aristocratical." Hutchinson labeled this presumption an attempt to undermine the prerogative by making the house the sole judge of its exercise. At this point, the council came to the defense of the house; the Court, it insisted, valued the prerogative fully as much as did the governor because the prerogative existed for the public good. If the removal of the Court damaged the interest of the province, then it became the responsibility of the Court to so inform the governor; and it was his duty to act upon this information. The decision to return the Court to Boston, the council agreed, remained with the governor; but his only proper source of guidance was the advice of the Court. Coming to the crux of the argument, the council observed that the charter gave the governor "full power" to summon, prorogue, or dissolve the Court, and the Crown had no business interfering in the decision.[23]

The council, Hutchinson replied, obviously did not understand the concept of the public good; that principle, he observed dryly, "is the great Purpose for which Government is instituted" and not merely the license for actions of the legislature.[24] Certain that a correct reading of the charter would leave no doubt about the propriety of the Crown's actions, he solicited a favorable legal opinion from Attorney General Jonathan Sewall. The term "full power" in the charter, Sewall explained, was intended "merely to exclude all claims from any Authority within the Colony"; and it in no way precluded the Crown's instructing the governor to exercise the prerogative in a particular manner. A year later, an anonymous writer, "Aequitas," probably Sewall himself, presented the most cogent constitutional defense of Hutchinson's conduct. He sought to determine "the end and design" of the governor's office under the charter and maintained that the charter, as a grant from the King, necessarily protected the royal prerogative. Although the governor exercised some of his powers at his own discretion and others according to expressed instructions, "all acts of prerogative should be in the Governor's name...for the sake of consistency." None of the governor's executive actions, "Aequitas" insisted, were immune from royal supervision for the simple reason that the Crown retained the power to dismiss a governor. Moreover, since the King had the power to dismiss a governor who

Part I: Ideas

failed to uphold royal policy, the province would be reduced to chaos if the King were not permitted to tell a governor what was expected of him. Royal instructions did require "unlimited obedience," "Aequitas" continued, and there was nothing sinister in that requirement; such power was "no farther extensive than is necessary to relieve the King" from continual involvement in Massachusetts affairs.[25]

This interpretation of the charter by Hutchinson and Sewall convinced the house to reconsider conspiratorial implications of its removal from Boston. Samuel Adams drafted the house's message, which was presented to the governor on August 1, 1770, and reiterated the chamber's resolution not to do business for fear that the King's ministers might misuse instructions to alienate the sovereign from his people and thus violate the terms of the compact between Massachusetts and the Crown. The house did not believe, Adams wrote; that the King had ordered the removal because no correspondence had been forwarded to prove this contention. He also denounced the constitutional opinions of Hutchinson's legal advisor. According to the charter, Adams argued, not even the king-in-council could settle disputes between the branches of the provincial legislature because there was no provision in the charter for such an appeal. The opinion of the attorney general, therefore, was not binding in Massachusetts. At this point in the argument, Adams introduced the strongest use of natural law yet attempted by the Court: because there was no provision in the charter to settle this dispute, the parties involved must turn to the only standard common to all, the public good. According to Locke, he continued, the people had the right to oppose all abusive exercises of legal and constitutional prerogatives of the Crown. Because there was no place on earth to appeal such abuses, the people could only "appeal to Heaven." Adams did not think such an appeal was necessary at that time, nor did he deny that royal instructions ought to be obeyed. They would cease to be binding, however, when they injured the people. These qualifying considerations did not weaken his argument, for once Hutchinson accepted the Court's standard of the public good, there was no need to push the argument further. The governor could judge what was good for the public, since the people could always inform him of any injury to them; and Hutchinson had merely to act upon this information. Adams added that the province had gone to great expense to raise a new town house in Boston. What assurance did men have that the "next Freak of a capricious Minister will not remove the Court to some other place"? On an even more alarming note, Adams boldly claimed that the house of representatives possessed the same rights in Massachusetts as the House of Commons in Great Britain; but now he feared that these rights, and the Massachusetts charter itself, were threatened by the "the subtle Machinations, and daring Encroachments of wicked Ministers."

The Removal of the Court from Boston

These sinister figures, Adams concluded, had given the Court ample reason to resist its removal. Consider, he said, the pattern of recent intimidation against Massachusetts—extended vice admiralty jurisdiction, swarms of customs officials, the Boston Massacre. Only a vigilant legislature stood between the people and further acts of tyranny.[26]

Hutchinson accepted this challenge to constitutional debate. The Court had vigorously restated the fundamental tenets of New England political theory: the ultimate responsibility of a magistrate to serve the interests of the people, and the duty of their representatives to thwart the efforts of a magistrate who became the tool of the crown or other special interest.[27] In the light of those principles, the Court's refusal to do business was a legitimate way of compelling Hutchinson to reconsider the interests of the province and dissuading him from continuing his assaults against the public good. Hutchinson did not contradict this interpretation of the compact; rather he sought to show that this dictum was not applicable to his removal of the Court from Boston. He first reviewed the precedents for the removal of the Court, the form of the writ for summoning the assembly, and the legal opinion that he had solicited. He dismissed the Court's use of Locke's compact theory, "detached as it is from the rest of the Treatise," because he knew of "no Attempts to enslave or destroy you." Rather than be drawn into a debate on the meaning of Locke's doctrines, Hutchinson presented his own understanding of the compact between the people and the crown.[28]

The central cause of the impasse, Hutchinson declared, was that the Court considered the "charter as a Compact between the Crown and the People of the Province" and wanted "one Party to the Compact to be held and not the other." He assured the Court that by calling it into session he had fulfilled his obligations under the charter and that it was the Court which, by refusing to reciprocate and proceed with its business, had failed to meet its obligations to the province. Moreover, he argued, the Court had chosen to define the charter in a manner which placed no burdens on itself and limited only the authority of the Crown and the governor. This devious conduct, he explained, not only was damaging to the immediate needs of the province but also was openly hostile to the operation of the Crown's prerogative. The Court now appeared to Hutchinson to be claiming a novel, unlimited power to decide whether any exercise of the prerogative served the interests of the province. Behind this ambition he perceived an ominous presumption: the notion that the Crown could not compel a governor to obey its instructions. Thus, he argued, the governor was repeatedly forced to use the one power at his disposal—the very one the Court wanted to limit—that of continuing to call the Court to meet in Cambridge so long as it refused to do business and denied the force of the prerogative. Until then, he warned, "it is not in my Power to remove you to Boston . . . without a further Signification of his Majesty's Pleasure." If he were convinced, however, "that removing the court from Boston was an Encroachment upon your [the Court's] natural or constitutional Rights, I would not urge my Commission or Instructions to justify...doing it; *but I must make my own Reason and Judgment My Rule and not yours.*"[29]

In Hutchinson's view, the compact between the Crown and the people could function only if the Court relinquished its role as an enemy of the prerogative. Once the Court acquired the power to exercise final review over any use of the prerogative—once it was freed from the responsibility of persuading the governor and securing his voluntary acquiescence—then the balance of power within the province would shift dangerously toward legislative domination over the crown. Recognizing that the removal issue had revealed fresh disagreements in Massachusetts about the proper location of power within the province, Hutchinson declared that if the Court's opinion were to prevail against the position of the Crown, then "to what Purpose was this or any other Reserve in the Charter made to the Crown?" With the words ringing in the legislators' ears, Hutchinson again prorogued the Court.[30]

Proroguing the Court settled nothing. When it was summoned again to Cambridge on September 26, 1770, Hancock presented Hutchinson with the house's request to return the Court to "its ancient and legal Seat." Hutchinson ignored this request and informed the house that it had pressing business, since many provincial statutes, particularly revenue laws, had expired. His request elicited no positive response, but what Hutchinson failed to accomplish by rhetoric, he advertently achieved by obeying another one of his instructions. On orders from General Gage, Castle William, overlooking Boston harbor, was occupied by British troops. In order to protest this provocative action, the house voted fifty-nine to twenty-nine to return to business. The representatives resolved that the garrisoning of Castle William, based on instructions from London, was another unconstitutional use of prerogative power. Only for this reason, the house agreed to transact routine business and to protest, at the same time, against Gage's order. When this work was completed, Hutchinson prorogued the Court. He remarked on this temporary victory; the house had failed to impeach his conduct or force him to give up any part of the crown's prerogative.[31]

The Court met at Cambridge twice in 1771, from April 3 to 25 and from May 29 to July 5. By this time Hutchinson's appointment as royal governor was official, and during both sessions the removal controversy merged with the beginning of a fresh conflict over his new, independent salary from the Crown. In 1769, the house had provoked Bernard to remove the Court to Cambridge when it refused to provide any funds for the operation of the administration, and in Cambridge the house voted unanimously to deny

The Removal of the Court from Boston

Bernard his salary. During the impasse over the removal of the Court in 1770, the house refused to pay Hutchinson's salary and expenses as lieutenant governor. In 1771, Hutchinson withheld his assent from bills compensating him £831 for his services as lieutenant governor and from a new grant of £1,300 to him as governor. When the house demanded an explanation on April 25, 1771, Hutchinson revealed that he was receiving an independent salary from the Crown.[32] In the face of this unprecedented challenge, Samuel Adams and James Otis fell to bickering over tactics. Adams wanted the house to refuse to do business outside of Boston; Otis, on May 29, 1771, impatiently replied that the governor had the power to assemble the Court "where he pleased," and he prevailed on the house to reject Adams' motion and send a conciliatory message to Hutchinson stressing the inconvenience of sitting in Cambridge.[33] This deviation scarcely represented what one observer called "Otis's Conversion to Toryism."[34] Nor did it indicate a fundamental division among the leaders of the house over the principles at stake in the removal controversy, for by June 18, Otis, Adams, Hancock, and Speaker Cushing reached agreement on a new message to Hutchinson. The message combined, in a unified argument, the house's objections against two uses of prerogative power—the removal from Boston and the governor's new, independent salary. The governor's power to assemble, prorogue, and dissolve the Court was so great—and in the past two years had been so much abused—that "the Safety of the People requires. . . a Check" on the executive. According to the charter, the house declared, the "free Gift" by the Court guaranteed that the people could influence a governor. Now the removal from Boston and the independent salary threatened "a free Assembly" subjugated to "arbitrary Edicts and Mandates."[35] On July 5, 1771, Hutchinson prorogued the Court and kept it prorogued until April 8, 1772, thereby eliminating repetition of protests in the journal of the house against his conduct. He also warned Hillsborough that the continued removal from Boston was beginning to hurt the Crown's interests because the Boston representatives were working to prevent any compromise of the dispute which would rob them of an effective grievance.[36]

Throughout the prorogation of the Court, Samuel Adams kept the issue alive in the pages of the Boston *Gazette*. Writing as "Candidus," he reminded his readers that "the Tyrants of Rome were Natives of Rome," just as Hutchinson was a native of Massachusetts. Royal instructions, he declared, could make the charter a scrap of paper. Indeed, by relinquishing his power to the secretary of state, Hutchinson had become a "*pimp* rather than a governor." Adams warned against attempts to lull the province into "that *quietude*. . . by which *slavery* is always preceded. . . ," for the people must not sleep while their "system of free government is changing." Under the pen name of "Valerius Popicola" ("Valerius, friend of the people"), Adams sharpened

Part I: Ideas

and restated his Lockean views. He argued that if the people of a state had not consented to the authority over them, no such authority existed. If Massachusetts were part of the body politic of Great Britain, it should be consulted in its law making; if Massachusetts were a separate body politic, it should make its own laws. Adams was quickly challenged on this point. "Those who see [the royal instructions] as an infringement of our Liberties," a Hutchinson supporter retorted, "seem to look upon this province as an absolutely free and independent state. . . . But this objection will vanish when it is considered that we are not more than a subordinate province." By seeking to deny the governor any "freedom or independence" in adhering to royal instruction, the writer continued, the Court was grasping for "absolute and uncontrollable" power.[37]

The struggle returned to the legislature when the house met in Cambridge on April 8, 1772. Worried by the length and direction of the controversy, Hutchinson was conciliatory and cautious. As he explained to Hillsborough, he was determined to return the Court to Boston for reasons of convenience if the Court would refrain from questioning the Crown's prerogative to determine its meeting place. He convinced Hancock to present a petition for removal to Boston along these lines, but the motion was soundly defeated.[38] The key to the situation, Hutchinson then concluded, lay in what the house could be induced to leave unsaid in their petitions. He was, however, determined not to omit from his own pronouncements a vindication of the royal prerogative, for "if I had said nothing to them of their denying the King's authority to instruct the Governor, I think they. . . would have triumphed in having carried their Point." Whatever his views on the prerogative, Hutchinson sincerely desired an end to the impasse. In early June 1772, in an interview with Hancock and Speaker Cushing, Hutchinson advised them that he would act upon any petition from the house which did not deny the King's authority to instruct the governor. He promised to overlook any other "frivolous objections" which the house might "insist upon. . . to save appearances," such as the inconvenience of meeting in Cambridge, the obligation of the governor to be guided solely by the public good, "and the like." According to Hutchinson's version of the interview, Hancock and Cushing agreed to these terms but warned that Samuel Adams might try to upset the arrangement by insisting on a denunciation of the prerogative. Hutchinson endorsed this strategy and cautioned them against Adams' "art and insidiousness."[39]

To no one's surprise, Adams did induce the house to insert into its address the accusation that the removal of the Court to Cambridge had been unnecessary. Hutchinson asked only for a clarification of the veiled accusation. The house replied that its message was sufficiently clear and required no explanation. Hutchinson could not retreat from this semantic dispute;

The Removal of the Court from Boston

"what appears to you to be sufficiently plain," he countered, "appears to me to be doubtful and equivocal." He could not determine with certainty whether the message denied the prerogative of the Crown to instruct the governor. But Hutchinson believed that Adams had outwitted him. Many representatives, he feared, were unaware that their message might be construed as questioning the prerogative, and they would accuse him of breaking his promise to return the Court to Boston if the house would ask him to do so solely for reasons of convenience. Pressed by his own supporters to act expediently, Hutchinson kept the house sitting for ten days and then summoned the council. He asked its members whether they considered the return of the Court to Boston to be consistent with the governor's obligations to the King. As Hutchinson anticipated, the council agreed that the step was legal, and the Court was recalled to Boston. Thus two years of conflict ended on an undecisive note. The Court was jubilant, but Hutchinson wrote to John Pownall that he had "Manifested to the people of the province" his "strict regard to the king's instructions," which he felt would strengthen him in his future contests with the Court.[40]

The controversy over the removal of the Court from Boston was at once an illuminating and perplexing episode in pre-Revolutionary Massachusetts politics. It was, clearly enough, one of the last of a long series of colonial protests against the use of royal instructions as a legal basis for harassment of a refractory assembly. The resourcefulness of Hutchinson and Bernard in interpreting the instructions in the most opportunistic manner and in defending their legality with painstaking precision underscores Leonard W. Labaree's contention that by the 1770s the instructions, even in the hands of an able governor, were archaic, inflexible methods of imperial administration.[41] Moreover, the controversy was almost certainly the major cause of the grievance in the Declaration of Independence accusing the King of calling "together legislative bodies at places unusual, uncomfortable, and distant from the repository of their public records for the sole purpose of fatiguing them into compliance with his measures."[42]

The struggle further modifies the deceptive appearance that the years 1770–1772 were a period of quiet in Massachusetts when resistance against British authority nearly collapsed.[43] Though it lacked the violence and explosive polemics of protests in the 1760s, the controversy over the removal of the Court revealed continuing and unresolved tension between British and colonial concepts of liberty and order. However, while the characterization of the early 1770s as a *quiet period* fails to account for that tension and consequently overlooks its potential for further political turmoil, it does rest upon some undeniable evidence. Boston's activist politicians did become increasingly divided over tactics in 1771 and 1772.[44] These disagreements influenced the later stages of the removal controversy in May 1771 when the

Court proceeded to do business despite Samuel Adams' objections and, a year later, when Hancock and Cushing negotiated secretly with Hutchinson. While his use of these differences was a tribute to Hutchinson's tenacity and skill, he knew that he could extract only limited advantage from his opponents' differences over tactics; and when the house only partially muted its attacks on the prerogative in June 1772, he seized the opportunity to be done with the dispute. On balance, then, the controversy might well appear to have reached its climax in August 1770 and, thereafter, to have become a stalemate for nearly two years while both Hutchinson and the Court searched for the terms of a face-saving but inconclusive retreat from positions each had unwisely chosen to defend. It might also appear that the Court protested its removal from Boston because it had no serious grievances left to agitate after nonimportation collapsed in October 1770.

Beneath this appearance of indecisiveness and triviality, however, the removal controversy was a protracted, serious inquiry into the nature of the prerogative. The development of the debate forced both of the participants to define more precisely their responsibilities and the principles which each believed should govern the use of power in provincial affairs. The most striking quality of the controversy—the extraordinary amount of time and effort expended on a relatively minor issue—is itself an important clue to the essential meaning of the dispute. The Court, torn between a traditional and novel mode of resistance,[45] preferred to construct an unsystematic set of tangible precedents. Its tenacious clinging in its messages to phrases like "according to usage" and "ancient and legal seat" emphasized the preservative, traditional sources of the Court's favorite ideas. Hutchinson's tenacity in rebutting these specific arguments, and the alarming implications of his version of prerogative power, compelled the Court to formulate a more comprehensive justification for resistance. The Court first argued that the removal was an attempt to give the instructions the force of law in Massachusetts, and then it discovered the more sinister intention of the crown to emasculate the assembly's will to resist other encroachments.

Hutchinson contributed substantially to this heightened awareness of the implications of the prerogative. His defense of it was a frightening recital, all the more because his dry, legalistic style was at once precise and suggestive. Unintentionally but vividly he depicted an intimate and constant communication between the ministry and the governor and a pervasive influence that was as far-reaching as a governor's receptiveness and malleability would allow it to become. This notion of the prerogative corresponded exactly with the conception of power which Bernard Bailyn has found in pre-Revolutionary ideology where "most commonly the discussion . . . centered on its essential aggressiveness: its endlessly propulsive tendency to expand itself beyond legitimate boundaries."[46] The Crown's attempt to punish Boston by removing the Court and, to a greater extent, Hutchinson's com-

The Removal of the Court from Boston

pelling demonstration of the political processes at work forced the Court to move beyond the defensive appeal to precedent and to articulate more fully than at any previous time the vague but sweeping doctrine that the prerogative could be used only to serve the public good, that the public good was equivalent to the happiness and security of the people, and that only the people's representatives could determine when their happiness and security were served or endangered. That idea was dynamic and contagious. New exercises of the prerogative starting in 1771—independent salaries, the garrisoning of Castle William, and Hutchinson's refusal to assent to a law which would have taxed Crown officials[47]—provoked the court to borrow extensively from the 1770 debates in order to construct, from traditional practice and the theory of compact, a new set of limitations on the use of the prerogative.

In early 1773, Hutchinson and the Court again debated a basic constitutional question—the extent of Parliamentary power—in their celebrated clash over the Boston Resolves. The removal controversy may have influenced that debate by conditioning both sides to eschew peripheral differences and to proceed at once to the heart of their disagreement about the meaning of the British constitution. Certainly the removal controversy reinforced the predisposition among public men in pre-Revolutionary Massachusetts—and during a period of constitutional strife—to conceive of institutions as players in a moral drama. Hutchinson regarded the removal as virtuous, disinterested discipline by the Crown of a willful colonial assembly; the Court questioned the virtue of any exercise of imperial authority which was based on such lofty presumptions. Some of the participants seemed to sense that the exposure of political evil and the execution of prudent countermeasures was an uncertain undertaking. For, as the dispute ended, an anxious undercurrent appeared in some of their assessments of the outcome. Hutchinson must have felt a sharp twinge of doubt when he predicted that the Court, in forthcoming battles over independent Crown salaries, would remember and respect the tenacity he had shown during the removal controversy. Likewise, Councillor James Bowdoin may have betrayed a certain nervous exhilaration as well as jubilance when he declared in October 1772 that "the removal of ye General Assembly to Boston, as well as from it, has proved alike ineffectual to bring them to an acquiescence with ministerial measures. The air of Cambridge & of Boston is equally unsuitable" to affect the vision of Massachusetts representatives.[48]

---

1. Previous treatments of the removal of the Court include Robert E. Brown, *Middle-Class Democracy and the Revolution in Massachusetts, 1691–1780* (Ithaca, N.Y., 1955), pp. 269–92; John Cary, *Joseph Warren: Physician, Politician, Patriot* (Urbana, Ill., 1961), pp. 101–2; Clifford K. Shipton, *Sibley's Harvard Graduates: Biographical*

Part I: Ideas

Sketches of Those Who Attended Harvard College. . . (14 vols., Boston, 1933–   ), vol. 8, pp. 188–91; John F. Burns, *Controversies betwen Royal Governors and their Assemblies in the Northern American Colonies* (Boston, 1923), pp. 195–210; John C. Miller, *Sam Adams: Pioneer in Propaganda* (Boston, 1936), pp. 242–53; Thomas Hutchinson, *The History of the Colony and Province of Massachusetts-Bay,* Lawrence Shaw Mayo, ed. (3 vols., Cambridge, 1936), vol. 3, pp. 202, 242, 256; Douglass Adair and John A. Schutz, eds., *Peter Oliver's Origin & Progress of the American Rebellion: A Tory View* (San Marino, 1961), pp. 99–100; Lawrence Henry Gipson, *The British Empire before the American Revolution* (14 vols., New York, 1958–1968), vol. 12, pp. 43–44. For a convenient collection of some of the major documents in the controversy, see Hutchinson, *History of the Colony and Province of Massachusetts-Bay,* vol. 3, pp. 370–404.

2. Lord Hillsborough to Francis Bernard, July 30, 1768, March 24, 1769, Instructions to Provincial Governors of Massachusetts, transcripts, vol. 8, pp. 2422–27, 2439–40 (Massachusetts Historical Society, Boston); *Journal of the Honorable House of Representatives of His Majesty's Province of the Massachusetts-Bay, in New England, Begun and Held at Boston, in the County of Suffolk, on Wednesday the Thirty-First of May, Annoque Domini, 1769* (Boston, 1769–1770), pp. 20, 56–60, 80–87; Bernard to Hillsborough, Aug. 6, 1768; Bernard to Richard Jackson, April 8, 1769; Bernard to John Pownall, April 23, 1769; Bernard to Hillsborough, May 15, 1769, Francis Bernard Papers, vol. 7, pp. 19–23, 163–66, 274–76, 282–85 (Harvard College Library, Cambridge). Quoted by permission, Harvard College Library.

3. Hillsborough to Thomas Hutchinson, Dec. 9, 1769, Instructions to Provincial Governors, VIII, 2449; Hutchinson to Thomas Gage, Feb. 25, 1770, Hutchinson Letterbooks (Massachusetts Historical Society, transcripts), Massachusetts Archives, vol. 26, pp. 445, 448 in Boston, where two regiments of British troops were stationed at the end of 1769.

4. Bernard to Hutchinson, Dec. 5, 1769, Bernard Papers, vol. 8, pp. 28–30.

5. Hillsborough to Hutchinson, July 6, 31, Aug. 4, 1770, Instructions to Provincial Governors, vol. 8, pp. 2462–64, 2467, 2469.

6. Hutchinson later alluded to a "conditional" instruction superseding the July and August 1770 dictates (Hutchinson, *History of the Colony and Province of Massachusetts-Bay,* vol. 3, p. 243), probably the instruction of July 3, 1771 (Instructions to Provincial Governors, vol. 8, pp. 2543–44). In June 1771, he had considered returning the Court to Boston, but the house's message of June 19, 1771, which attacked the prerogative, forced him to change his mind. Hutchinson to Israel Williams, Dec. 2, 1771, Israel Williams Papers (Massachusetts Historical Society, Boston). It is unclear from the letter to Williams whether the message of June 19 provoked the crown to rescind Hutchinson's discretionary authority or whether the July 3, 1771, instruction subsequently convinced him that the house's message eliminated, for the time being, conditions under which he could use his discretion. No further instructions which indicated the extent of his discretion have been found except one drafted ten days before he finally summoned the Court to Boston. It was received too late to have affected that decision. It referred to unspecified "Conditions upon which you *alone* are authorized to assemble" the Court at Boston (Instructions to Provincial Governors, vol. 8, pp. 2565–66) and probably noted the terms of the July 3, 1771, instruction. See also Hutchinson's "Account and Defense of his conduct and actions in Massachusetts, 1764–1774," pp. 4–7 (Massachusetts Historical Society, Boston).

7. Peter Orlando Hutchinson, comp., *The Diary and Letters of His Excellency Thomas Hutchinson* (2 vols., London, 1883–1886), vol. 1, pp. 525–26.

The Removal of the Court from Boston

8. Instructions to Provincial Governors, vol. 8, p. 2428; Bernard to Hutchinson, Dec. 5, 1769, Bernard Papers, vol. 8, pp. 28–30.

9. Malcolm Freiberg, "How to Become a Colonial Governor: Thomas Hutchinson of Massachusetts," *Review of Politics,* 21 (Oct. 1959): 655–56; Hutchinson to Pownall, March 21, 1770; Hutchinson to Pownall, June 8, 1770, Massachusetts Archives, vol. 26, pp. 464, 502–03, and Boston *Gazette,* June 19, 1775; Hutchinson to Bernard, March 25, 1770, Hutchinson Letterbooks, vol. 26, pp. 471–72, and Boston *Gazette,* June 5, 1775.

10. Hutchinson, *History of the Colony and Province of Massachusetts-Bay,* vol. 3, p. 243; Hutchinson to Pownall, July 27, 1770, Massachusetts Archives, vol. 26, p. 524; Hutchinson to Thomas Whately, Oct. 3, 1770, ibid., vol. 27, pp. 11–12, 21.

11. The Harvard Corporation soon complained that the use of the College for so controversial a purpose encroached upon the independence of the institution; only after Hutchinson's adroit intervention with the Board of Overseers, of which he was a member, did that body decline by a vote of eight to seven to make a similar protest. Harvard Corporation to Hutchinson, May 3, 1770; Hutchinson to Harvard Corporation, May 14, 1770, Miscellaneous Manuscripts, vol. 13 (Massachusetts Historical Society, Boston); Hutchinson to Hillsborough, May 3, 1770, Massachusetts Archives, vol. 26, pp. 476–77; Samuel Eliot Morison, *Three Centuries of Harvard, 1636–1936* (Cambridge, Mass., 1946), pp. 136–37. For Hutchinson's comments on the meeting of the overseers on May 1, 1770, see transcript, UA II, 27.70, Harvard University Archives; Hutchinson to Bernard, May 3, 1770, Massachusetts Archives, vol. 25, pp. 416–17; Shipton, *Sibley's Harvard Graduates,* vol. 10, pp. 149–50.

12. *Journal of the. . . House of Representatives of. . . Massachusetts-Bay. . . 1769,* pp. 90–97.

13. Ibid., pp. 97–99; Massachusetts *Gazette,* March 29, 1770. The issue was debated further in "Verus," Massachusetts *Gazette and Boston Weekly News-Letter,* May 16, 1771, and [Benjamin Prescott] *A Free and Calm Consideration of the Unhappy Misunderstandings and Debates. . . Between. . . Parliament and. . . Colonies* (Salem, Mass., 1774), pp. 50–51.

14. *Journal of the. . . House of Representatives of. . . Massachusetts-Bay. . . 1769,* pp. 99–102.

15. Ibid., pp. 139, 178–81.

16. *Boston Town Records, 1770 through 1777* (Boston, 1887), 27–32. John Cary, *Joseph Warren,* 101, identified Quincy as the author of the legal arguments in the resolves. William Blackstone, *Commentaries on the Laws of England* (4 vols., Philadelphia, 1771–1772), vol. 1, p. 252. Quincy did not identify Blackstone as the author of this quotation, but merely referred to "our lawbooks"; the quotation is correct. Blackstone credited the definition to Locke— *"For Prerogative is nothing but the Power of doing publick good without a Rule."* See Peter Laslett, ed., *John Locke: Two Treatises on Government* (Cambridge, Eng., 1960), p. 396.

17. Hutchinson to [?], May 22, 1770; Hutchinson to Bernard, March 25, 1770, Massachusetts Archives, vol. 26, pp. 489–90, 471–72.

18. *Journal of the Honorable House of Representatives of His Majesty's Province of Massachusetts-Bay in New-England, Begun and Held at Harvard-College in Cambridge in the County of Middlesex, on Wednesday the Thirtieth Day of May, Annoque Domini, 1770* (Boston, 1770–1771), pp. 6–7.

19. Ibid., pp. 12–13.

20. Ibid., pp. 6–7, 10–11, 15–22.

21. Ibid., pp. 23–32. In 1729–1730, the house met variously at Cambridge, Salem, Roxbury, and George Tavern on Boston Neck, and in 1737 at Salisbury from Au-

gust 10 to October 20; it is interesting to note that in 1637, at the height of the Antinomian controversy, John Winthrop managed to have the General Court removed from Boston, which was the center of Anne Hutchinson's supporters, to Newton (later Cambridge), where he regained the office of governor by defeating Mrs. Hutchinson's ally, Sir Henry Vane.

22. Hutchinson to Pownall, May 30, 1771, June 8, 1770; Hutchinson to Hillsborough, June 8, 1770; Hutchinson to Thomas Hood, June 8, 1770, Massachusetts Archives, vol. 27, p. 174, vol. 26, pp. 502-3, 504. At this point Hutchinson, deeply involved in efforts to secure a delay of the Boston Massacre trials, commented that "a jovial celebration of the Festival at Boston in opposition to me for carrying the General Court to Cambridge" had "diverted" public attention away from radical demands for an immediate trial of Captain Preston and his soldiers. The unusually sarcastic tone of that remark suggests, however, that at this time Hutchinson did not really minimize the seriousness of the removal controversy. L. Kinvin Wroth and Hiller B. Zobel, eds., *Legal Papers of John Adams* (3 vols., Cambridge, Mass., 1965), vol. 3, p. 12.

23. *Journal of the... House of Representatives of... Massachusetts-Bay... 1770*, pp. 25-31, 32-37, 39-43.

24. Ibid., pp. 49-51.

25. Ibid., pp. 58-59. The relevant passage in the charter stated: "the Governour ...shall have full power and Authority from time to time as he shall Judge necessary to adjourne Prorogue and dissolve all Great and General Courts or Assemblyes met and convened as aforesaid." Francis N. Thorp, ed., *The Federal and State Constitutions, Colonial Charters and other Organic Laws... 1492-1908* (7 vols., Washington, 1909), vol. 3, p. 1879. "Aequitas," Massachusetts *Gazette and Boston Weekly News-Letter*, July 18, 1771. See also "Constitutionalists" and "Publius," ibid., Feb. 21, May 23, 1771; Catherine B. Mayo, ed., *Additions to... Hutchinson's History of Massachusetts Bay* (Worcester, 1949), p. 39.

26. *Journal of the... House of Representatives of... Massachusetts-Bay... 1770*, pp. 63-71; Harry Alonzo Cushing, ed., *The Writings of Samuel Adams* (4 vols., New York, 1904-1908), vol. 2, pp. 19-35.

27. For a searching analysis of New England Lockean sermons on restraining the magistrate, see Richard Buel, Jr., "Democracy and the American Revolution: A Frame of Reference," *William and Mary Quarterly*, 21 (April 1964): 169-70.

28. *Journal of the... House of Representatives of... Massachusetts-Bay... 1770*, pp. 58-61, 73-78.

29. Ibid. (italics added).

30. Ibid.

31. Brown, *Middle-Class Democracy*, 275-76; *Journal of the... House of Representatives of ...Massachusettrs-Bay...1770*, pp. 80-82, 85-87, 89-91, 97-99, 170-82. Henry Young Brown to Hutchinson, Nov. 28, 1770, Massachusetts Archives, vol. 25, pp. 453-54.

32. Gipson, *The British Empire before the American Revolution*, vol. 12, p. 44.

33. *Journal of the... House of Representatives of... Massachusetts-Bay... 1769*, pp. 20, 42; *Journal of the Honorable House of Representatives of His Majesty's Province of Massachusetts-Bay in New England, Begun and Held at Harvard-College in Cambridge in the County of Middlesex, on Wednesday the Twenty-Ninth Day of May, Annoque Domini, 1771* (Boston, 1771-1772), 242; Shipton, *Sibley's Harvard Graduates*, vol. 11, p. 282.

34. A remark by John Chandler, quoted in John Adams' diary, entry for June 2,

The Removal of the Court from Boston

1771, L. H. Butterfield and others, eds., *Diary and Autobiography of John Adams* (4 vols., Cambridge, Mass., 1961), vol. 2, p. 20.

35. *Journal of the. . . House of Representatives of. . .Massachusetts-Bay. . .1771*, pp. 62–64.

36. Ibid., 177; Hutchinson to [?], June 5, 1771; Hutchinson to Hillsborough, June 22, 1771; Hutchinson to Pownall, June 22, 1771; Hutchinson to Jackson or Whately [?], July 19, 1771, Massachusetts Archives, vol. 27, pp. 180–81, 188–89, 197–98.

37. "Candidus," Boston *Gazette*, Sept. 9, 23, 30, Oct. 14, 1771; "Valerius Popicola," ibid., Oct. 28, 1771; Miller, *Sam Adams*, p. 253; Cushing, *Writings of Samuel Adams*, vol. 2, pp. 204–12, 222–29, 237–45, 256–64; "Chronus," [Henry Caner] Massachusetts *Gazette and Boston Weekly News-Letter*, Jan. 2, 1772.

38. *Journal of the. . . House of Representatives of. . .Massachusetts-Bay. . .1771*, pp. 119–20; Samuel Adams to James Warren, April 13, 1772, Massachusetts Historical Society, *Collections*, 72 (Boston, 1917), 10–11. For Hutchinson's strategy prior to the session, see his letters to Pownall, Oct. 14, 1771, and to Hillsborough, March 12, 1772, Massachusetts Archives, vol. 27, pp. 240, 301–2.

39. Hutchinson to Hillsborough, April 10, 1772, Massachusetts Archives, vol. 27, pp. 315–16; Hutchinson to Pownall, June 15, 1772, Massachusetts Historical Society, *Proceedings*, 19 (Boston, 1881–1882): 138.

40. Hutchinson to Pownall, June 15, 1772, Massachusetts Historical Society, *Proceedings*, vol. 19, p. 138; Hutchinson to Hillsborough, June 15, 1772; Hutchinson to James Gambier, June 30, 1772, Massachusetts Archives, vol. 27, pp. 344, 354–55; Hillsborough to Hutchinson, Aug. 7, 1772, Instructions to Provincial Governors, vol. 8, pp. 2568–69.

41. Leonard Woods Labaree, *Royal Government in America: A Study of the British Colonial System Before 1783* (New Haven, Conn., 1930), pp. 446–48.

42. On two other occasions during the reign of George III, an assembly was removed from its traditional seat—in South Carolina in 1772, when the Commons House was moved from Charleston to Beaufort during the Wilkes fund controversy, and again in Massachusetts in May 1774, when General Gage, Hutchinson's successor, removed the Court in Salem. See Jack, P. Greene, "Bridge to Revolution: The Wilkes Fund Controversy in South Carolina, 1769–1775," *Journal of Southern History*, 29 (Feb. 1963): 37; Gipson, *The British Empire before the American Revolution*, vol. 12, p. 150. Of these disputes, the 1770 removal of the Court was by far the most widely known. It was discussed in Boston in 1775, when some of Hutchinson's stolen correspondence relating to the affair was published. See Boston *Gazette*, June 5, 1775. When Hutchinson read the Declaration of Independence, he assumed that it referred to his removal of the Court; and his wry *Structures upon the Declaration of the Congress at Philadelphia* (London, 1776), pp. 14–15, asked how the Court could have been "fatigued" while idly refusing to do business.

43. See John C. Miller, *The Origins of the American Revolution* (Boston, 1943), pp. 315–25.

44. Cary, *Joseph Warren*, pp. 98–113.

45. The same ambivalence is discussed in Richard D. Brown, "Massachusetts Towns Reply to the Boston Committee of Correspondence, 1773,; *William and Mary Quarterly*, 25 (Jan. 1968): 36–38.

46. Bernard Bailyn, *The Ideological Origins of the American Revolution* (Cambridge, Mass., 1967), p. 56.

Part I: Ideas

47. See Gipson, *The British Empire before the American Revolution,* vol. 12, pp. 43–47.

48. James Bowdoin to Pownall, Oct. 24, 1772, Massachusetts Historical Society, *Collections,* sixth series, 9 (Boston, 1897): 297. See the discussions of the Crown's prerogative as a source of anxiety, instability, and conflict from the 1730s to the 1750s and the moral implications of those struggles in Bernard Bailyn, *The Origins of American Politics* (New York, 1968), pp. 69–73, 136–52.

4

"THE SCANDALOUS HISTORY OF SIR EGERTON LEIGH"

"I am a down-right *Placeman*," Egerton Leigh declared in 1773. Shortly thereafter, with equal candor, Thomas Lynch, a delegate from South Carolina to the First Continental Congress, and a man of sound judgment, described him as the greatest "Rascall among all the Kings Friends."[1] That South Carolinians of Lynch's stature had come to regard the terms placeman and rascal as virtually synonymous was largely because Leigh appeared to share both roles, and his notorious quarrel over vice-admiralty matters with the merchant Henry Laurens, though not always fully understood, has long been familiar to students of early American history.[2] What has hitherto been generally overlooked, however, is that Leigh was one of the most able Crown servants in the colony prior to the Revolution and that his early achievements appeared to establish firmly his position in local society. Indeed, the contrast between this early promise and later disgrace has the fascination of classical tragedy as well as considerable historical significance.

Certainly, Leigh was not the only Crown officeholder to find the difficulties of the pre-Revolutionary period insurmountable, but his unique vantage point and qualifications made him an unusually perceptive interpreter of the forces which helped to destroy him. His career, his awareness of the political hostility which he aroused, and his introspective contemplation of his own dilemma, illustrate the complexity of loyalist motivation and, in addition, illuminate several facets of the pre-Revolutionary period in South Carolina.

In 1753, at the age of twenty, Leigh arrived in South Carolina with his fa-

Part I: Ideas

ther, the newly appointed chief justice. Doubtless under the latter's benign aegis, Leigh quickly launched a brilliant career. He began to practice law immediately and, aided by a short term as clerk of the Court of Common Pleas—a position which gave him valuable contacts among the legal profession—he rapidly built up a very successful private practice.[3] With equal speed, he accumulated public honors and offices. In January 1755 he was elected to the Commons House of Assembly by St. Peter's parish; re-elected in 1757, he retained this position until January 1760 when he took a seat on the Council.[4] In the meantime, on November 3, 1755, he was appointed surveyor general of the province. Six years later he became judge of the Charleston Vice-Admiralty Court, and in 1765 he became the attorney general.[5]

Wealth and social position accompanied his professional rise. From 1756 to 1765 his private law practice yielded between £1,000 and £1,200 sterling per year, and his official positions probably more than doubled this amount. As a result his income was among the largest in the colony.[6] Although somewhat more aggressive in acquiring offices than land, between 1757 and 1763 he accumulated grants totaling 1,800 acres, bought a 500 acre plantation on the Santee River, and purchased more than 2 acres in Ansonboro, a rapidly developing northern suburb of Charleston.[7] Moreover, in 1756 he married Martha Bremar, the daughter of Martha and Francis Bremar. The elder Martha was Henry Laurens's sister; Francis had been a merchant associate of Laurens and a member of the Commons House.[8] If the marriage to Laurens's niece did not bring immediate wealth to Leigh—which it probably did not—it did help to cement a friendship between the two men and thereby insure that for more than a decade Leigh would handle much of Laurens's legal business.[9] Leigh, a cultured man whose versatile talents included considerable ability as a musician as well as a poet and prose writer, rented a house in Charleston and furnished it with an extensive library, which soon totaled more than 800 volumes, a large organ, and a magnificent collection of paintings, including works by Veronese and Correggio.[10] The parishioners of St. Philip's elected him a vestryman, and he became a commissioner of the provincial free school in Charleston. In 1765 the local Masons elected him deputy grand master and heir apparent to the provincial grand master, Benjamin Smith, the respected speaker of the Commons House of Assembly.[11]

It was an amazing performance. In a dozen years Leigh, at the age of thirty-two, had vaulted into the very top ranks of local society. Only a fortuitous combination of circumstances could account for such phenomenal success. A relative lack of competition helped, for there was a dearth of educated men to fill public offices in the colony. Family connections certainly contributed: Egerton's father, Peter, had been high bailiff of Westminster before becoming chief justice of South Carolina. Despite later stories of misconduct as high bailiff—none of which was proved—the elder Leigh seems to have retained sufficient influence at Whitehall to further his son's advancement, and his name was usually mentioned in solicitations in behalf of the young Leigh.[12]

Hard work also furthered Egerton Leigh's career. He allocated his time carefully and therefore paid more attention to his private law practice and the lucrative duties of the surveyor generalship than he did to responsibilities which he discharged gratis, such as service in the Commons. During his term in the House he seldom appeared when attendance was voluntary, though he performed required duties conscientiously enough to become a relatively prominent figure.[13] Somewhat surprisingly, although his power to appoint deputy surveyors—and he had squadrons of them—gave him control of considerable patronage, Leigh does not appear at this time to have been interested in using this power to advance his career.[14] Perhaps he did not need to or rather aimed at goals where popular support was of little value. Certainly he succeeded in impressing men who had the political and economic power to help him. High regard for his ability and character seems to have been the most important cause of his rapid professional advancement. Governor William Henry Lyttelton's enthusiastic recommendation of him as a rising young lawyer of "unblemished reputation," not influential family connections, secured Leigh's appointment to the Council.[15] Even after the break between the two friends, Laurens continued to respect Leigh's natural ability, although he vigorously condemned his judgment and his morals. For example, during the admiralty affair Laurens, a sternly moral but shrewd judge of men, noted that "if he had resolution enough to with stand the temptations of high Life [he] would be an admirable Man." What Laurens probably realized was that Leigh had mortgaged his future income for present consumption. Nevertheless, Laurens had earlier trusted his friend implicitly. When Leigh went to England in 1764, Laurens wrote merchant correspondents there, recommending him as a worthy man "for whome I bear the highest regard" and authorizing them to lend him whatever sums he might need, up to the limits of Lauren's own credit.[16]

The Stamp Act crisis, however, triggered severe financial and political problems for Leigh. Its most immediate impact was to cut off practically all of his income for nearly six months. The inability to obtain stamps brought business in the Court of Commons Pleas to a standstill, closed the Vice-Admiralty Court, and prevented the granting of lands. But a sense of duty, or perhaps the hope of future reward, influenced Leigh more than concern over his immediate loss of income. Alone among the lawyers of Charleston in the spring of 1766 he argued against reopening the Court of Common

Part I: Ideas

Pleas without stamped paper. When Chief Justice Charles Shinner reported to the ministry on the conduct of local officials during the crisis, he censured virtually everyone except Leigh.[17] But opposition to opening the court endeared him to few. When the nature of Shinner's report became public knowledge, gossip quite naturally (and probably correctly) marked Leigh as the instigator of Shinner's accusations and dealt his popularity another serious blow. Leigh's private law practice never recovered.[18] Consequently, he became dependent upon his Crown offices for financial rewards and a sense of importance. The need to retain these pursuits therefore obsessed him, but his tenaciousness increasingly appeared to put private interest before the public welfare, thus further estranging him from the local community. In short, he was caught in a vicious circle.

The next step in Leigh's downfall was also a by-product of the Stamp Act crisis. In the spring of 1766 the commons, hoping that the Rockingham ministry might be willing to make further concessions to the colonies, undertook a comprehensive review of various problems confronting South Carolina. Leigh's recent role had made him and his offices conspicuous. Among other sources of concern, the House therefore noted that Leigh and some of his fellow royal officers held positions which were partly designed to check each other. A man who sought to occupy simultaneously all of Leigh's offices risked entangling the colony, as well as himself, in many unnecessary difficulties—Laurens warned his friend against the pitfall. The Commons House, always wary of power which did not appear properly limited, took more direct action by ordering Charles Garth, its agent in London, to ask the ministry to remove Leigh from some of his offices.[19] Leigh ignored the friendly advice, attributed the actions of the Commons purely to resentment at his conduct during the Stamp Act crisis, and mobilized his friends in London in his behalf. They apparently succeeded. Lord Shelburne, who actually sympathized with the attitude of the House, informed Garth that Leigh could not be deprived of any of his offices because no charges of misconduct had been brought against him. It was, however, a Pyrrhic victory for Leigh.[20]

In the spring of 1767 a new customs collector, Daniel Moore, a former member of Parliament for the borough of Great Marlow, arrived in Charleston and opened Pandora's box. It is possible that Moore was primarily dedicated to serving his country by tightening up the customs service in South Carolina, but it is probable that he was more interested in enriching himself by the same means.[21] At any rate, he adopted questionable practices which may have actually violated the law. Enraged local merchants responded with an avalanche of suits, complaints, and informations against him in the Courts of Common Pleas, General Sessions, and Vice-Admiralty. Within six months Moore fled to England, but not before his ac-

Sir Egerton Leigh

tivities brought into the Vice-Admiralty Court what the *South Carolina Gazette* correctly termed "as difficult causes as perhaps ever came before that court in America."[22] In all likelihood no one could have coped with them successfully. Certainly Leigh failed, although within the limits set by the desire to protect his position he tried to render just and equitable verdicts.

Four cases marked Leigh's progress into an ever-deepening morass. On June 19, 1767, he released the *Active,* a coasting vessel seized for failing to clear properly. The crux of Leigh's decision was his statement that because the navigation acts were not intended to "lay any unnecessary Restraint" on legitimate commerce, they should not be rigidly applied to intracolonial trade.[23] The decision was certainly reasonable and Leigh believed it to be praiseworthy, but officialdom thought otherwise. Concerned about the precedent which the decision might set, the Lords of the Treasury referred the matter to the British attorney and solicitor generals who considered the verdict much too lenient.[24] Leigh had overreached himself, and even before he learned of the full reaction to his decision, he realized that unless he gave more support to customs officials he would jeopardize his judgeship.[25] In the next case he therefore relied upon a technicality to acquit Moore of a charge filed by local merchants that he had demanded illegal fees. Leigh, however, believed that Moore's underhanded conduct merited a sharp reprimand.[26] The remaining cases involved the *Broughton Island Packet* and the *Wambaw,* two coasting schooners belonging to Henry Laurens, which had been seized under almost identical circumstances because they had not cleared as Moore demanded. But the ballast in the *Wambaw* was saleable; that aboard the *Broughton Island Packet* was not. The difference enabled Leigh to engineer a compromise by condemning the former vessel and releasing the latter. Moreover, Leigh neglected to declare "a probable cause of seizure," i.e., that reasonable grounds had existed for believing that the discharged schooner had been operating in violation of the law.[27] The omission opened the way for Laurens to recover his losses on the one vessel by suing for damages in the case of the other—something that Laurens's lawyers immediately recognized. Given the context of the whole affair and the fact that Leigh was an experienced judge, it is difficult to believe that his apparent oversight was unintentional.[28]

Leigh's attempt to make his compromise as equitable as possible proved to be a fatal mistake. Laurens sued George Roupell, the customs searcher who had made the actual seizure. Although Roupell had been a member of the Commons House and for nearly twenty years a respected customs official,[29] he was now unable to find a private lawyer to defend him and Leigh, as attorney general, consequently acted for his fellow Crown officer. However, as Roupell later complained to the customs commissioners, "he had left such an opening when Judge, that the attorney general could not close it

Part I: Ideas

again," and the jury awarded Laurens a judgment which Roupell was unable to pay. Nor did the temporary collector who succeeded Moore, Roger Peter Handaside Hatley, feel free to pay the sum from customs funds without the authorization of his superiors. Roupell thus faced going to jail,[30] but on June 17, 1768, Hatley deliberately delayed receiving a bond for goods already aboard the *Ann,* a large vessel belonging partly to Laurens, so that Roupell could seize it. Acting through intermediaries, Roupell then offered to release the ship if Laurens would surrender his demand for damages. Laurens refused, and Leigh faced a serious dilemma.[31] On the one hand, because local customs officials had been filing a stream of complaints against him,[32] he could not hope to retain his office unless he protected Roupell. On the other hand, because the officers had so obviously resorted to subterfuge, it was extremely difficult to justify declaring a probable cause of seizure. The problem appeared almost insoluble, but Leigh devised a rather ingenious way out. He forced Roupell to take the seldom used oath of calumny, a declaration that his actions were not motivated by malice. The bond had not been posted; the vessel was technically in violation of the law; Roupell swore that he had acted in good faith; *ipso facto* there was a probable cause of seizure; and on July 11, 1768, Leigh so certified when he discharged the vessel, noting that he had a "Strong Suspicion that there was more of design and Surprise on the part of some officers than of any intention to commit fraud on the part of the Claimant. . . ."[33]

Throughout the whole series of cases Leigh had really acted as an arbitrator and, considering the pressures upon him, a reasonably fair one. At the time many South Carolinians may have understood this, and the *South Carolina Gazette,* a newspaper not noted for its partiality to officers of the Admiralty Court, reported that the "equitable decree" regarding the *Ann* "seems to have given general satisfaction."[34] But in attempting to protect himself while extricating everyone else from their own difficulties, Leigh had succeeded chiefly in making himself vulnerable for, as Roupell put it in a complaint to the customs commissioners, "no Judge of Admiralty can make a Court of Equity of it upon all occasions, which for this year past has been the case."[35]

Laurens understood the situation as well as Roupell and was equally dissatisfied. He attacked Leigh in a pamphlet entitled *Extracts from the Proceedings of the Court of Vice-Admiralty.* Leigh defended himself with *The Man Unmasked,* a personal attack on Laurens who in turn countered with a new edition of the *Extracts* which contained an appendix in reply to Leigh. These pamphlets cannot be dismissed as mere scurrilous polemics. In a sense both Leigh and Laurens were fighting for professional and political survival. Each took the matter with utmost seriousness, and the pamphlets therefore reveal much about the men involved.

Sir Egerton Leigh

Leigh clearly expected that Laurens would understand the pressures that he was under and make allowances for them: that, given the circumstances, he had done the best he could for him and that the part of a relative and a friend was to help one through a difficult situation by remaining quiet. Knowing full well that he was vulnerable—throughout the entire proceedings he had tried to stifle complaints against his decisions—and knowing that Laurens knew this, Leigh was not only panic-stricken at being pilloried in the press, he was also horrified at Laurens's apparent ingratitude and Iago-like betrayal. He had, Leigh declared, violated their long friendship and family ties and cruelly endangered the livelihood of Leigh's wife, seven children, and mother-in-law. "Every man who reads his book, must perceive the motive," Leigh explained. "Under the specious shew of an *exalted kind of virtue,* which regards no law, no friendship, no alliances, no ties of blood," Laurens had attempted "to gain a *popular name*" and to sacrifice "the fame of a man in the meridian of his days."[36]

It was true that Laurens for various reasons had found himself out of step with a good part of the community during the early 1760's and that he realized that his conduct during the admiralty affair redeemed him in the eyes of many persons.[37] Nevertheless, in attributing Laurens's behavior to a lust for popularity, Leigh considerably oversimplified the matter. Laurens had been unfairly treated by the customs officers; the whole affair had been very expensive and time-consuming; it had forced him to postpone an intended trip to England; and he was a busy man whose attitude toward the use of time was the essence of the Puritan ethic. Equally important, while the *Ann* was loading, he left Charleston for his Georgia plantations after writing to his correspondents in England, "As I have been very attentive to the general Interest I beg you will not be under any apprehensions of mismanagement on Account of my absence. . . . " While he was gone, goods were put aboard the ship that led to its seizure. Moreover, Laurens had earlier lost his temper at Moore, who was an elderly man, and twisted his nose on a crowded street—a widely publicized episode that mortified Laurens after he had cooled down.[38] In short, he had good reason to be irate over the whole business and to feel that both his reputation as a merchant and his self-respect as a man of honor were at stake. Most important, all of these personal considerations contributed to his willingness to perform what he considered to be his duty. There can be no doubt that throughout his entire career Laurens possessed an amazingly deep commitment to the public welfare and a heroic sense of duty, though like other human beings he could interpret the one and exercise the other from his own limited vantage point. He and his contemporary South Carolinians were profoundly skeptical of the ability of fallible mortals to use power wisely. Because neither kings nor commoners were divine their power should be hedged about by proper limits. As a sin-

Part I: Ideas

gle judge in a court without a jury, Leigh's powers were potentially dangerous. That he had placed his own self-interest above his duty in failing to curb the customs officers proved that he could not be trusted with these powers. Thus self-interest and personal considerations combined to reinforce Laurens's belief that the admiralty jurisdiction as it was constituted in America invited arbitrary exercises of power. Friend or no friend, Leigh and his court had to be attacked for the sake of the commonweal.[39]

It would be a mistake to dismiss Laurens's point of view as a mere rationalization. It would be equally erroneous to see Leigh's reaction as entirely a matter of wounded feelings or of tactical maneuver designed to discredit Laurens. Fundamentally, what was at issue were two basically different conceptions of what constituted morality in a public officeholder. To Leigh morality was something personal, intimate, almost clannish. The preservation of family ties and the protection of friends took precedence over abstract considerations of right and wrong, while ingratitude was the most heinous of sins. For Laurens the priority was reversed: virtue, duty, and the common good transcended all other considerations, even the obligations of friendship and family.

Irrespective of which might be considered a higher form of ethics, Leigh's system was poorly adapted to the glare of publicity, and the episode of the vice-admiralty quarrel proved a disaster to him. Laurens made a point of demonstrating the inherent conflicts between Leigh's multiple roles which involved him at various times in the same cases as a private lawyer, as attorney general, and as judge. Roupell made the same point in complaints to the customs commissioners and succeeded where the whole Commons House had earlier failed. The ministry directed Leigh to resign either as Vice-Admiralty judge or attorney general. Leigh resigned the less lucrative judgeship and did his best to make the resignation appear voluntary, but without much success.[40] Two years later Leigh also gave up his private practice in the Court of Chancery on which he sat as a member of the Council. The reason for his action is not entirely clear, but it is worth noting that one of the parties in his last case was another Crown officer, George Saxby, the receiver general of quitrents. Perhaps Leigh was forced to resign; perhaps, remembering the admiralty affair, he thought it prudent. Whatever the reason, he did not give up much—his chancery business was already very small.[41]

More important than the loss of judgeship was the increasing isolation from the community that his declining private practice reflected. Part of his alienation was the result of his stand during the Stamp Act crisis, part came from his questionable conduct and the adverse publicity of the admiralty cases, and part was largely a matter of personality. Insecure and therefore hypersensitive, flamboyant, witty, erudite, and arrogant, he possessed an

Sir Egerton Leigh

unfortunate knack for unnecessarily irritating people. For example, while he was presiding over the cases of the merchants against Moore, a rumor reached him that the merchants had acted as a group in order to intimidate him by their combined wealth and influence. Infuriated, Leigh unleashed a barrage of sarcastic accusations before checking the accuracy of his information, which was false. Understandably, the merchants were offended.[42]

Whatever its causes, the growing hostility toward Leigh increasingly meant that his sins were magnified and his good deeds overlooked. Although by the late 1760s the road was not entirely downhill, Leigh was now so estranged from the local leaders that his minor triumphs—unlike his earlier successes—often appeared to be victories of an outsider, achieved at the expense of the community. While still judge, he had responded to complaints against supposedly exorbitant charges in the Vice-Admiralty Court by reducing fees, but he received little credit for his action. Conversely, although the Commons House seemed to begrudge him every penny, he forced it to more than double the salary first offered to him in lieu of fees under a new court system planned for the back country. The reason for his success as a negotiator was his credible threat to secure disallowance of the act establishing the courts unless he was more adequately compensated. The price of his victory was a conviction among many South Carolinians that he did indeed put his private interest before the public welfare.[43] A success of a different kind, for which he paid a different price, was his purchase in 1767 of a fine plantation, 553 acres seven miles up the Cooper River from Charleston. Significantly, he seems to have named it "The Retreat." However, it proved to be more of a headache than a consolation. Its purchase price put a severe strain on his dwindling income and he sold it within four years.[44] Even his election as grand master of the local Masons in January 1768 was less of an achievement than it might have appeared to be, for as deputy provincial grand master since 1765 Leigh was already in line to succeed Benjamin Smith when he retired in 1767 because of ill-health.[45]

Despite these apparent successes, Leigh was only too well aware that his fortunes had suffered an amazing reversal since 1765. Quite understandably he blamed Laurens for many of his troubles, but Leigh was too intelligent not to realize that the source of his difficulties went much deeper: that the tensions of the last few years had made it impossible for Crown officers to function effectively unless they had the power to command respect. Impotent threats only brought contempt, as Leigh had painfully discovered when he futilely tried to block publication of Laurens's *Extracts* by threatening to cite him for contempt of court and sue for libel.[46] Public support made Laurens impregnable; the lack of it rendered Leigh vulnerable.

Leigh sought refuge behind the mysteries of the law. He maintained that Laurens had revealed his ignorance of the law when he had accused the

Part I: Ideas

Vice-Admiralty judge of inconsistent rulings in the cases of the *Wambaw* and the *Broughton Island Packet*. The difference between the cases, Leigh replied, was perfectly apparent to his trained legal eye. If Laurens could not see that difference, it only proved that he was "in a strange element, clearly out of his depth, perplexed by an enquiry foreign to the whole study and labour of his life." Leigh's definition of his craft involved more than mere technical knowledge and practice. Law was a calling requiring an elaborate initiation. Outsiders could never be expected to comprehend its wisdom. Laurens's attacks on Leigh only reassured him how "every departure, from the regular system to which we are bred. . .from that track which nature or our parents chose for us. . .will only involve us in a. . .perplexity of inextricable mazes."[47] Leigh's plea for the higher wisdom of lawyers revealed major weaknesses which he most wanted to disguise. In his eyes, indecision became judicial deliberation. The contempt with which men viewed his conduct became the ignorance of laymen about legal processes. The widespread sympathy among South Carolina leaders for Laurens's plight became blindness to Leigh's right as a royal official to deference and respect.

Laurens's criticisms, Leigh argued further, were not merely personal differences; they undermined the whole structure of law and the administration of justice. Sheltering himself within legal tradition, he tried to explain how judicial processes worked. The king was the source of justice, distributing it through the realm through the work of judges, all fallible men. The system of appeal—as well as precedent and procedure—served to correct judges' human errors. Inevitably, he explained, defeated parties accused the judge of bias. When they did so, they set themselves above the law and subverted the constitution. Attacks on judges endangered the community because slandered jurists had no means of retaliation. Laurens, Leigh concluded, misunderstood both the relation between the courts and society and the actual merits of his own case. Actually, he had been treated very well, Leigh observed. He therefore had no real grounds for complaint, and his accusations were "wild, inconsistent, irregular, and strange."[48]

In the final analysis, however, Leigh's defense rested on a plea that his professional dignity entitled him to a special construction of his actions. "When seizures are made," he explained, "the [Vice-Admiralty] judge is presumed to be totally indifferent to the parties in the dispute; charity supposes likewise that he is influenced only by his sense of duty."[49] If he had made errors, they were errors of judgment, not of evil intent. Brought before the bar of public opinion, he could, in effect, only avow that his intentions had been good and plead for mercy. For a proud and sensitive man such impotence must have been a humiliating, frustrating experience.

What was so galling was that he could not bring most South Carolinians

Sir Egerton Leigh

to recognize his own wise and constructive propensities. The trouble seemed to be that most persons did not understand the principles of human behavior. Men were difficult to analyze because they were a "mixture of so much *goodness* and so much *baseness*...a compound of opposite *qualities, humours,* and *inclinations.*" When faced with this problem, the average man, Leigh believed, simply counted a person's good and bad qualities, deducting one total from the other "as we do in vulgar arithmetic." Leigh proceeded differently: "I...sift out...the first ruling principle of the man, and then...carry in my eye his leading passion, which I separate from the other parts of his character, and then observe how far his other qualities, good and bad, are brought to support *that.*"[50]

Recognition from the Crown, he hoped, would help him command respect because it would compel men to take seriously his "leading passion" of service to the King and thereby dissuade them from simply compiling his alleged misdeeds. Perhaps the triumph of a peerage could redeem everything. In the spring of 1771 he therefore set sail for England where he pestered the King's advisor, the Earl of Rochford, to recommend him. Receiving little encouragement, he finally resorted to a presumptuous maneuver. He told Rochford that if the King did not grant him a royal honor before his ship sailed for South Carolina in ten or twelve days, he would then return to Charleston "under a patient Expectation that Royal Favour will be extended to me in due time." The twelve days passed without a summons from the palace, but Rochford did not disabuse Leigh of the presumption that he could force the King's hand in this manner. Six weeks later, on September 14, 1772, George III granted his hard pressed servant a baronetcy, though not a peerage.[51]

While in England Leigh also seems to have received other favors. At least he made pregnant a girl in his household, an orphan who was his own ward, his wife's sister, and Henry Laurens's niece. Who seduced whom is a question that will probably always remain unanswerable.[52] Nevertheless, two points can and should be made. First, a kind of poetic injustice was involved: Leigh believed that Laurens had attempted to destroy his reputation and had thereby violated family ties, while Leigh's incestuous conduct violated family ties and struck at the reputation of Laurens's family. Second, Leigh's attempts to hide the affair were astonishingly clumsy. He and the girl returned separately to South Carolina. When her time to deliver was near, he put her aboard a vessel bound for England whose captain was an acquaintance of Laurens. Although Leigh enjoined the girl under threat of dire penalties not to contact her uncle, it seems almost incredible that a man of his intelligence did not realize that Laurens would learn of the affair. Indeed, Laurens himself realized as much when he wrote, "Nothing is too

Part I: Ideas

Wicked for him to *attempt*, even when Detection and Judgement are at his Threshold—He is the most Wicked Man and the greatest Fool that ever I heard or Read of, in a Man of tolerable Education and Sense."[53]

Not only Laurens but all of Charleston soon discovered what had happened. Before the vessel was out to sea the girl went into labor. When the captain attempted to put her ashore, Leigh prevented it. She gave birth with no midwife in attendance, and the baby died within the week. Laurens termed it murder and suspected that Leigh had hoped that without proper care the mother would die as well.[54]

Whether or not Laurens's suspicions were justified, Leigh's conduct was indefensible, and he became a social pariah, reduced to associating chiefly with Fenwick Bull, another recently fallen Crown officer who had been horsewhipped and ostracized for attempting to bribe a jockey into fixing a horse race.[55] No baronetcy could help Leigh now—it could only further disgust South Carolinians with the administration that appeared to honor him. (Laurens correctly suspected that Leigh had probably purchased his title, but by this point in the pre-Revolutionary controversy, most colonial observers simply regarded the title as a genuine expression of the Crown's esteem for Leigh.) Thus John Adams recorded in the diary which he kept during the First Continental Congress: "He [Thomas Lynch] entertained us with the scandalous History of Sir Egerton Leigh—the Story of his Wife's Sister, . . . and all that. There is not says Lynch a greater Rascall among all the Kings Friends. He has great Merit, in this Reign."[56]

Whatever merit he possessed, Leigh had become ineffectual, and—certainly in South Carolina—a positive liability as a servant of the Crown. Although the powers and prestige of the Council had been waning for more than a decade, it had been a consistent source of support for royal officers who tried to uphold imperial measures. When Leigh became the senior member and president, the Council and its measures were identified with a man who was already considered to be beyond the pale. Moreover, because he led the upper house into imprudent, if not irresponsible, actions, there appeared to be some foundation for the charge that Council "Business is generally done by a small Junto, under the Direction of a man desperate in Fortune, abandoned in Principle, and ruined in Reputation."[57] Leigh's presidency therefore materially accelerated the complete eclipse of the South Carolina Royal Council.

The final round of the battle between the Commons House and the Council stemmed from the Wilkes fund controversy which arose in 1769 when the Commons dispatched a donation from provincial funds to the Society of Supporters for the Bill of Rights in England, a group supporting John Wilkes. Again, Leigh found himself drawn into controversies begun by other men. In 1773 he tried to take the initiative after the Crown and successive governors had failed to induce the Commons to relinquish its claim to sole control of provincial expenditures. For nearly four years the Crown had forbidden governors to assent to a tax bill unless it included a clause prohibiting the treasurer from transmitting public funds out of the province.[58] On his return from England Leigh took matters into his own hands. Acting on information supplied by Henry Perroneau, one of the public treasurers, he prodded the Council to prepare a report which blamed the depleted state of the provincial treasury on the Commons for its refusal to enact an acceptable money bill. Somewhat later, two members of the Council—John and William Henry Drayton—prepared a report criticizing the recent conduct of the upper house and, in effect, praising the Commons for its stand. The Draytons' manifesto appeared in the *South Carolina Gazette*. Infuriated at this opposition, Leigh as president of the Council ordered the arrest of the paper's printer, Thomas Powell, for violating the privileges of the upper house.[59] The Commons exploded in protest, and two local justices of the peace—both members of the Commons—immediately ordered Powell's release on the grounds that because the councilors held their positions at the pleasure of the Crown, the Council was in reality an appendage of the executive and therefore not an independent house of the legislature possessing the power of commitment for contempt. Powell and one of his supporters then sued Leigh but lost when the chief justice, a member of the Council, ruled that that body was an upper house of the provincial legislature and within its rights in enforcing its privileges.[60] But the Commons House transmitted a vigorous denunciation of the Council's actions to the ministry and most South Carolinians continued to believe that the justices of the peace had the better of the argument. As a result of its apparently unwarranted and arbitrary behavior, the Council sank even lower in public estimation.[61]

In the meantime, the Powell affair had made Leigh's own position completely intolerable. During a meeting of the upper house the volatile William Henry Drayton reportedly called Leigh a damn fool to his face—a remark which the journal does not record. It does show, however, that the members felt it necessary at this time to adopt a series of "Remembrances for Order and Decency to be kept in the Upper House of Assembly," one of which stipulated that "all personal sharp and taxing Speeches [ought to] be forborn." Worse yet, Edward Rutledge, who made his name as a patriotic lawyer by representing Powell during the proceedings, denounced Leigh unmercifully in open court. On top of all these difficulties, in the spring of 1773 the ministry ordered a temporary embargo on the granting of lands in all royal colonies, and Leigh's income as surveyor general vanished.[62] What was to be gained by remaining in South Carolina was obviously no longer worth the price. Therefore, Leigh arranged for an allowance of £500 sterling per year from James Simpson who would act as attorney general in Leigh's absence. Then, having apparently delayed his departure in an unsuccessful attempt to avoid encountering Laurens in London, Leigh sailed for England on June 19, 1774.[63]

While waiting to depart he wrote an account of political events in South Carolina and sent the manuscript to London where in January 1774 it was anonymously published as a pamphlet entitled *Considerations on Certain Political Transactions of the Province of South Carolina.* Leigh's defense of the Council and attack upon the conduct of the lower house enraged Henry Laurens, who correctly guessed the author's identity. Laurens and Ralph Izard, also then in London, therefore enlisted Izard's friend, Arthur Lee, to compose an *Answer to the Considerations on Certain Political Transactions of the Province of South Carolina.*[64]

Even Dr. Alexander Garden, who was relatively unsympathetic to the Commons in the Wilkes fund controversy, thought that Lee's *Answer* was an effective rebuttal, though he considered Egerton Leigh the better literary stylist.[65] Nevertheless, even though his position was too extreme for a future loyalist like Garden, Leigh's analysis of the situation in South Carolina was shrewd and perceptive. There was good reason for the quality of his observations. While he was a member of the Commons House it had been engaged in one of its periodic controversies with the upper house, and Leigh had served on a committee appointed to report whether or not the Council ought to be considered an upper house.[66] His service on this committee, his general experience in the Commons, and his membership in the Council gave him unusual insight into the workings of the political system in the colony. As a result, his analysis of the Wilkes fund controversy contained a highly sophisticated study of the nature of political change in South Carolina, and in particular it went to the heart of the matter in its discussion of the Commons's ascendancy from the 1720s to 1770s. Stripped of Leigh's attempts at self-justification, his pamphlet presented an analytical explanation of how the Commons House expanded its power. He took pains to delineate specific elements in the collective behavior of the assemblymen: the steady accumulation of power throughout the history of the legislature, the careful nurturing of precedents by the Commons, the tenacity with which assemblymen performed their functions and clung to their powers, the gratification they derived from the common endeavor, the absolute impasse between the Commons and the Crown which the additional instruction on provincial finance imposed on their struggle, the dependence of the Council's status as an upper house upon form rather than function, the hopeless tactical position of the Council once Powell had been released, and the supreme importance which the Council placed on its dignity after the bases for that dignity had disappeared.

Sir Egerton Leigh

As an opponent of the Commons, Leigh, significantly, acknowledged primacy of constitutional principle as a motivation of the House's actions in the Wilkes fund controversy. He based his case on the undesirability and impropriety of the Commons's extension of its fiscal powers "beyond the original. . .intention of those from whom they derive their whole authority." Every political power, he reminded the assemblymen, had in its nature some limit beyond which it ought not to be extended. The constant temptations of men "to be misled by passion, fancy, or caprice" made these limits necessary and justified the Crown and Council in opposing the Wilkes fund grant or any repetition of it.[67] Neither conspiracy nor self-interest had any central place in Leigh's indictment. Rather the Commons's action had proceeded from folly, ignorance, and childish fascination with "a *factious* Club of Men. . .at the London Tavern"—as he styled the pro-Wilkes society. Leigh readily conceded the accuracy of the Commons's body of precedents, dating back to 1737, for their power to appropriate public funds. "In order to combat these Facts," he argued, "let us. . .reflect what slow advances *Infant Societies* of Men make towards Regularity or Perfection." The feeble efforts of early provincial government to cope with its problems scarcely justified subsequent attempts by the Commons to spend public funds on any purpose whatever. These admitted "Precedents, therefore, of new Communities are of very little weight." Most early examples of spending by the Commons dealt with mundane matters like the salaries of the clergy or the encouragement of silk production.[68] By admitting the legalistic nature of the Commons's appeal to its early development, Leigh recognized the central fact about the province's political history, and he thereby deprived himself of grounds for strong rebuttal. He denounced the exercise of the Commons's power; he could not, however, deny the existence of that power.

Leigh not only comprehended the constitutional ingredients of the Commons's ascendancy; he also understood its dynamic character. The success of its efforts and the sheer pleasure of maneuver and struggle reinforced the ambitions of its members and produced "baneful effects." Noting the constant agitation of provincial politics since the Stamp Act crisis, he explained that "human nature. . .cannot bear a constant Tide of flattering Successes without becoming Insolently Saucy, and Arrogantly Vain." This emotional dimension of politics explained why the Wilkes fund controversy had proceeded from one impasse to another in "*Geometric Progression.*" As it developed, both the Commons and Council, he recalled, held tightly to their commitments. The Council insisted that as an upper house it could refuse assent to money bills, while the assemblymen remained "tenacious in their Rights as they conceived them." The additional instruction, prohibiting the governor from assenting to any money bill which did not forbid the treasurer to send money out of the province, prevented any compromise and reinforced the Council's intransigent position. The additional instruction confirmed a situation to which men on both sides were already committed. Thus the issue became "Whether the King is to recall...his Instruction; or the People submit to a check for an unconstitutional Application of the Public Treasure." "Justice as well as Prudence," he declared, "require us to yield the point." A gesture of obeisance by South Carolina, Leigh realized in 1773, was needed to restore the vigor of British authority in the province.[69]

Leigh derived his accurate assessment of the changes in South Carolina politics which, in part, had destroyed him politically and would contribute substantially to the coming of the Revolution there from the same self-centered and rigid quality of mind which blinded him to his opponents' values. He realized that the protests against the Council's arrest of Powell were also a personal attack against his exercise of the Council's power. Vainly seeking the support of Lieutenant Governor William Bull, he called the suit by Powell and one of his supporters against him "the unprecedented Insult which is intended to be cast on the Second or Middle branch of the Legislature [the Council]...for an Act done by me as President."[70] Leigh insisted that his chief motive in arresting Powell was to uphold the dignity of the Council and thereby preserve the constitution of the province. That dignity, apart from an admittedly shadowy similarity with the British House of Lords, consisted of the sacrifices made by its members. The lack of emoluments, public scorn of its proceedings, danger of arbitrary dismissal, and, now, the Wilkes fund controversy completed the sacrificial process in which Leigh took such pride. The Council, he pleaded, could not hope to maintain itself as a viable institution much longer if men in the province could publicly violate its prerogatives, if no court would enforce its decisions, and if men looked on it as an agent of oppression. "What security can such a Branch of the Legislature have," he demanded, "when...General Opinion proclaims, that a Place in Council is a kind of alienation from the concerns and interest of the People?"[71] He was incredulous that South Carolinians should consider him as alienated from their society, but at the same time he retained an especially acute awareness that in performing what he considered an honorable function in the politics of the province he had helped place himself, the Council, and the interests of the Crown directly in the way of the consuming flame of political opposition.

In part, Leigh had written his pamphlet in the hope of vindicating the Council and himself against the accusations of the Commons House. He also doubtless hoped that his performance would attract the favorable attention of the ministry, but his success was meager. Everyone was preoccupied by the chain of events that followed the Boston Tea Party and neither the *Considerations* nor its author aroused much interest.[72] Languishing in Lon-

Sir Egerton Leigh

don, he petitioned Lord Dartmouth, secretary of state for American affairs, for a position in one of the middle or northern colonies. Long residence in South Carolina, he claimed, had "so effected the state of his Nerves" that his return there would be fatal. Nevertheless, along with other councilors then in England, he was given the choice of returning or resigning his position. He resigned.[73] After the conquest of Charleston, however, he went back to South Carolina, and became a member of the military commandant's advisory council, the Board of Police, and an intendant of the city.[74] He also recommended to the ministry that civil government be reestablished as soon as possible and that, because of his experience, he be appointed governor. Neither event occurred; instead Leigh, who had been ill for some time, died in Charleston on September 15, 1781.[75]

The pathos and scandal in Leigh's career should not be allowed to obscure its historical significance. Clearly, his actions and, ultimately, his mere presence, helped to disenchant South Carolinians with imperial authorities and their policy. Eventually, through the circulation of pamphlets and by word of mouth, Leigh became notorious throughout the colonies. As a result, he contributed significantly to the growing American hostility toward the Vice-Admiralty Courts and to the increasing feeling that Great Britain and her servants were corrupt.

The obvious question, however, is how a man of Leigh's ability, to all intents and purposes firmly entrenched in local society, could have gotten himself into such a predicament. One plausible explanation might be that events beyond their control placed all Crown servants in untenable situations; another might stress Leigh's apparent immorality. Neither interpretation is quite adequate. Leigh was not merely a passive victim of forces beyond his control. Rather, as the pre-Revolutionary movement embroiled him in difficulty, he seems almost suicidally to have rushed to meet his fate. Nor was he entirely immoral. It is difficult to believe that Laurens and others would have trusted him initially if he had been an unmitigated scoundrel. Apart from his relationship with his sister-in-law—an aberration more deserving of the clinical compassion of a psychiatrist then condemnation by a historian—none of Leigh's actions could be termed iniquitous by an impartial observer. He did occasionally use poor judgment and in a few cases violated propriety—something to which he seemed oblivious. This quality of ethical obtuseness is indeed a key to explaining much of Leigh's behavior. Like his self-destructiveness, to which it was closely related, this trait manifested itself chiefly in Leigh's inability to protect an appropriate public image in a society where image and reputation mattered enormously. Being a perceptive man, he recognized that his difficulties, as well as those of other Crown officials, arose fundamentally from a lack of public support. Being something of an intellectual, he sought to resolve symbolically those dilem-

Part I: Ideas

mas which he could not resolve in actuality. So when his actual power failed him, he loved to replay the scene on paper—a medium in which he had more control. In the process, of course, he hoped that his pamphlets would vindicate him, shame his detractors, and thereby regain for him the power which he believed he deserved to possess. However, the results of his efforts were exactly the opposite of what he intended.

These attempts at self-justification were more than the self-pitying afterthoughts of a discredited officeholder. Throughout the pre-Revolutionary controversy, Leigh struggled in his own tenacious way to understand the political culture of South Carolina and, in the light of the reverses he had suffered there, to understand himself. He could not help but broadcast the conclusion that he was a uniquely gifted bureaucratic and judicial operator. His presumption to a special legal insight into matters of vice-admiralty law which was denied to laymen, his belief that only his intelligence and sense of the dramatic could save the Council from further degradation, and his conviction that attacks upon himself were attempts to destroy the institutions which he served were not only defense mechanisms. They were also expressions of his pride as a placeman and the products of his sustained effort at political analysis and self-examination. His pride and intellectual determination thus drove him to accentuate the very presumptions about himself and about British authority which South Carolinians most detested and impelled him to equate their resulting hostility with a leveling process which he alone could diagnose and denounce.

Although his approach was hardly calculated to win applause in South Carolina, Leigh was correct in realizing that profound changes had occurred in the character of local politics during the preceding quarter of a century. What he did not realize was that the dominant position of the Commons House of Assembly was associated with the development of a particular climate of opinion in which his own political instincts were unreliable. His success, and that of the family in which he was brought up, had depended on the ability to impress a small number of individuals who possessed the power to grant or withhold preferment. Ability, good intentions, and loyalty to one's patron were qualities which enabled one to navigate this political world successfully. Leigh's apologia, then, condemned ingratitude and disloyalty to family and friend as the greatest of sins; purity in those areas, he seemed to think, excused admitted lapses in judgment. Where political power was controlled by small factional groups, such a defense was at least relevant and might have been effective.

In South Carolina it was worse than irrelevant. Effective political power depended less on imperial than upon local popular support, and for nearly a generation, though the pre-Revolutionary period accelerated the trend, South Carolinians had reserved their esteem for those politicians who ap-

Sir Egerton Leigh

peared to put the public welfare above all else. Laurens, a product of the local political environment, understood this; Leigh, a product of a different system, never did. Consequently, when the tensions of the 1760s undercut the position of Crown officers, he had no effective way to protect himself. In fact, his attempts to defend himself instead of confounding his critics merely served to condemn him by his own words, for they revealed that he subscribed to a different set of political mores. Lest anyone should miss these implications, Laurens hammered the point home when he replied to the charge of family disloyalty. "As far as human Strength will assist me," he wrote, "I am never influenced in Favour of any Man contrary to the publick Good, from so poor a Consideration *only* as his *Alliance to me.*" These words could well serve as Leigh's political epitaph, for if, as he charged, Laurens was not at home in the technicalities of the law, Leigh was equally out of his element in the political atmosphere of pre-Revolutionary South Carolina.[76]

The point here is not to draw an invidious distinction between differing sets of political ethics, but rather to demonstrate that a difference did exist.[77] When rents began to appear in the fabric that bound royal officials and local leaders together into a coherent whole, it became clear that in many cases they spoke a different language. Thus attempts at communication often failed. Instead of resolving differences, moral considerations frequently accentuated them. Isolated and introspective, Leigh sensed more acutely than most of his contemporaries that this failure of communication had occurred. As a result, his writings depict the anguish of a misunderstood villain in a complex moral struggle and provide poignant, illuminating insight into facets of the personal and intellectual dilemma of many loyalists on the eve of the Revolution.

1. [Sir Egerton Leigh], *Considerations on Certain Political Transactions of the Province of South Carolina* (London, 1774), 2; entry of Aug. 31, 1774, in L. H. Butterfield, et al., eds., *The Diary and Autobiography of John Adams* (Cambridge, Mass., 1961), vol. 2, p. 118. The authors wish to thank Wylma Wates of the South Carolina Archives Department for calling their attention to the latter reference.
2. For standard treatments of this affair, see David D. Wallace, *The Life of Henry Laurens* (New York, 1915), pp. 137–49, and Oliver M. Dickerson, *The Navigation Acts and the American Revolution* (Philadelphia, 1951), pp. 224–31. Two more recent works, Thomas C. Barrow, *Trade and Empire: The British Customs Service in Colonial America, 1660–1775* (Cambridge, Mass., 1967), pp. 206–10, 234–35, and Carl Ubbelohde, *The Vice-Admiralty Courts and the American Revolution* (Chapel Hill, N.C., 1960), pp. 107–14, provide brief accounts that anticipate some points which we emphasize.
3. H. Hale Bellot, "The Leighs in South Carolina," *Transactions of the Royal Historical Society*, 5th Ser., 6 (1956): 175; Aug. 12, Nov. 6, 1754, Miscellaneous Records, KK, 76, 113, S.C. Archives Department, Columbia, S.C.; Governor William

Part I: Ideas

Henry Lyttelton to Board of Trade, Apr. 14, 1759, Transcripts of Records Relating to South Carolina in the British Public Record Office, vol. 28, p. 188, S.C. Archives. Hereafter these transcripts will be cited as Trans., S.C. Records.

4. It is not clear that at the time of his election Leigh held property in St. Peter's, a rural district relatively remote from Charleston. Indeed, on Jan. 24, 1755, he purchased the first real estate that he is known to have owned in South Carolina, two lots in Charleston, for which he paid £2,000 South Carolina currency. Less than one week later he was elected to the Assembly. It hardly seems a coincidence that the election law stipulated that a member of the Commons House must possess a freehold of 500 acres and 10 slaves or £1,000 worth of buildings, lands, or town lots. Two other men had been elected for the parish and failed to qualify; Leigh, who was elected unanimously, was therefore the third choice. In all probability, a relatively small number of voters turned to him because, as a resident of Charleston and a man of ability who was willing to serve, he represented an available candidate. See Charleston County Deeds, Vol. PP, 236–37, on microfilm at S.C. Archives; Thomas Cooper and David McCord, eds., *The Statutes at Large of South Carolina* (Columbia, S.C., 1838), vol. 3, p. 137; Nov. 13, 1754, Jan. 8, Feb. 6, 7, 1755, South Carolina Commons Journals, vol. 30, Pt. 1, pp. 28–29, 60, 62, 216–18, 226, in S.C. Archives; Oct. 6, 1757, South Carolina Commons Journals, Colonial Office Group, Class 5, Piece 474, Public Record Office; and Jan. 11, 1760, South Carolina Council Journals, vol. 28, p. 154, S.C. Archives.

5. Nov. 3, 1755, Oct. 2, 1761, Jan. 31, 1765, Misc. Records, KK, 402, LL, 405, MM, 277.

6. Egerton Leigh, Memorial to Lord Dartmouth, Mar. 2, 1775, Dartmouth Papers, II, 1174, William Salt Library, Stafford, England. Although it is impossible to give a precise figure for the worth of each of Leigh's offices, a rough idea can be obtained from the fact that James Simpson, who replaced Leigh as attorney general in 1771, claimed to have received more than £2,000 sterling per year from a private practice worth £700, the attorney generalship, and the office of clerk of the Council. The vice-admiralty position was not considered lucrative. See James Simpson's case in Examinations in London: Memorials, Schedules of Losses, and Evidence, South Carolina Claimants, American Loyalists, Audit Office Transcripts, vol. 54, p. 213, Manuscript Division, New York Public Library, New York, hereafter cited as Loyalists' Trans.; and Lieutenant Governor William Bull to Lord Hillsborough, Oct. 16, 1768, ,Trans., S.C. Records, vol. 32, p. 55.

7. In 1770 he added an additional 100 acres. See grants on May 21, 1757, Dec. 5, 1759, May 18, 1763, Nov. 9, 1770, Pre-Revolutionary Grants, vol. 8, pp. 4, 480, vol. 11, p. 62, vol. 21, p. 283, S.C. Archives; Sept. 30, 1758, July 2, 1775, Sept. 9, 1757, July 27, 1761, Charleston County Deeds, TT, 338–339, SS, 52, 114, XX, 288–291, microfilm, S.C. Archives. See also M. Eugene Sirmans, "The South Carolina Royal Council, 1720–1763," *William and Mary Quarterly,* 3d Ser., 18 (1961): 373–92.

8. Bellot, "Leighs in South Carolina," *T.R.H.S.,* 175; Joseph W. Barnwell, ed., "Correspondence of Henry Laurens," *South Carolina Historical and Genealogical Magazine,* 29 (1928): 103; the entry of Jan. 17, 1744/5, in James H. Easterby and Ruth Green, eds., *The Colonial Records of South Carolina: The Journals of the Commons House of Assembly, 1736–1750,* 5 (Columbia, S.C., 1955): 277.

9. See Laurens to Francis Bremar, March. 27, 1748, in Barnwell, ed., "Correspondence of Henry Laurens," *S.C. Hist. and Geneal. Mag.,* 31 (1930): 222, and will of Francis Bremar, May 16, 1760, Charleston County Wills, Works Progress Ad-

Sir Egerton Leigh

ministration Transcripts, vol. 8, pp. 482–83, S.C. Archives. For Leigh as Laurens's lawyer, see Henry Laurens to Lachlan McIntosh, May 19, 1763, Laurens to Elias Ball, Oct. 5, 1765, and Laurens to Inglis and Hall, Dec. 12, 1767, Philip M. Hamer and George C. Rogers, eds., *The Papers of Henry Laurens* (Columbia, S.C., 1968–), Vol. 3, pp. 454–55; Vol. 5, pp. 19, 503–4. Hereafer cited as *Laurens Papers.*

10. *South Carolina Gazette* (Charleston), Dec. 3, 1772, Feb. 28, 1771; "Historical Notes," *S. C. Hist. and Geneal. Mag.,* 11 (1910): 133–34.

11. *S. C. Gazette* (Charleston), Dec. 16, 1760; *South Carolina Gazette and Country Journal* (Charleston), Dec. 31, 1765.

12. Bull to Hillsborough, Aug. 7, 1771, Trans., S.C. Records, vol. 33, p. 80; Bellot, "Leighs in South Carolina," *T.R.H.S.,* 169–174; Lyttelton to Board of Trade, Apr. 14, 1759, Trans., S. C. Records, vol. 28, p. 188; Leigh, Memorial to Dartmouth, Mar. 2, 1775, Dartmouth Papers, II, 1174.

13. For his attendance in the House, see Feb. 7, 1755 to Oct. 13, 1759, S.C. Commons Journals, vols. 30–33, passim. On the basis of the importance and amount of committee work which he performed, Leigh reached the second rank of leadership in the 1757–1758 session, Jack P. Greene, *The Quest for Power: The Lower Houses of Assembly in the Southern Royal Colonies, 1689–1776* (Chapel Hill, N.C., 1963), p. 481. For Leigh's most important committee assignments, see March. 5, 7, Apr. 11, 12, 1755, June 22, 1756, May 16, Dec. 8, 1758, Jan. 31, 1759, S.C. Commons Journals, vol. 30, Pt. 1, pp. 293, 314, 449, 457, vol. 31, Pt. 1, p. 204, vol. 32, pp. 220 [*sic*], 38, 97–98.

14. For a listing, see entries for Leigh in the manuscript index to the Misc. Records.

15. Lyttelton to the Board of Trade, Apr. 14, 1759, Trans., S.C. Records, vol. 28, p. 188; Privy Council, June 26, 1759, ibid., pp. 201–02; Jan. 11, 1760, S.C. Council Journals, p. 154.

16. Laurens to Edwards Pierce, Mar. 31, 1773, Laurens Papers, VII, 82; Laurens to William Fisher, Aug. 1, 1768, Letters and Papers Regarding the Ship *Ann*, Etting: Large Miscellaneous Manuscripts, 24, Historical Society of Pennsylvania, Philadelphia; Laurens to Isaac King, Apr. 3, May 7, 1764, *Laurens Papers,* vol. 4, pp. 268–70; vol. 5, pp. 180–84.

17. For an account of the effects of the crisis, see Robert M. Weir, "Liberty and Property and No Stamps: South Carolina and the Stamp Act Crisis" (unpubl. Ph.D. diss., Western Reserve University, 1966). For Shinner's comments, see his report enclosed in Governor Lord Charles Montagu to the Board of Trade, May 6, 1766, Trans., S.C. Records, vol. 31, p. 134.

18. Laurens to John L. Gervais, Sept. 1, 1766, *Laurens Papers,* vol. 5, pp. 180–84. Leigh, Memorial to Dartmouth, Mar. 2, 1775, Dartmouth Papers, II, 1174.

19. June 24, 1766, S.C. Commons Journals, vol. 37, Pt. 1, p. 175; Laurens to William Fisher, Aug. 1, 1768, Letters and Papers Regarding the Ship *Ann,* 24; Committee of Correspondence to Garth, July 2, 1766, Charles Garth Letter Book, 1766–1775, 2, S.C. Archives.

20. Garth to Committee of Correspondence, Sept. 26, 1766, Jan. 31, Mar. 12, 1767, ibid., pp. 14, 25, 28.

21. *S. C. Gazette,* Mar. 23, 1767. For a brief biography of Moore—which omits his service in South Carolina—see Sir Lewis Namier and John Brooke, *The History of Parliament: The House of Commons, 1754–1790* (New York, 1964), vol. 3, pp. 160–61. For a more sympathetic treatment of Moore than ours, see Barrow, *Trade and Empire,* pp. 204–09; for a more hostile account, the South Carolina merchants' ver-

Part I: Ideas

sion of his activities, see *A Representation of Facts, Relative to the Conduct of Daniel Moore, Esquire; Collector of His Majesty's Customs at Charles-Town, in South Carolina* (Charleston, 1767).

22. Ibid., passim; Montagu to Lord Shelburne, Oct. 5, 1767, Trans., S.C. Records, vol. 31, p. 414; S.C. *Gazette*, Sept. 19, 1768.

23. "Case," Treasury Group, Class I, Piece 465, Photostats, Library of Congress.

24. Sir Egerton Leigh, *The Man Unmasked: or, The World Undeceived in the Author of a Late Pamphlet entitled "Extracts from the Proceedings of the High Court of Vice-Admiralty in Charlestown, South Carolina &c." with Suitable Remarks* (Charleston, 1769), p. 96; "Case," T. 1/465, Lib. of Cong. Photosts.

25. For complaints against Leigh, see Barrow, *Trade and Empire*, p. 318.

26. See Laurens to James Habersham, Sept. 5, 1767, *Laurens Papers*, vol. 5, pp. 292–99.

27. Ibid.

28. Laurens to George Appleby, to James Habersham, May 24, 1768, Sept. 5, 1767, *Laurens Papers*, vol. 5, pp. 687–89.

29. Feb. 26, 1755, S. C. Commons Journals, vol. 30, Pt. I, 249–50. Roupell was also an artist of considerable local renown. See Anna Wells Rutledge, "Artists in the Life of Charleston Through Colony and State to Reconstruction," *Transactions of the American Philosophical Society*, vol. 39, Pt. 2 (1949): 118–19; Carl Bridenbaugh, *Myths and Realities: Societies of the Colonial South* (Baton Rouge, La., 1952), p. 107.

30. George Roupell to Commissioners of the Customs, July 11, 1768, enclosed in Commissioners of the Customs in America to Lords Commissioners of Treasury, Aug. 25, 1768, T. 1/465, Lib. of Cong. Photosts.; May 12, 1768, Charleston County, Records of the Court of Common Pleas, 1763–1769, Works, Prog. Adm. Trans., 244.

31. Transcripts of Proceedings in the Case of the *Ann*, T 1/465, 7, 14, 16, Lib. of Cong. Photosts.; Henry Laurens, *Extracts from Proceedings of the High Court of Admiralty*, 2d ed. (Charleston, 1769), passim; Henry Laurens, *Extracts from the Proceedings of the Court of Vice-Admiralty in Charles-Town, South Carolina* (Philadelphia, 1768), 9. Items in these sources pertaining to Laurens have been published in the *Laurens Papers*.

32. For citations to this correspondence, see Barrow, *Trade and Empire*, p. 318.

33. Trans. of Proc. of the *Ann*, T. 1/465, 10, 24–25, 28, Lib. of Cong. Photosts.

34. *S.C. Gazette*, July 11, 1768. Robert Wells, the publisher of the leading rival newspaper, *South Carolina and American General Gazette*, was marshall of the Vice-Admiralty Court. See Wells's case in Loyalists' Trans., vol. 56, p. 548.

35. Roupell to Commissioners of Customs, July 11, 1768, enclosed in Commissioners of Customs in America to Lords Commissioners of Treasury, Aug. 25, 1768, T. 1/465, Lib. of Cong. Photosts.

36. Trans. of Proc. of the *Ann*, T. I/465, 25–26, 28, Lib. of Cong. Photosts: Laurens to William Fisher, Aug. 1, 1768, Letters and Papers Regarding the Ship *Ann*, 24; Leigh, *The Man Unmasked*, pp. 20–21, 27–28.

37. For Lauren's difficulties during the Cherokee War and the Stamp Act Crisis, see Wallace, *Life of Henry Laurens*, 103–06, 116–20, and Laurens to James Habersham, Sept. 5, 1767, *Laurens Papers*, vol. 5, pp. 292–99.

38. Laurens to William Fisher, Aug. 1, 1768, Letters and Papers Regarding the Ship *Ann*, p. 24; Laurens to William Cowles & Co., to Ross and Mills, to James Habersham, June 7, 1768, Oct. 8, 14, 1767, *Laurens Papers*, vol. 5, pp. 718, 335–41, 364–67.

Sir Egerton Leigh

39. Laurens to William Cowles & Co. and William Freeman, Aug. 8, 1768, vol. 6, pp. 57–61; Wallace, *Life of Henry Laurens,* passim; Laurens, *Extracts, 1st ed., passim; Laurens to William Fisher, Aug. 1, 1768, Letters and Papers Regarding the Ship Ann,* p. 24.

40. Laurens, *Extracts,* 2d ed., passim; Commissioners of Customs in America to Lords Commissioners of Treasury, Aug. 25, 1768, and enclosure of George Roupell to Commissioners of Customs, July 11, 1768, T. 1/465, Lib. of Cong. Photosts.; Commissioners of Customs in America to Lords Commissioners of Treasury, Dec. 16, 1768, T. 1/465, Lib. of Cong. Photosts.; Bull to Hillsborough, Oct. 16, 1768, Trans., S. C. Records, vol. 32, p. 54; Leigh, *The Many Unmasked,* p. 100.

41. Bull to Hillsborough, Nov. 30, 1770, Trans., S. C. Records, vol. 32, p. 376; A. K. Gregorie and J. N. Frierson, eds., *Records of the Court of Chancery of South Carolina, 1671–1779* (Washington, D. C., 1950), 577 and passim.

42. Laurens to James Habersham, Sept. 5, 1767, *Laurens Papers,* Vol. 5, pp. 92–99.

43. Mar. 16, 1768, Aug. 1, 1769, S. C. Commons Journals, vol. 37, Pt. 2, 588, vol. 38, Pt. 1, 102; Bellot, "Leighs in South Carolina," *T.R.H.S.,* p. 181; Laurens, *Extracts,* 2d ed., Appendix, pp. 20–22.

44. Henry A. M. Smith, "Charleston and Charleston Neck: The Original Grantees and the Settlements along the Ashley and Cooper Rivers," *S.C. Hist. and Geneal. Mag.,* 19 (1918): 59.

45. In Jan. 1768, before the pamphlet war with Laurens, the local lodge petitioned the Duke of Beaufort to appoint Leigh grand master; his official installation did not come until two years later. "Historical Notes," *S.C. Hist. and Geneal. Mag.,* 4 (1903): 313; *S.C. and American General Gazette,* Jan. 1, 1768; *S.C. Gazette,* Mar. 8, 1770.

46. Laurens to William Cowles & Co. and William Freeman, Aug. 8, 1768, *Laurens Papers,* vol. 6, pp. 57–61; Leigh, *The Man Unmasked,* pp. 70–71.

47. Ibid., 7–10, 40–41.

48. Ibid., 12–19.

49. Ibid., pp. 43–44, 77–89, 100–01, 122–23.

50. Ibid., pp. 19–25. The concept of a "ruling passion" was fairly common in eighteenth-century literature, but Leigh cited Laurence Sterne as the source of his own sophisticated version of the doctrine. Sterne's most famous work, and the one to which Leigh probably referred, was *The Life and Opinions of Tristram Shandy.* For an introduction to Sterne and his use of Lockean psychology, see Albert C. Baugh, ed., *A Literary History of England* (New York, 1948), pp. 1022–26.

51. Leigh to [the Earl of Rochford], July 29, 1772, State Papers, Domestic, Class 37, Piece 9, 63, and Class 44, Piece 379, 384–385, Public Record Office; Leigh's patent as baronet indicated that he had made a sizeable contribution to the Crown which was a major factor in his receipt of the honor; the patent said nothing of his service in South Carolina but commended him for contributing a sum sufficient to support thirty troops in Ulster for three years, Leigh Family Papers, CR 162/576, Warwick Record Office, Warwick, England.

52. Although the girl changed her story several times and Leigh at first denied his complicity, he eventually confessed during a face-to-face confrontation with Laurens and offered to make a monetary settlement, an offer which Laurens did not accept. Henry Laurens to Leigh, to James Laurens, Jan. 30, 1773, Sept. 15, 1774, *Laurens Papers,* vol. 8, pp. 556–63, vol. 9, pp. 559–61. Historians have always chivalrously assumed that Leigh was the aggressor; nevertheless there is reason to

Part I: Ideas

suspect that the girl was something of a hellion in her own right. See Henry Laurens to James Laurens, postscript of Feb. 10, 1772 to. Feb. 6, 1772 letter; *Laurens Papers,* vol. 8, p. 175.

53. *S. C. Gazette,* July 2, 1772, Oct. 22, 1772; Laurens to Leigh, to Edwards Pierce, Jan. 30, 1773, Mar. 31, 1773, *Laurens Papers,* vol. 8, pp. 556-63, 654-55.

54. Laurens to Leigh, Jan. 30, 1773, ibid., pp. 556-63.

55. Henry Laurens to John Laurens, Jan. 28, 1774, ibid., vol. 9, pp. 258-59. Bull, who had been a notary public and register of mesne conveyances until his disgrace, was apparently not related to lieutenant Governor William Bull; the latter was a native of South Carolina, the former of England, *S. C. Gazette,* Feb. 9, 1769.

56. Henry Laurens to James Laurens, Oct. 5, 1772, *Laurens Papers,* vol. 8, pp. 490-96; Butterfield, *The Diary and Autobiography of John Adams,* vol. 2, pp. 117-18.

57. Jackson Turner Main, *The Upper House in Revolutionary America, 1763-1788* (Madison, Wis., 1967), pp. 11-20. [Arthur Lee], *Answer to Considerations on Certain Political Transactions of the Province of South Carolina* (London, 1774), p. 60. On Leigh as a liability to the Crown by 1773, see also Marvin R. Zahniser, *Charles Cotesworth Pinckney* (Chapel Hill, N.C., 1967), p. 29.

58. Jack P. Greene, "Bridge to Revolution: The Wilkes fund Controversy in South Carolina, 1769-1775," *Journal of Southern History,* 29 (1963): 19-52.

59. S.C. Council to Bull, Aug. 23, 1773, C.O. 5/395, 117-20; Leigh's warrant for Powell's arrest, Aug. 31, 1773, Bull to Lord Dartmouth, Sept. 18, 1773, ibid., 151, 133-38.

60. S.C. Council to George III, Sept. 9, 1773, Leigh to Bull, Sept. 18, Oct. 16, 1773, ibid., 163, 179-82.

61. Sept. 8, 1773, S.C. Commons Journals, vol. 39, p. 88, Committee of Correspondence to Garth, Sept. 16, 1773, Garth Letter Book, 1766-1775, 153-54.

62. Henry Laurens to John Laurens, Nov. 19, 1773, *Laurens Papers,* vol. 9, pp. 152-54. Sept. 1, 1773, S.C. Upper House Journals, C. O. 5/478, 20; May 31, 1773, S.C. Council Journals, vol. 37, pp. 178-79; Leigh, Memorial to Dartmouth, Mar. 2, 1775, Dartmouth Papers, II, 1174.

63. James Simpson's case, Loyalists' Trans., LIV, 240; Laurens to Edwards Pierce, Dec. 65, 1773, *Laurens Papers,* vol. 9, pp. 193-94; *S.C. Gaz.,* June 20, 1774.

64. Greene, "Bridge to Revolution," p. 45.

65. Laurens to Ralph Izard, Sept. 20, 1774. *Laurens Papers,* vol. 9, pp. 565-70.

66. For an account of this controvresy, see M. Eugene Sirmans, *Colonial South Carolina: A Political History, 1663-1763* (Chapel Hill, N.C., 1966), pp. 301-09. The committee, after requesting more time to study the matter, was eventually discharged without making a final report. Nov. 25, 27, 1755, Apr. 22, 1756, S.C. Commons Journals, 31, Pt. 1, pp. 10, 15-16, 192.

67. Leigh, *Considerations,* pp. 18-20.

68. Ibid. Ian R. Christie, *Wilkes, Wyvill, and Reform: The Parliamentary Reform Movement in British Politics, 1760-1785* (London, 1962), pp. 33-49; Leigh, *Considerations,* pp. 26-27.

69. Ibid., pp. 3, 17, 30.

70. Leigh to Bull, Sept. 18, 1773, C. O. 5/395, 163.

71. Leigh, *Considerations,* p. 54.

72. Greene, "Bridge to Revolution," p. 48.

73. Leigh, Memorial to Dartmouth, Mar. 2, 1775, Dartmouth Papers, II, 1174; John Pownall to Leigh, May 16, 1775, Trans., S.C. Records, vol. 35, p. 114; Leigh to Dartmouth, June 26, 1775, Dartmouth Papers, 1339.

Sir Egerton Leigh

74. Feb. 20, 1781, Misc. Records, SS, 382–83; Miscellaneous Proceedings of the Board of Police, 1780–1781, C. O. 5/520, 62 ff.

75. Leigh to Hillsborough, Feb. 25, 1781, Trans., S.C. Records, vol. 36, p. 112; Mabel L. Webber, ed., "Death Notices from the *South Carolina and American General Gazette,* and its Continuation the *Royal Gazette,* May 1766–June 1782," *S.C. Hist. and Geneal. Mag.,* 17 (1916): 160.

76. Laurens, *Extracts,* 2d ed., Appendix, 33.

77. See also John Higham's suggestions that the Revolution be reinterpreted "as a problem in political ethics," in "Beyond Consensus: the Historian as Moral Critic," *American Historical Review,* 67 (1962): 623.

5

"I HAVE DEDUCED YOUR RIGHTS":

Joseph Galloway's Concept of His Role, 1774–1775

1

On September 28, 1774, Joseph Galloway proposed to the First Continental Congress his solution to the imperial crisis. His famous Plan of Union envisioned the creation of an American branch of the British Parliament possessing concurrent jurisdiction over all colonial legislation. Although the delegates debated the proposal and postponed further consideration by a narrow vote, Congress repudiated Galloway's cautious approach by endorsing the Suffolk Resolves, adopting non-importation, and allegedly expunging the Plan of Union from the Journal of Congress. Historians have rescued the Plan from oblivion, some fascinated by the intrinsic merit of its ideas on imperial reform and others intrigued with the light it throws on the perplexing problem of loyalist motivation.[1] Yet Galloway's writings of 1774 and 1775 have not been fully utilized, and these sources remain the best historical account of his feelings and motives. His *Candid Examination of the Mutual Claims of Great Britain and the Colonies...*[2] not only contained the first published version of the Plan of Union and Galloway's arguments in its behalf, but also denounced the constitutional arguments of his critics, diagnosed their ethical and intellectual sins, and presented a truly candid view of his own injured pride and quest for distinction. When John Dickinson and Charles Thomson, his longtime political enemies, attacked the *Candid Examination,* Galloway responded with a bitter *Reply...*[3] which drew together brilliantly the tangled threads of his argument.

William H. Nelson and David L. Jacobson have shown that Galloway's

Joseph Galloway's Concept

chief concern in 1774–1775 was his consuming desire to exclude Dickinson from prominence.[4] At the heart of this mutual antagonism were their different assumptions about the province's interests and the ways of preserving colonial liberty. Dickinson opposed Galloway's scheme to make Pennsylvania into a royal colony and denounced successive British encroachments in the 1760s, because he sensed a growing and pervasive conspiracy to subvert colonial liberty.[5] As Speaker of the Assembly from 1766 to 1774, Galloway became increasingly concerned that resistance against British policy would upset the delicate balance within Pennsylvania politics and jeopardize his own power.

In a curious way, competition with Dickinson may have stunted Galloway's own development as a whiggish defender of constitutional liberty in America. During a struggle, in 1760, with the proprietors over judicial tenure, he had defended the independence of the judiciary on broad, libertarian grounds.[6] In 1766 and 1770 he privately denounced British restrictions on colonial currency as inexcusable deprivations of liberty.[7] His breadth of vision contracted as he came to fear that British encroachments would keep Pennsylvania politics in turmoil and encourage the appetites of his own political rivals. He came to believe that his dominance was an essential prerequisite to the defense of Pennsylvania's interests.[8] His opposition to non-importation as well as his contempt for Dickinson's constitutional views led to the defeat of Galloway and his faction in Philadelphia in the Assembly election of 1770, forcing him to rely on his home county of Bucks for a seat in the Assembly and on assemblymen from outside of Philadelphia for his reelection as Speaker. These events vindicated his conviction that colonial resistance against British policy only served to feed the ambitions of dangerous men.[9]

The crisis of 1774, as Jacobson has demonstrated, brought this struggle for preeminence to an abrupt conclusion. Dickinson dominated the meetings in Philadelphia during May and June which led to the calling of a Provincial Congress in July, and his *Essay on the Constitutional Power of Great Britain* strongly influenced the Congress's recommendations to the Assembly. Under Speaker Galloway's influence, the Assembly ignored the proposals advanced by the Congress, excluded Dickinson and his supporters from the delegation to Continental Congress, and instructed those delegates to devise a "Plan" of reconciliation and to oppose any pronouncements "indecent or disrespectful to the Mother State."[10] Delegates to the Congress arriving in late August and early September, 1774, found Galloway acting as a self-appointed chairman of local arrangements for the Congress while Pennsylvania seethed with rumors of Galloway's treachery and ambition. The erosion of Galloway's influence in provincial politics culminated in October when Philadelphia elected Dickinson to a seat in the Assembly, and the Assembly in turn removed Galloway as Speaker and named Dickinson a delegate to the Congress.[11]

Recent studies of these events, especially those by Nelson and Jacobson, have properly concentrated on Galloway's statements and writings from July 1774, when he began to reveal his proposals for imperial reform, until April 1775, when he finally withdrew from the pre-Revolutionary debate. These sources provide a more accurate guide to his pre-Revolutionary motives than does his retrospective *Political and Historical Reflections on . . . the American Rebellion.*[12] His writings of 1774–1775 deserve reconsideration, not only because they depict his well-known ambition and haughtiness as well as the ingenuity and resourcefulness of his Plan, but also because they abound with implicit and explicit testimony about the role he was playing, the inner struggle he experienced as he perceived the collapse of his strategy, and the compulsion he then felt to salve his own ego and vindicate both the utility and validity of his proposals. Nelson touched briefly, and suggestively, on this problem when he hinted that Galloway's "disabling vanity" crippled his energetic, imaginative quest for reconciliation.[13] Surviving sources— including a recently published Galloway letter of July 1774, which delineated in fresh detail his assumptions about his role—permit a reconstruction of Galloway's own comprehension of this experience. No writer has yet made extensive use of personal testimony in the *Candid Examination* and *Reply.* To use Galloway's polemical pamphlets as guides to his personality is, of course, risky, and some of the following analysis is, admittedly, speculative. What is not speculative is that the portrait of Galloway's motives in his pamphlets is corroborated by his surviving correspondence, several revealing quotations in John Adams's diary, and other sources.

Galloway's view of his own dilemma—his conception of his role and attempts to cope with the collapse of his political effectiveness—involved several elements. First, there was the structure of his famous imperial ideas, and next his persistent attempts to reconcile the disparate elements in his argument. Further, there were moral issues which the triumph of his enemies forced him to consider. Finally, the pattern of his introspection and intransigence, as it gradually developed, served to relate and connect all of these factors.

2

On September 8, 1774, Galloway sat on a committee of Congress listening to a debate on the sources of colonial liberty. Most involved in the discussion were four delegates: Richard Henry Lee and John Jay argued that the colonies were distinct political communities voluntarily associated with

Joseph Galloway's Concept

the British state, while John Rutledge and James Duane took the more limited position that the colonies were extensions of the British political system. At stake was the wording of the Congress's statement on colonial rights; Lee, Jay,[14] and others wanted to base the American cause on the natural law right of a people to constitute a government as well as on English common law precedents protecting the rights of the subject. Duane and Rutledge considered natural law a dangerous ground and pleaded that the English constitution alone would serve as the basis of colonial remonstrance.

Only after these differences had emerged did Galloway enter the debate—apparently speaking at much greater length than the others he attempted to provide irrefutable support for Duane and Rutledge's position. Congress should not base its appeals on natural law, he argued, because the colonies had been from the earliest settlement politically organized societies rather than ones which had emerged from a state of nature. Therefore, only the constitutional history of England provided a credible explanation of colonial rights. "The Essence" of the constitution was the representation in Parliament of the proprietors of land in the realm and their consent to legislation binding the inhabitants of those lands. Because the first settlers in America occupied territory not so represented, no law of Parliament enacted since the establishment of the colonies necessarily bound the colonists. Even Lord North, Galloway concluded, would concede the validity of these arguments if he made an effort to inform himself of the history of the constitution. Strong language! Galloway quickly acknowledged its radical implications: "I am well aware that my Arguments tend to an Independency of the Colonies and militate against the Maxim that there must be some absolute Power to draw together all the Wills and strengths of the Empire."[15]

That admission represented the crux of Galloway's problem during his direct involvement in the pre-Revolutionary debate, from July 1774 to April 1775. Throughout that period he tried to sustain two distinct lines of argument containing the very contradictory implications he confessed to the committee of Congress. *Representation* was the key to the imperial problem; therefore, the exercise of Parliamentary jurisdiction over the colonies was a grievous anomaly which justified colonial opposition to the British policy. At the same time the *subordinate* status of the colonists within the Empire sharply circumscribed the permissible limits of colonial remonstrance. He felt confident that he alone could reconcile those two truths and in so doing promote the only possible solution to the imperial controversy. It is plausible to argue that Galloway stressed the need for some form of colonial representation in the councils of the Empire until October 1774 as a means of attracting support for his Plan of Union and that he lapsed into negative talk of subordination only after the delegates rejected his positive proposals. There was, of course, a distinct change in emphasis between the summer of

Part I: Ideas

1774 and spring of 1775, but only of emphasis and not of substance. Galloway continued to insist throughout the 1774–1775 period that his doctrines of representation and subordination could be reconciled. His unpublished memorandum on the imperial constitutional problem, "Arguments on Both Sides...," urged their compatibility. His statements in Congress and subsequent pamphlets dealt at length with both colonial rights and obligations. Perhaps the depth of his commitment to both doctrines was best illustrated when a friend in New York, Samuel Verplanck, sent him copies of polemical tory pamphlets, in all likelihood those of Samuel Seabury and Thomas Bradbury Chandler. After complimenting them for their insistence on colonial obedience, he complained that "they do not show the rights of the American Subject or even acknowledge that we do have any. They do not own that we have any Grievance and consequently nothing is pointed out as a Constitutional Remedy."[16]

Though withdrawn and secretive at the opening of Congress, Galloway was excited and sustained by his belief that "I stand here almost alone" in seeing both sides of the imperial dispute; "perhaps were I to remove to your great Capitol," London, he wrote to the English politician and colonial agent, Richard Jackson, "where the most important Matters are decided, I should not be less so." The margin for error in seeking to resolve the differences between Britain and the colonies, he told Jackson, was perilously small. Fundamental to the problem of colonial discontent was the burgeoning population of the colonies which would probably grow by tenfold in the coming century. It was inconceivable, he added, that Parliament could continue to exercise unlimited jurisdiction over so populous and expanding a society.[17]

His *Candid Examination* elaborated on these dangers. The "circumstances" of the colonies—their territorial extent, distance from Britain, and numerous harbors and ports—encouraged colonial autonomy and should behoove Britain to offer the colonies tempting inducements to remain within the Empire. More pressing was his concern that "the genius" and "temper" of the Americans required tactful handling for "no people in the world have higher notions of liberty."[18] Therefore the inability of the colonists to share in the process of imperial lawmaking violated "Reason," "Common Sense," and "the Principles of the English Government." "Is it unreasonable," he asked, "to expect...Discontent will not fill the Breasts of Americans?" In retrospect, Galloway regretted that the British government had not begun constitutional reform of the Empire at the close of the Seven Years' War by guaranteeing to the colonists "the same Rights and Privileges ...enjoyed by the Subjects in Britain." The ministry and Parliament should have then seen the need for such a settlement if for no other reason than the difficulty experienced in obtaining fiscal support from colonial as-

Joseph Galloway's Concept

semblies during the War. Similarly, he believed, the colonists had squandered their opportunities during the previous decade by ridiculing the notion of colonial representation in Parliament which, while impractical, was a theoretically sound proposal deserving respectful consideration. Instead the colonists had poisoned future relations with the mother country by "tracing American Rights up to Sources from which they never came."

The dynamics of Britain's increasingly assertive policy and the growing intransigence of the colonists perplexed Galloway and instinctively he wished these new forces would cease functioning until he could implement a solution. "Is it not high Time," he asked Jackson, "that both Countries should retreat a little and take other Ground seeing That which they are now upon is likely to prove dangerous and distressing to Both?" Even if he could persuade the colonists to seek conciliation, he warned Jackson, nothing could be accomplished unless Parliament showed a willingness to modify its claims of unlimited supremacy: "I cannot find that there is the least Disposition in the People of this Country to submit to the parliamentary Jurisdiction under the present System of Government and the Share they hold in it."[19] That precarious balance—the necessity for simultaneous "retreat" on both sides—entirely engrossed Galloway and helped account for his withdrawn behavior at the outset of the Congress.

Galloway's confidence that he could effect reconciliation sprang from his assumption that scrupulous wording of the colonists' petition to the Crown could induce the ministry to accept negotiation without appearing to force its hand. He proposed to accomplish this feat by a studious appeal to the rights of Englishmen. From the composition of the first Saxon Witan, feudal courts, and Parliaments under Edward II, all proprietors of land had possessed an integral role in the enactment of legislation binding the inhabitants of the realm. Only by an accident of history were the inhabitants of the colonies left unrepresented. The first settlers had not permanently surrendered that right, but had merely accepted Parliamentary supervision from "extreme necessity." Therefore, he concluded, the constitutional solution was for Parliament to introduce some form of representation. Until this change was accomplished, British authority in America would remain valid only in theory, and would be in practice, "as absolute and despotic" as that of any continental monarch. In the meantime, he wanted Britain to hold its power in abeyance. As a practical matter, "Parliament ought not, *as the Colonies are at present circumstanced,* to bind them by its Legislative Authority." On this basis reconciliation consisted of prodding Britain gently to adopt restraint by having colonial demands clothed in language which would not offend British sensibilities. Any disinclination to obey Parliament, he warned, would imply disrespect of the very institution which had the power to make needed changes in the status of the colonies. However, he acknowledged,

Part I: Ideas

some implied colonial defiance was unavoidable. "Yet when that denial shall be accompanied with an express desire of establishing a political *Union* with the *Mother Country*," he exulted, having discovered the goal of this tortuous maneuver, "such a denial does not carry with it any Thing unjust, offensive, or indelicate."[20]

His *Candid Examination* refined the techniques of reconciliation by demonstrating how statements of colonial rights could be embodied in the rhetoric of obedience. His suggested model petition to Parliament acknowledged the necessity of a supreme authority within every state before it pointed to the sacrifices and hazards endured by the colonists in settling a wilderness and increasing the "wealth and power" of Britain. He attributed the limitations of colonial liberty to historical accident: "by such settlement" the colonies had "lost the enjoyment of, though not the right to, some of the first and most excellent privileges of Englishmen," the representation of their lands in Parliament and capacity to "participate in the supreme legislative authority." By emphasizing the constitutional flaw in the structure of the Empire, his petition minimized the significance of specific colonial grievances regarding Parliamentary taxation, commercial policy, and interference with colonial self-government. Certainly, he conceded, those British policies had caused "great discontent. . . in the breasts of his Majesty's faithful American subjects"; however, the petition assured Britain that this discontent was chiefly regrettable because it eroded "that harmony which ought to subsist between the members of the same community." Finally, he insisted that the whole justification for colonial petition was the fact that only Parliament could remedy the situation. Colonial disunity and the absence of institutions representative of the colonies as a whole prevented any colonial contribution to the costs of imperial defense. Parliament possessed the power of restoring to the colonies a voice in Parliament and thereby enabling them to respond to the needs of the parent state.[21]

Galloway sought to enhance the attractiveness of this approach by projecting its future consequences. Legislative union with Britain would not only exempt the colonies from onerous Parliamentary restrictions, it would enable the colonies to contribute to the cost of the empire without any loss of freedom. On these terms, reconciliation would produce lasting stability in the colonies by eliminating at one stroke existing colonial grievances and giving the colonies "the best of all political securities," a perpetual exemption from further British restrictions on trade and manufacturing. Critical to this stabilizing process was a new procedure, "a capacity of discharging with justice and punctuality all [colonial] duties to the [British] State." This solution aimed at the transformation of the British Empire by the "uniting of two great countries by the firmest hands of political freedom into one grand and illustrious Empire."[22]

Joseph Galloway's Concept

Galloway's Plan of Union sought to reconcile the requirements of colonial liberty with the closer integration of the Empire. Its preamble spurned the notion that the colonies were autonomous communities within the Empire. Its purpose, "the establishment of a Political Union," was defined both as the repair of disunity among the colonies and the creation of a durable connection between them and the parent state. It conceded the impracticality of colonial representation in Parliament and sought Parliament's approval of a plan which would simultaneously consolidate the capacities of the Empire to meet common dangers, advance the "interest of both countries," and preserve the "rights and liberties of America."[23] To secure these ends, the Plan would have created a continental legislature, a "Grand Council," whose delegates would be chosen by provincial assemblies for three-year terms, and the assemblies would retain control over their internal affairs. The Plan would have enlarged the scope of royal authority through the creation of a "President General," appointed and serving at the pleasure of the Crown and vested with extensive administrative and executive power which he would exercise with the "advice and consent" of the Grand Council. He could withhold his assent from bills passed by the Council. All colonial legislation would require the approval of both Parliament and the Council.[24]

The closest equivalent to Galloway's Plan of Union was a proposal for an American parliament drafted in 1767 by William Smith, Jr., a New York Councillor and historian.[25] Both men were certainly familiar with Benjamin Franklin's Albany Plan for a union for the American colonies (1754) and revamped for their own purposes its recommendations for a continental assembly and royally appointed Governor General.[26] Franklin, in 1775, repudiated Galloway's Plan and argued that British policy since the Declaratory Act had so altered the imperial relationship as to make any extension of British administration in America undesirable. Galloway, for contrasting reasons, also recognized that colonial suspicion of British policy rendered the Albany Plan obsolete and for this reason called for a legislative union with the British Parliament.[27] That very innovation, however, provoked Franklin's acerbic comment, "when I consider the extreme corruption prevalent among all orders of men in this old, rotten state [he was then in England], and the glorious public virtue so predominant in our rising country, I cannot but apprehend more mischief than benefit from a closer union. ...It seems like Mezentius' coupling and binding together the dead and the living."[28] Franklin's treatise on population may well have exercised a more pervasive influence on Galloway and Smith than did his Albany Plan. Both men were fascinated with the impact of burgeoning colonial population on American self-assertiveness and imperial relations.[29] In addition, both men devised their proposals in response to the pre-Revolutionary con-

Part I: Ideas

troversy as means of healing the breach in the Empire and both ultimately became loyalists. Smith indeed was excited when he heard rumors of Galloway's Plan, noting in July 1774 that "at Philadelphia a Plan is digesting for an American Constitution. I know not the Out lines of it. I hope it is for a Parliament and to meet here annually."[30]

Though Galloway's and Smith's plans contained similar proposals, they were based on quite different assumptions about constitutional doctrine and the nature of imperial politics. The two documents also differed on a fundamental issue. Smith's legislature would have bypassed Parliament and dealt directly with the Crown in matters of imperial finance; Galloway sought a legislative union in which the British Parliament and its American branch would share concurrent jurisdiction over colonial affairs. Smith prefaced his plan with an analysis of imperial relations which was far more pragmatic and flexible than Galloway's. Smith abhorred the use of abstract constitutional principles because these interfered with constructive discussion.[31] Where Galloway spoke sketchily in 1774 about an increased political stature for the colonists under the Plan of Union, Smith propounded an expansive view of the future of American politics. He envisioned a time when population growth and westward expansion would make the colonies Britain's equal; his imperial constitution was to be a practical step in adjusting imperial relations during a generation of change from subordination to parity.

Galloway conceived of the Plan of Union as an instrument for his own public vindication, whereas Smith shunned any open participation in the controversies of 1774–1775. He preferred to work quietly among acquaintances in New York. His letters to friends in the Second Continental Congress suggested elaborate and subtle ground rules governing any attempts to negotiate with Britain and put forward his plan for an American parliament as a basis for negotiation. However, unlike Galloway's approach to reconciliation, Smith's imperatives were entirely tactical and revealed a clinical sense of political communication: "feeling the pulse" of the ministry, proceeding "without a Word about Rights," and exercising exquisite tact and timing.[32] Galloway was much too concerned with questions of doctrine and with his own self-justification to bother with these questions of tactics and protocol. The two men, then, suggested similar proposals for imperial reform, but proceeded from very different assumptions about constitutional doctrine and the mechanics of reconciliation.

As the late Richard Koebner demonstrated, ideas about the nature of the Empire underwent a bewildering transformation in 1774–1775.[33] Writers as diverse as Richard Cartwright, Dean Tucker, John Adams, Thomas Jefferson, Edmund Burke, and George III sought to define the structure of the Empire, praised its benefits, and called for vigorous steps to preserve it.

Joseph Galloway's Concept

What they lacked was a meaningful vocabulary to describe the Empire's internal stresses. In seeking to articulate their respective diagnoses they endowed concepts like "power," "liberty," "rights," and "reconciliation" with a host of contrasting meanings. Koebner made passing reference to Galloway's Plan as "a new constructive solution."[34] Had he chosen to discuss Galloway in the detail he lavished on other writers, Koebner would certainly have found additional support for his view that imperial concepts in 1774–1775 were derived more from the initial presuppositions of their authors than from any consensus about the meaning of the term "British Empire."

Galloway's "grand and illustrious Empire" referred not to the familiar Empire of the past but rather to a future relationship which only the Plan of Union could bring into being. Created under the same pressures which inspired other equally novel imperial concepts on the eve of revolution, Galloway's view could easily have appeared overwhelmingly original to its author and only part of a cacophonous blur to his audience.

3

Galloway's reputation as a skilled theorist was established as early as 1897 by Moses Coit Tyler's *Literary History of the American Revolution*. Julian P. Boyd's study of the Plans of Union added substance to that view. Nelson's account astutely shifted the emphasis away from the Plan of Union and toward Galloway's conception of representation. "In perceiving that Parliament was a territorial assembly with no rightful claim to control lands which were not represented," Nelson concluded, "Galloway went to the heart, not of the political, but of the constitutional impasse between Britain and America."[35]

The gap between constitutional and political acumen merits further consideration, and Galloway's doctrine of subordination provides a key to his difficulties at reconciling theory and practice. His strictures on obedience rested on a series of distinct propositions which he never integrated into an effective argument. First, he endeavored to establish the inseparability of the authority of the Crown and Parliament. Further, he insisted on the necessity of a supreme authority within every state. Finally, he sought to prove that the colonies were, of necessity, integral parts of the British state. The logical connection between these propositions was clear enough, but they lacked the unifying purpose and ingenuity which he had brought to the problem of representation. So elaborate and didactic were his writings on these issues that he was never able to reconcile, in a straightforward manner, the colonial right to representation in the legislative processes of the Empire with the need for a single supreme source of power lodged in the hands of

Parliament and the Crown. He could only plead that the contradiction would cease to exist once his Plan of Union became a reality. Long before he had reached that conclusion, his assumptions about subordination in his *Candid Examination* had spread confusion and distrust. "Mr. G[alloway] has spent (I think) his first 20 pages in laying a wrong foundation and the super-structure he has raised on it falls of itself," Ebenezer Hazard wrote to Silas Deane, sensing Galloway's vulnerability. "He has taken for granted a very principle part of the dispute, *viz.,* our being *within the Realm*—a monstrous proposition."[36]

Hazard, of course, distinguished between the British realm and the British Empire, a distinction which Galloway did not deny. The Plan of Union and its accompanying theory of representation acknowledged that the colonies possessed, by historical accident and present circumstances, a different relationship to Parliament than did the lands of the realm. What he insisted upon was that subordination was as important a bond of the Empire as the colonists' right to representation in imperial legislative processes. The subordination which Hazard considered monstrous was what Galloway sought to pacify and render innocuous by imperial reform.

The unpublished "Thoughts on Both Sides..." laid the initial foundation for Galloway's theory of subordination when he insisted that the colonies owed simultaneous obedience to both the Crown and Parliament. To refute the argument that colonial charters obligated the colonists to obey the Crown alone, he argued that charters assumed the first settlers in America to have been "Members" of the British state who "did implicitly agree and consent...to yield Obedience to the supreme Authority of the State." If the King could exempt the colonists from obedience to Parliament, Galloway argued, he could as easily "discharge the whole People of *Great Britain* from their Obedience" and thereby "dissolve the Constitution."[37] Colonial petitions to the Crown which ignored Parliament, he asserted in the *Candid Examination,* "involve the cause of America in an inextricable absurdity" by acknowledging the authority of the Crown but denying other equally inherent constitutional principles.[38]

No doctrine of political theory, he declared, was more "firmly established" than the necessity of a supreme authority within every state. That argument, he apparently came to realize, depended on more than the concurrent authority of the King and Parliament. He had to demonstrate that the political order of the colonies was subject to all manner of deadly misfortunes against which the supreme legislative authority of Parliament was the only antidote. Carefully arranged citations from Burlamaqui, Tully, Locke, and Acherley all identified the legislative power as the cement of society and obedience as the only alternative to political disintegration.[39] This characterization of Parliament's power as a solitary line of defense against chaos

Joseph Galloway's Concept

was, for Galloway, a comparatively forthright way of claiming that the colonies were in fact part of the British state. Either they were part of the British state, he reasoned, or they were "so many independent Communities, in a state of nature" and bound by no authority whatever.[40] In this condition, colonial governments fell under Pufendorf's stricture, "with regard to lawful bodies,...whatever rights and whatever power they have over their members are all defined and limited by the supreme power, and cannot be opposed to or prevail against it. For otherwise, were there a body not subject to limitation by the supreme civil power, there would be a state within a state."[41] Galloway found further doctrinal support in Locke's statement, *"whoever. . . enjoys any part of the Land"* within a state *"must take it with the Condition. . . of submitting to the Government of the Commonwealth."*[42] Finally, Galloway argued, the rights of the colonists carried "reciprocal" and unavoidable duties; "shall Americans have the right to withdraw from the performance of duties," he demanded "and the state be bound to continue *them* in the enjoyment of all their rights?"[43]

Galloway's purpose in explaining the meaning of subordination was, in part, to eliminate all alternatives to his Plan of Union as solutions to the imperial crisis. But these strictures only involved him in his most pointed exchange with his detractors, Dickinson and Thomson. They attacked the rigidity of his definition of subordination, which insisted that the colonies were either fully independent states like Hanover or France or else they remained "complete members of the [British] State."[44] Such an arbitrary definition of the bases for subordination, Dickinson and Thomson retorted, reduced the colonies to the level of "mere Corporations."[45] "I confess I do not understand what you mean by a 'mere corporation,'" Galloway replied. A corporation, he explained, was a respectable political entity, a dependent community within a sovereign state. Pufendorf insisted on the subordinate status of such communities with respect to the governing power. Indeed a subordinate community not bound by a supreme authority was "a *monster,* a thing *out* of nature." By focusing on the abnormality of autonomous subordinate communities, Galloway instinctively shifted the argument away from the primary issue—whether the colonies were in fact within the boundaries of the British state.[46]

Confident that he established the propriety of applying the term "corporation" to the status of the colonies, Galloway continued the discussion on his own terms. The natural characteristic of a subordinate community was the power to exercise local police power.[47] It simply did not follow, he lectured Dickinson and Thomson, that a community could expand local police power into full legislative authority. Now he was prepared to confront one of Dickinson's and Thomson's chief contentions: that the colonial assemblies were not subordinate because they exercised within their provinces jurisdic-

Part I: Ideas

tion as complete as that of Parliament within Great Britain. The Pennsylvania Assembly, he retorted, possessed no such unbridled authority. It could not enact laws repugnant to those of Britain; its laws had to conform as closely as possible to British law; none of its enactments could interfere in any way with the enforcement of Parliamentary laws. Surely, he concluded, a legislative body so circumscribed was scarcely supreme. On the contrary, colonial assemblies differed in no way from the units of English local governments, "corporations" like Bristol or the City of London. After all, he reminded his critics, both Bristol and London were represented in Parliament. Dickinson's and Thomson's claim that colonial assemblies were supreme within their respective provinces clarified their intentions, Galloway concluded, thanking his adversaries "for *blabbing this long concealed and most important secret*" and revealing for the first time "the cloven foot, . . . the black scheme of Independence . . . exhibited in all its horrid deformity."[48]

Virtually the only reference to "independence" in the pre-Revolutionary debate—at least prior to 1775—were in these exasperated accusations by Galloway and other critics of colonial resistance. Among the most important practical consequences of their writings was to raise the spectre of independence at the very time that the leaders of resistance were attempting to re-define Parliamentary supremacy in terms compatible with colonial autonomy.

Bernard Bailyn's *The Ideological Origins of the American Revolution,* sets Galloway's constitutionalism in context.[49] His strictures on subordination restated what had been, until the 1760's, an orthodox view in the Anglo-American world. It was the English "Whig conception of a sovereign Parliament" which had been hammered out in the struggles of the seventeenth century, given classic form in Blackstone, and embodied most bluntly in the Declaratory Act. "How to qualify, undermine, or reinterpret this tenet of English political theory was the central intellectual problem that confronted the leaders of the American cause," Bailyn explained. "It is a classic instance of the creative adjustment of ideas to reality. For if in England the concept of sovereignty was not only logical but realistic, it was far from that in the colonies."[50] Dickinson's *Essay on the Constitutional Power of Great Britain* was one of the foremost efforts to accomplish this trick by devising separate spheres in which Parliamentary authority and colonial autonomy could operate. Dickinson's argument—which, it will be recalled, was drafted in a vain attempt to influence the Pennsylvania delegation to Congress later dominated by Galloway—argued that "the sovereignty over these colonies must be limited" and that "there must be . . . a line" drawn clearly designating the limits of Parliamentary jurisdiction.[51]

In October 1774 Congress adopted this position in its Fourth Resolve which acknowledged Parliament's control over imperial commerce and reserved to the provincial assemblies "exclusive right of legislation... in all cases of taxation and internal policy."[52] It was this solution to the problem of sovereignty which led Galloway to define most clearly his differences with Dickinson and Thomson: "you first took into your *learned* heads, philosopher-like, to conceive that the supreme legislative authority, which is indivisible to its nature, was like matter, divisible *ad infinitum;* and under this profound mistake, you began with splitting and dividing it, until by one slice after another, you have hacked and pared it away to less than an atom."[53]

4

Galloway's doctrines of representation and subordination and his contentious style of argument were a cumbersome apparatus which he carried proudly. But refusing to jettison arguments he could not convey effectively, he was progressively isolated by his erudition from the public discussion he longed to dominate. "He is a man of integrity" and "improved understanding, but he is too fond of *system*," Rev. John Vardill, a New York tory, said of Galloway in a letter to an English official in 1778, to which he added, "his natural warmth of temper, inflamed by the oppressions and indignities he has suffered, will render you cautious in trusting his representations."[54] This same rigidity in the structure of his ideas and fluid, volatile self-consciousness was already apparent in Galloway's writings in early 1775. Such was his resourcefulness that as his intellectual position became increasingly vulnerable and misunderstood, he turned his attention inward and contemplated with growing fascination his peculiar role as a critic of colonial resistance. "I... have laid before you the constitutional extent of parliamentary jurisdiction," he declared at the close of his *Candid Examination:* "I have... *deduced* your rights, ... and explained your duties. I have pointed out the mode which... you ought to pursue for a restoration of those rights."[55] This didactic posture was the essence of his concept of his role; it drew together in his mind the complex threads of his arguments and set his whole endeavor in perspective.

That concept of his role was implicit in all of Galloway's conduct in 1774–1775. He assumed that situations should hold still and men stand attentive while he brought the power of his mind and the persuasion of his pen to bear on the problem. "Parliament ought not, as the colonies are at present circumstanced, to bind them by its Legislative Authority," he pleaded in July 1774, "both Countries should retreat a little and take other Ground."[56] All of his secretive preparation in August and September 1774 demonstrated—as Nelson adroitly concluded—that "Galloway conceived of

Part I: Ideas

the Continental Congress as a constitutional convention; indeed, as *his* constitutional convention."[57] As the delegates deviated from Galloway's scenario, he adapted his approach accordingly by enlarging his role and gambling everything on the hope that his brilliant speech in behalf of his Plan would compel his critics to accept his leadership or admit that their own motives were selfish and disruptive. He sought to shield himself from personal attack by identifying himself entirely with the manifest virtues and disinterestedness of his Plan.

The last thing he expected was that his enemies would oppose his Plan by ignoring its substantial provisions. During the final stages of the Congress, an unidentified Virginia delegate, almost certainly Patrick Henry, taunted Galloway that his Plan was "big with destruction to America" and challenged him to debate its merits. Desperate to get the Plan reconsidered by Congress, Galloway agreed on the condition that the debate be part of its proceedings. The clash never materialized, but Galloway was shocked to hear that the Virginia delegates were at the same time openly talking of their intention to have the Plan expunged from the Journal of Congress.[58] When Dickinson and Thomson chided him for refusing to debate with Henry about his Plan "when he had been for months haranguing and caballing about it,"[59] Galloway concluded that trickery and deceit were the only replies he would receive to his serious proposals. "Your assaults have not even ruffled its scarf-skin," he said of attacks on his Plan more in chagrin than triumph. His accusation that, "It stands like an impregnable bulwark in the path of your independence and you do not know how to remove it,"[60] did not conceal his disappointment that his enemies had not tried to "remove it," that they did not consider his Plan the central issue in the debate, and that they preferred to discuss British abuses which he overlooked and to impugn his dedication to colonial liberty.

At the heart of these tactics Galloway perceived the sin of "sophistry," the twisting of words about colonial rights without regard for the inherent limitations of colonial institutions, and the reinterpretation of colonial interests in terms of men's imaginations and ambitions. When Dickinson and Henry engaged in these practices, he conceded, they may have done so unwittingly, out of "perverseness," but they violated the ethical standards of "honour and candour" which should govern polemical debate and thereby forfeited the respect of "sensible and honest men." Techniques of boldness, clever construction of arguments, and ideological finesse, in his view, had become ends in themselves, blinding men to the fact that "sophistry" could not "render. . . 'supreme' and independent what is in in its nature limited, subordinate, and dependent."[61]

This intellectual confusion explained to Galloway's satisfaction the success of the movement toward colonial resistance. Not content with their own

Joseph Galloway's Concept

disobedience, whig leaders felt compelled to spread their guilt more widely by stampeding into rebellion men "whose leisure and abilities will not suffer them to inquire into...fallacious doctrines."[62] A decade earlier he had used the same argument to explain why members of his own political faction joined the resistance to the Stamp Act. "Our Friends were inclined to unite with those Wretches," he had then written, "not seeing their Design of bringing us to an Act which would Crown all the Violent Measures they had...taken against the Power of Parliament."[63] Now in the light of his experience in the First Continental Congress and his inquiry into the morality of his opponents' conduct, Galloway believed he had isolated the source of disorder. His *Candid Examination* closed with a question calculated to unmask it: "are you *still* resolved," he asked of his readers, "to surrender up your reason to the miserable sophistry and jargon of designing men?"[64]

Galloway's diagnosis of whig "sophistry" marked the end of his attempt to play a meaningful role in the pre-Revolutionary debate. In May 1775, he asked to be removed as a delegate to the Second Continental Congress; and by June he considered himself "retired...from the distressing and ungrateful Drudgery of Public Life."[65] The superstructure of ideas he had constructed during the previous year was fraught with internal stresses. He had worked with tireless industry to resolve apparent contradictions in his doctrines of representation and subordination. He only could have succeeded if his audience had sympathized with his basic purposes: to "deduce" colonial rights singlehandedly from arbitrarily chosen premises and then to neutralize colonial discontent with a Plan so ingenious and dramatic as to compel assent. That concept of his role, and the experiences from which it crystallized, comprised the moral and emotional basis for his subsequent loyalism.

AUTHOR'S NOTE (1988): In the original article I accepted Galloway's claim that his Plan of Union had been "expunged" from the journal of the Continental Congress. For procedural reasons, the Plan never became a part of the record of the Congress, see Paul H. Smith, ed., *Letters of Delegates to Congress, 1774–1789* (Washington, D.C., 1976), vol. 1, pp. 112–13, 116–17.

1. Julian P. Boyd, *Anglo-American Union: Joseph Galloway's Plans to Preserve the British Empire, 1774–1788* (Philadelphia, 1941); William H. Nelson, *The American Tory* (Oxford, 1961), pp. 47–69; David L. Jacobson, "John Dickinson and Joseph Galloway, 1764–1776: A Study in Contrasts" (unpublished Ph.D. dissertation, Princeton University, 1959), and *John Dickinson and the Revolution in Pennsylvania, 1761–1776* (Berkeley and Los Angeles, 1965), chapter 5; Max Savelle, "Nationalism and Other Loyalties in the American Revolution," *American Historical Review*, 67 (1962): 910; Moses Coit Tyler, *Literary History of the American Revolution* (New York, 1897), vol. 1, pp. 369–83.

Part I: Ideas

2. [Joseph Galloway], *A Candid Examination of the Mutual Claims of Great Britain, and the Colonies: with a plan of Accommodation, on constitutional principles* (New York, 1775).
3. [Joseph Galloway], *A Reply to an Address to the Author of a Pamphlet, entitled, "A Candid Examination," &c. By the Author of the Candid Examination* (Nwe York, 1775).
4. Nelson, *The American Tory*, pp. 47–48, pp. 54–69; Jacobson, "Dickinson and Galloway," pp. 178–204, and *John Dickinson and the Revolution*, pp. 83–85.
5. See Bernard Bailyn, ed., *Pamphlets of the American Revolution, 1750–1776* (Cambridge, Mass., 1965), vol. 1, pp. 660–65, and Jacobson's articles, "John Dickinson's Fight against Royal Government, 1764," *William and Mary Quarterly*, third series, 19 (1962): 64–85, and "The Puzzle of 'Pacificus,' " *Pennsylvania History*, 31 (1964): 406–18.
6. Bailyn, ed., *Pamphlets of the American Revolution*, vol. 1, pp. 249–72.
7. Galloway to Benjamin Franklin, January 13 and June 16, 1766, June 21, 1770, Jared Sparks, ed., *The Works of Benjamin Franklin* (Boston, 1836–1840), vol. 7, pp. 303–5, 321–25, 481–83.
8. On Galloway's political strength and tactics in the late-1760s, see Benjamin H. Newcomb, "Effects of the Stamp Act on Colonial Pennsylvania Politics," *William and Mary Quarterly*, third series, 23 (1966): 257–72.
9. Jacobson, *John Dickinson and the Revolution in Pennsylvania*, pp. 66–69.
10. Jacobson, "Dickinson and Galloway," pp. 178–79; *Pennsylvania Archives*, 8 Series, vol. 8, p. 7100.
11. William Bradford to James Madison, August 1, 1774, William M. E. Rachal and William T. Hutchinson, eds., *The Papers of James Madison* (Chicago, 1962), vol. 1, pp. 117–19; Silas Deane to his wife, September 5–6, 1774, in Edmund C. Burnett, ed., *Letters of Members of the Continental Congress* (Washington, D. C., 1921–1936), vol. 1, p. 11; Jacobson, *John Dickinson and the Revolution in Pennsylvannia*, pp. 80–81.
12. The only surviving copy of Galloway's speech to Congress of September 28, 1774, proposing the Plan of Union is the draft in his *Historical and Political Reflections on the Rise and Progress of the American Rebellion...*(London, 1780), pp. 41–44. John Adams's notes on Galloway's speech reveal, as Julian P. Boyd has demonstrated, that the 1780 version was heavily revised for its English readers and is not a reliable source for Galloway's ideas in 1774, see *Anglo-American Union*, pp. 35–36, and Lyman Butterfield et al., eds., *The Diary and Autobiography of John Adams* (Cambridge, Mass., 1961), vol. 2, pp. 141–44. Merrill Jensen reprinted a striking passage from *Historical and Political Reflections* in *American Colonial Documents to 1776* (London, 1955), pp. 801–3, which depicted the motives of Galloway's enemies in Congress in terms similar to those he used in 1775; however, this passage places somewhat more emphasis on the "republican" character of their beliefs and economic factors—"declining fortunes" and "debt to British merchants"—than his 1775 analysis of whig motives.
13. Nelson, *The American Tory*, p. 54.
14. When Galloway presented his Plan, Duane, Edward Rutledge, and Jay spoke in its defense, provoking Patrick Henry's outburst to John Adams about his "horrid Opinion" of "Galloway, Jay, and the Rutledges" and "their System," *Diary and Autobiography of John Adams*, vol. 2, p. 151. Jay's support of Galloway's Plan raises a curious problem, for in the committee on colonial rights and grievances he led the attack against the objections of John Rutledge, Duane, and Galloway who wanted to restrict Congress to the use of English constitutional precedents. Congress, Jay

insisted then, should "recur to the Law of Nature" as well because "there is no Allegiance without Protection. And Emigrants have a Right to erect what Government they please." (Ibid., p. 128).

15. Ibid., pp. 129-30.

16. "Arguments on Both Sides in the Dispute Between Great Britain and her Colonies...," *Archives of New Jersey,* vol. 10, pp. 483-92; Galloway to Verplanck, February 14, 1775, *Pennsylvania Magazine of History and Biography,* 21 (1897): 480-81.

17. Galloway to Richard Jackson, August 10, 1774 (a copied extract in Jackson's handwriting enclosed in Jackson to Lord Dartmouth, December 21, 1774), Dartmouth Papers, II, 1031, William Salt Library, Stafford, England, printed in Jack P. Greene, ed., *A Documentary History of American Life,* vol. II, *Colonies to Nation, 1773-1789* (New York, 1967), pp. 239-41.

18. Galloway, *Candid Examination,* pp. 42-43.

19. Galloway to Jackson, August 10, 1774, Greene, ed., *Colonies to Nation,* pp. 239-41.

20. "Arguments on Both Sides...," *Archives of New Jersey,* vol. 10, pp. 483-92.

21. *Candid Examination,* pp. 59-61.

22. *Reply,* pp. 6-8.

23. The introductory resolution is printed in *Candid Examination,* 53, and another version is "Resolutions intended to be offered by Mr. Galloway & seconded by J[ames] D[uane] for Promoting a Plan of Union between G. B. & A.," with the notation, "But as the Plan itself was rejected by the Congress; the Resolves became fruitless & were not proposed," James Duane Papers, New York Historical Society.

24. Boyd, *Anglo-American Union,* pp. 112-14; for a further discussion of the Plan and comparison with subsequent versions, see ibid., pp. 34-37, 85-111, and Nelson, "The Last Hopes of the American Loyalists," *Canadian Historical Review,* 32 (1951): 40-42.

25. Robert M. Calhoon, ed., "William Smith Jr.'s Alternative to the American Revolution," *William and Mary Quarterly,* third series, 22 (1965): 105-18.

26. Galloway, of course, must have known the Albany Plan well from his long association with Franklin, and Smith's father, William Smith, Sr., was a member of the committee at the Albany Congress which approved Franklin's proposal; see Leonard W. Labaree et al., eds., *The Papers of Benjamin Franklin* (New Haven, 1962), vol. 5, p. 376 n. 6, and pp. 417-18 n. 4.

27. One critic accused Galloway of plagiarizing Franklin (*Pennsylvania Journal,* April 5, 1775), and Galloway retorted that his Plan differed materially from Franklin's, especially in its provision for a "political union" with Great Britain (*Pennsylvania Gazette,* April 26, 1775); for further discussion see Nelson, *The American Tory,* p. 60, no. 23, Boyd, "Joseph Galloway's Plans of Union...," *Pennsylvania Magazine of History and Biography,* 64 (1940): 503, n. 34, and Labaree, et al., *The Papers of Benjamin Franklin,* vol. 5, pp. 417-18, n. 4.

28. Franklin to Galloway, February 25, 1775, in Samuel Eliot Morison, ed., *Sources and Documents Illustrating the American Revolution, 1774-1788...* (Oxford, 1923), pp. 137-39.

29. For documentation see Calhoon, ed., "William Smith's Alternative...," p. 117, n. 18.

30. Smith to Philip Schuyler, July 23, 1774, in William H. W. Sabine, ed., *Historical Memoirs from...1763 to...1776 of William Smith...* (New York, 1956), p. 190.

31. Calhoon, ed., "William Smith's Alternative...," p. 113.

Part I: Ideas

32. Smith to Schuyler, May 16, 1775, and Smith to Lewis Morris, June 5, 1775, in Sabine, ed., *Historical Memoirs*, pp. 224-25, 228-27c.
33. Richard Koebner, *Empire* (Cambridge, England, 1961), pp. 194-238.
34. Ibid., p. 209.
35. Nelson, *The American Tory*, p. 59.
36. Ebenezer Hazard (in New York) to Silas Deane, April 7, 1775, Connecticut Historical Society *Collections*, 2 (1870): 211-13.
37. "Arguments on Both Sides...," pp. 478-81.
38. *Candid Examination*, p. 26.
39. Ibid., pp. 4-5.
40. Ibid., p. 10.
41. Ibid., pp. 29, 21-22; Samuel Pufendorf, *De Jure Naturae et Gentium Libri Octo*, C. H. and W. A. Oldfather, trans. (*Publications of the Carnegie Endowment for International Peace* [Oxford and London, 1934]), vol. 2, p. 996; on Pufendorf's utility to both sides in the pre-Revolutionary debate, see Leonard Krieger, *The Politics of Discretion: Pufendorf and the Acceptance of Natural Law* (London and Chicago, 1965). Galloway found in Pufendorf an explanation of the necessary limits placed on subordinate communities, and James Otis, Samuel Adams, and Alexander Hamilton cited his dictum that "colonies may be...planted in different ways. For either they remain a part of the state from which they were sent forth, or they are obligated to show respect to the mother state and to uphold its majesty...by a kind of unequal treaty, or, finally, they treat with it on equal terms and right." (*De Jure Naturae*, vol. 2, p. 1356; Krieger, *Politics of Discretion*, pp. 260-61, 302-3.)
42. Peter Laslett, ed., *John Locke's Two Treatises on Government* (Cambridge, Eng., 1960), p. 366; *Candid Examination*, pp. 14-15.
43. Ibid., pp. 13, 24.
44. Ibid., p. 5.
45. *Pennsylvania Journal*, March 8, 1775.
46. *Reply*, pp. 25-26.
47. Galloway's service in 1777-1778 as General William Howe's Superintendent General for Police in Philadelphia amplified his understanding of this idea. He strived with considerable administrative and political ingenuity to expand the office into a powerful executive position from which he might rally and dominate loyal sentiment and thereby demonstrate how benevolent, strong-minded colonial administration could—in conjunction with effective military measures—break the back of the Revolution. He viewed the police power of a provincial government as the cutting edge of imperial policy and as a means of achieving the same kind of reconciliation he had first proposed in 1774. See John M. Coleman's study of Galloway's concept of his role in 1777-1779, "Joseph Galloway and the British Occupation of Philadelphia," *Pennsylvania History*, 30 (1963): 272, 274, 279-80, 288-93.
48. *Reply*, pp. 26-27, 15-16, 4-5.
49. Bailyn, *The Ideological Origins of the American Revolution* (Cambridge, Mass., 1967), pp. 201-203.
50. Ibid., 223; *Reply*, p. 20.
51. *Pennsylvania Archives*, 2 Series, vol. 3, pp. 528, 594; Bailyn, *Ideological Origins*, 223.
52. W. C. Ford, ed., *Journals of the Continental Congress, 1774-1789* (Washington, 1904), vol. 1, p. 68.
53. *Reply*, p. 20.

Joseph Galloway's Concept

54. [Vardill] to [William Eden], April 11, 1778, quoted in Coleman, "Joseph Galloway and the British Occupation of Philadelphia," pp. 281–82.
55. *Candid Examination,* p. 61.
56. See above note 19.
57. Nelson, *The American Tory,* p. 48.
58. *Reply,* pp. 33–34.
59. *Pennsylvania Gazette,* March 8, 1775.
60. "To the Public," ibid., April 26, 1775; *Reply,* pp. 35–36.
61. Ibid., pp. 41–42, 3–4.
62. *Reply,* pp. 24–25. Mary E. Blagg, "Tory Political Theory in America, 1765–1776" (unpublished Ph.D. dissertation, Duke University, 1954), esp. pp. 115, 118.
63. Galloway to William Franklin, November 14, 1765, Leonard W. Labaree, ed., *The Papers of Benjamin Franklin* (New Haven, 1950–   ), vol. 12, pp. 372–75; Newcomb, "Effects of the Stamp Act on Colonial Pennsylvania Politics," p. 269.
64. *Candid Examination,* p. 62.
65. Galloway to Verplanck, June 24, 1775, *PMHB,* vol. 21, p. 483.

6

"UNHINGING FORMER INTIMACIES":

*Robert Beverley's Perception of the
Pre-Revolutionary Controversy, 1761–1775*

1

Considering the enormous amount of scholarly writing that has been done on the causes of the American Revolution and the motives of men who supported and opposed colonial resistance, little is known of the dilemma of men who felt immobilized by doubt or uncertainty during the crisis of 1774–1775. The subject deserves attention, all the more now in light of Bernard Bailyn's pioneering analysis of the "interior view" of Revolutionary ideas..."the assumptions, beliefs, and ideas...that lay behind the manifest events of the time."[1]

The plight of the uncommitted was recognized at the time, even by men who were themselves wholly committed to the Revolutionary cause. "I say, gentlemen, there are men among us who are not enemies to their country, who are friends to all America,...[who] acknowledge that we are greatly aggrieved and oppressed," Henry Laurens told the South Carolina Provincial Congress on July 4, 1775, "but they cannot, they dare not, for many reasons, subscribe to the [non-importation] Association....Other men there are who are no less friendly to America...but who think we have precipitated a measure which ought to have been delayed." Laurens refused to "anathemize" these "good men."[2] Such a man was Richard Wells, a Philadelphia moderate, who affirmed that the colonies could not submit to Parliamentary dictation and yet searched for a means of avoiding rash or violent resistance. "When an individual shall dare to step forth with his private opinion and offer to public notice on affairs of the utmost importance

Robert Beverley's Perception

to his country, much does he risque in the attempt.... Hard is the *middle* path to find." Yearning for political wisdom which he feared he did not possess. Wells continued, *"I contend with a zeal which convinces me that I am right* that ...our passions cannot always remain upon the stretch; we shall gently relax...and heedlessly and gradually slide down the hill of opposition; our rulers will become tyrants; and from a country of happy freeman, we shall degenerate into a land of abject slaves."[3] The Reverend Jeremy Belknap of Dover, New Hampshire, an Old Light Congregationalist, refused to sign a non-importation "Covenant" in July 1774, "because tyranny in one shape is as odious to me as tyranny in another." The Covenant had been drafted in Boston and distributed from Portsmouth to the towns of New Hampshire "without any legal authority" from the people asked to sign it. "Here is no liberty of conscience nor right of private judgment." A year later Belknap was a member of a Committee of Safety and a militia chaplain, but the moment of crisis in 1774 found him immobilized.[4] An Anglican cleric in Philadelphia, William Smith, preached a militia sermon in June 1775 condemning alike "passive submission" to Parliament and "licentious opposition" by ambitious factions against British authority; when, however, the logic of his argument compelled him to prescribe an ethical course for men to follow during the crisis, Smith acknowledged and then evaded the issue: "To draw the line and say where submission ends and resistance begins is not the province of ministers of Christ.... Pulpit casuistry is too feeble to direct or controul here."[5]

Running through these pathetic, candid self-appraisals was a suspicion that political endeavor was neither a meaningful form of human activity nor an effective means of achieving social change. This apolitical skepticism hardened as the pre-Revolutionary controversy grew in intensity and made the opponents of colonial resistance feel increasingly vulnerable and immobilized. Few of these critics of the pre-Revolutionary movement left enough personal testimony to enable historians to explore the interrelationships between their attitudes. One who did was Robert Beverley, a Virginia planter who was neutral during the war. While nearly all of his contemporaries among the Virginia gentry received thorough training in local government and actively participated in resistance against British policies, Beverley avoided the duties of government throughout the pre-Revolutionary period and could not comprehend why his fellow Virginia aristocrats reacted so vigorously to British encroachments. He became a critic of colonial resistance in a colony where whig leaders achieved a remarkable unity. Though himself a third generation planter-aristocrat, he refused to align himself with men of identical social and economic background. He felt ill at ease in political discussion, even within his own family, though he lived in a society which valued political discourse. Beverley's situation was, therefore, a paradox which he did not fully comprehend and which other men misunderstood.[6]

Beverley worried about what made him different from other men and tried to adjust his behavior toward conformity. However, he also valued his vantage point outside of politics and above its temptations and emotions. From this position he tried to join in the pre-Revolutionary debate, to point out flaws in whig reasoning and tactics. At the same time, he refused to compromise his impartiality by joining in the activity of Virginia politics. To complicate his confused situation still more, many Virginians took offense at his apparently carping advice, and their hostility confirmed his worst suspicions about the corroding effect of politics upon such values as trust, tolerance, and good will. Thus he felt a simultaneous pull toward active participation in the pre-Revolutionary debate and aversion to its emotion and discord.

2

Beverley felt vaguely out of place when he returned to Virginia at the age of twenty-three in 1761 after spending ten formulative years acquiring an English education. He described one of his first impressions as "an aversion to slavery: 'tis something so very contrary to humanity that I am really ashamed of my country...and if I ever bid adieu to Virginia, it will be from that cause alone."[7] He sent detailed instructions to his coachmaker in London for a "post chariot,...light green upon silver";[8] resolved to put his newly inherited estates on a sound footing and eliminate his debts and then return permanently to England, where "I solemnly averr I had much rather be an inhabitant...upon £500 per annum than to blaze away here upon four times the sum."[9] Gradually he reconciled himself to settling permanently in Virginia, perhaps because of the weight of his debt to English merchants and his marriage two years later to Maria Carter, the daughter of Landon Carter of Sabine Hall.

He never felt at ease among the Carters, though by every external qualification he was fully their social equal. Perhaps he never had a chance; even before Beverley's marriage the family regarded him with suspicion, and Landon Carter heard warnings from his brother that Beverley was immature and irresponsible.[10] Beverley continued to abstain from the drudgery of work in local government in Virginia, assuming none of the posts of vestryman, justice of the peace, or member of the House of Burgesses expected of the planter elite, depriving himself of the opportunity to learn the vocabulary and concepts of political practice. His only recorded interest in public office before 1787 was to ask Landon Carter in 1772 to recommend him for

Robert Beverley's Perception

a possible vacancy on the moribund royal Council.[11] Nothing came of his passing interest in a Council seat, and his disagreements with his father-in-law were enervating experiences, dissipating what little interest he had in political activity. At the close of one of their arguments, when Carter apparently tried to remain cordial, Beverley compulsively replied, "There was not the least need for apology in your last letter. There can be no real [trust?] if we must send every letter with professions and apologies that we would be thought sincere."[12]

As public discussion dealt increasingly with opposition to British policy, his sense of inadequacy heightened. During the tense month of August 1774, for example, he wrote to Carter, ". . . you put an improper construction on my words in making me say that I am resolved to carry my political opinions to the grave." "I meant to say," he explained, that the arguments he had heard in favor of resisting British authority had not *yet* changed his mind. "This is what I intended to say, and if I made use of other sentiments, it was a mistake." Pleading his open-mindedness, he insisted on his right to resist novel opinions as well as his duty to change his mind in the face of convincing evidence: ". . . it [is] the highest folly to be attached blindly to any particular notions or servilely to change opinions," he concluded in defense of his indecisive approach to political issues.[13]

Landon Carter was, of course, by 1774 a deeply embittered man, disappointed in his children and violently hostile toward his son, Robert Wormeley Carter; he would have been a difficult father-in-law for the most congenial young man. Carter's choice of insults, however, and Beverley's reactions to them reveal elements of the younger man's self-image. "Your comparison of your soil and my temper may possibly be applicable enough," he complained to Carter, "but I scarce know a man to whom this comparison may not be extended with equal propriety, for I find very few amongst us who are willing to sacrifice any opinions. . . to adopt others of a different complexion."[14]

Perhaps in an effort to make amends for his neglect of politics, he occasionally made random comments from the sidelines. At first these gestures did him no harm. In 1763 he labeled British restrictions on Virginia currency "a very genteel. . . method of repaying our *ridiculous* and overzealous loyalty in the course of the late war." During the Stamp Act crisis he wrote to Landon Carter, "It cannot be conceived that two millions of free born people will sink tamely into slavery, or give up part of their liberties without making some effort to preserve it." He even suggested expedients which the Burgesses might adopt—renewed remonstrance and then closing the courts—but seemed to sense how little these proposals compensated for his inactivity in the controversy. His letter to Carter ended plaintively, "I am afraid I have transgressed upon your patience, . . . however. . . I will make no

Part I: Ideas

further apology. . . . You may . . . spend a moment or two reading my non-sense, for 'tis possible it may create a smile to find that *I have become a politician.*"[15] He soon abandoned this hesitant endorsement of resistance against British measures, refused to subscribe to the non-importation association after the passage of the Townshend duties, and expressed anger when men accused him of a "sinister purpose" where he believed he had acted out of principle.[16] In 1771, when Carter snorted his disapproval of Lord Dunmore's appointment as governor, Beverley interjected his reasons for reserving judgment. "I do not think it absolutely necessary that every governor . . . should be excessively learned or profoundly wise." Instead he considered a "good heart" more important than intellect, and he proposed to take Dunmore's good sense and integrity for granted until he saw evidence to the contrary. Lord Botetourt, he recalled, had overcome inexperience and achieved success in his performance as governor. "I . . . judge men," he concluded, "as I find them . . . I think it rather cruel to forbode otherwise."[17]

Beverley's insistence on judging men as he found them masked his lack of information on which to found a judgment. Behind a genuine attempt at detached thoughtfulness, he did not know how to think through political issues. Others might come to quick judgments about British intentions, he conceded, but he wanted to reflect longer. The purpose of prolonged contemplation, he implied, was a sense of inner satisfaction which he acquired from making independent judgments.

3

"At present the country is in a most unhappy state of anarchy and misrule," Beverley wrote to John Backhouse of Liverpool in July 1775; "all I can do is to remain . . . a sorrowful spectator of these tumultuous times."[18] He hoped he could remain a static observer on the fringe of Virginia's intense political activity and enjoy the tranquility he would find in neutrality. From that vantage point, however, he could not avoid making occasional comments on politics, and the hostility which these aroused spurred him to defend himself and extend his criticism of whig tactics. His aloofness and political naïveté, as well as his compulsiveness, tended to hide another side of his introspective personality—his acute curiosity about the consequences of emotionalism and agitation on the conduct of politically active Virginians in 1774–1775. "In the ardour of commotions," he observed, "the passions become so inflamed and the tempers so much prejudiced, that frequently measures of the most salutary nature are rejected as the effects of pusillanimity or treachery."[19] Beverley was not only isolated and immobilized by that turmoil, but he also understood how anxiety and stress[20]

Robert Beverley's Perception

among Virginia's ruling elite could accelerate the pace of events and limit the options open to political leaders. Certainly he believed that his reason and judgment had revealed to him an atmosphere in which those rational tools were of little use. While that assessment may have been a subtle and even sophisticated one, Beverley himself was not the kind of facile thinker who could pursue the implications of this sobering insight. He preferred instead to make a virtue of indecision. "In all combustions of this kind," he predicted, "the impartial world will find errors and faults on both sides."[21]

Nothing soothed Beverley's anxiety more than finding equivalent injustice in both British and colonial conduct. At the outset of a long letter to William Fitzhugh in July 1775, he put the best possible face on colonial grievances. He acknowledged the colonies' exemption from British taxation. He conceded that the operation of vice-admiralty courts as well as the penal provisions of the Coercive Acts infringed on the right of trial by jury in a defendant's own locality. He condemned the suspension of the New York Assembly in 1767.[22] But here his concession to the whig position ended. The Boston tea party, he feared, had fatally compromised the integrity of colonial principles. In discussing the tumult in Boston, he brooded over the excesses of both sides. Avoiding the obvious issue of authority versus disobedience, he weighed instead a variety of extenuating circumstances which suggested to him that both sides were wrong, yet each had some justification for its actions. Clearly, Boston had the right to oppose implementation of the Tea Act, but the violent destruction of the tea itself did not sound to him like a deed motivated by patriotism. Because many men there stood to lose money under the East India Company's monopoly, he queried Fitzhugh, "Let me ask how far the destruction of the tea was influenced by virtuous principles." The ministry, he cautioned, ought first to have asked for restitution for the tea before considering harsher penalties. Thus torn, he could only "lament that this unnatural civil war took rise from such a cause."[23]

However, because the crisis in Boston did exist and did involve Virginians, Beverley sought pretexts which would justify continued submission. Virginia could not complain too loudly about the treatment of Boston, he suggested incorrectly, because it had "beheld with silence and unconcern" the suspension of the New York Assembly in 1767 and thereby compromised its capacity to defend the preservation of Massachusetts' representative institutions. Nor, he added, could the colonies claim that the colonial charters protected their assemblies from arbitrary suspension. Charter rights seemed to him conditional on good behavior. Quickly retreating from such a positive statement, he doubted whether the destruction of the tea in itself merited so severe a penalty. Still, he went on, the people of Massachusetts had only themselves to blame because "their constitution...rests so entirely with the people that they are perpetually engaged in tumults and cabals."[24]

Patriot agitators and the emotional quality of their appeals alarmed Beverley much more than the underlying constitutional issues of the pre-Revolutionary crisis. Demagoguery provided him with a phenomenon he could analyze endlessly, pass judgment upon, and blame for all public disorder. The tone of patriot polemics explained to his satisfaction why a constitutional dispute had grown into an emotional contagion endangering his society. At the outset of the controversy each side, he believed, had nervously exaggerated its claims. "Extravagant encomiums" and "illiberal abuse" at once became the medium of discussion. Agitators quickly took advantage of the situation and perpetuated the use of emotional and ill-considered rhetoric. Caught in a trap of their own making, responsible colonial leaders could not retreat or compromise without arousing cries of cowardice or treachery. The tone of patriot propaganda also suggested several concrete consequences of the controversy. The functioning of the British constitution, Beverley explained, depended on men's restraint and willingness to forego personal advantage when they engaged in politics. The militant tone of patriot appeals suggested to him that "ambition, corruption, [and] faction" had seriously blemished the operation of the constitution in Virginia. Emotional rhetoric, moreover, foreclosed the possibility of reconciliation because it artificially inflated men's estimates of their own power and exaggerated the rightness of their position. Under its influence Beverley's acquaintances simply would not listen to his arguments about the true interest of the colonies. Finally, emotional whig arguments only needlessly antagonized British officials. Virginian attacks on Lord Dunmore illustrated this danger. Conceding that Dunmore was a bad governor and ignorant of the colony's interests and rights, Beverley argued that vilifying him served no useful purpose. "May it not be presumed. . . that he has met with some unmerited, illiberal treatment? If he has, resentment is natural to all men, and most probably he may be supposed to retaliate."[25]

The alacrity with which patriot agitators exploited their advantages—such as Dunmore's indiscretions—excited Beverley's curiosity about their motives. "I have long apprehended," he told Fitzhugh, "that we had some men amongst us who, from the beginning, have been artfully endeavouring to blow up the seeds of dissatisfaction that they might gradually and wickedly prepare the minds of men for a change of government." These militants, he suspected, had no concrete program. Instead they felt only a vague anticipation that a republic might be more congenial to their restless temperaments than the ordered society of a limited monarchy. Patriot leaders therefore recognized no debt to what Beverley considered the province's traditions of law enforcement, and their committees of safety in many in-

Robert Beverley's Perception

stances have "tyrannized over the liberty of mankind, and trampled upon the very appearance of humanity and justice."[26] Still more suggestive about the motives of agitation, in Beverley's eyes, was the conduct of colonial printers in publishing anti-British tracts and their ambition to "flatter our prejudices and fascinate our understandings."[27] Typically, he came to no definite conclusions about the motives of agitators. Their conduct suggested to him their lack of appreciation of colonial political traditions, their inability to select concrete goals, and their willingness to undermine the liberties of their critics. Unable to proceed beyond these indefinite suggestions about their motives, he relied on the imagery of disease to satisfy his desire for explanation. He returned repeatedly to the "inflamed" condition of their minds and those of their converts. The printers' ambition to "fascinate our understandings" indicated, suggestively, the nature of the sickness.

The resort to emotional persuasion and the encouragement of intimidation made, in Beverley's eyes, the colonial defense of liberty ambiguous. Throughout the controversy that ambiguity made him feel more comfortable in his own precarious neutrality. Even when he tried to put the best possible face on the colonists' cause in a letter to an English merchant in September 1774, he underlined its ambiguity. "I profess myself strongly for moderate though not submissive measures," he explained. The colonists' wanted "liberty, not licentiousness [nor] independence." If pushed too far they might try to develop their own manufacturing capacity, but such austerity would be unpleasant. "I would not have you infer from hence that this measure is the object of our choice," he cautioned his correspondent. "It is a step which cruelty, injustice, and necessity have driven us to." Quickly he qualified himself: "independence we desire not, as we are conscious it must be as serious to ourselves as to you, and must involve us in endless misery." In this light he reassured the merchant about the purposes of the non-importation association initiated by the First Continental Congress. It was not an act of defiance, but a safety-valve, "a means of extricating many people from their present distresses."[28] Beverley's inability to take a resolute position on the validity of colonial grievances or the propriety of non-importation was rooted in his yearning for repose. "Little more is required," he declared, "to bring this dreadful dispute to a fortunate and honorable issue... than to consider ourselves as members of the British Empire."[29] Only tactics "of the negative cast," he warned Fitzhugh, could serve the cause of liberty.[30]

Throughout the year of crisis in Virginia, roughly between the summers of 1774 and 1775, he tried to find something constructive to say. When he did so he moved erratically from one suggestion to another, uncertain of his facts or their meaning to politically conscious Virginians. He praised the period of relative calm during Lord Botetourt's term as governor (1768–

1770) and deduced from that example an argument for restraint in dealing with Britain. He dwelled on a host of dangers created by the controversy. As an alternative he proposed a scheme of negotiated reconciliation which seemed to him to go to the heart of the imperial problem. His compulsion to speak on these issues, if even to a small audience of other planters, occurred in fits and starts during his period of general avoidance of political activity. The process became all the more painful as his relations with Landon Carter continued to deteriorate. "I heard perhaps a pretended excuse from Blandfield [Beverley's estate] for its coolness to Sabine Hall," Carter wrote in his diary in August 1775. "It seems the conceited wise one attempted, in his trammelled way of condemning all measures publikly fallen upon to support our liberties."[31]

To Carter's astonishment Beverley saw no oppressive pattern in recent British policy and he separated Virginia's political interests in the controversy from those of other colonies. No British encroachment had occurred in Virginia, he declared, since 1770, when Parliament had partially repealed the Townshend duties. So restricted was his definition of a British encroachment that he saw no danger to Virginia's liberty in the Tea Act or Coercive Acts. Having disposed of more recent developments, he turned to consider Lord Botetourt's term as royal governor and depicted it as a happy interlude during which discontent evaporated. Citing two pieces of evidence, which seemed to him conclusive, he recalled Botetourt's speech announcing partial repeal of the Townshend duties and the Burgesses' conciliatory reply. He also called attention to the statue which the Burgesses purchased to honor Botetourt. These considerations, he concluded, "ought in some measure to have restrained our passion for laying aside government."[32] These suggestions revealed Beverley's skepticism about the cumulative dangers of British policies and about the durability of colonial unity. He therefore feared that colonial retaliation would jeopardize colonial interests, especially Virginia's, far more than a continuation of their present difficulties. Non-importation, for example, was particularly dangerous. British merchants, he warned, would not consider an embargo as a temporary delay in the payment of planter debts but as an absolute repudiation of those obligations; non-importation would not only destroy the planters' credit standing, it would needlessly ruin "nine-tenths of the persons engaged in this trade." Finally, it would not deprive the British treasury of needed revenues because Parliament had enacted the Tea Act "more . . . as a precedent" than as a revenue measure.[33]

As an alternative to these precipitate actions, Beverley proposed a plan of negotiated reconciliation which constituted his most forthright contribution to the pre-Revolutionary debate and the furthermost extent of his reluctant participation in it. In the summer of 1774 he had presented a version of his

Robert Beverley's Perception

plan to a meeting of freeholders in Essex County. The colonies, he urged, should send a delegation of prominent colonists with mercantile experience to London, which would reiterate colonial opposition to Parliamentary taxation but temper that stand with the offer of an annual contribution to the cost of imperial defense. The negotiators should reaffirm colonial sympathy for the plight of Boston and request repeal of the Coercive Acts. If the ministry did not respond sympathetically to these suggestions, they should appeal directly to the British electorate.[34] The Essex freeholders declined to endorse Beverley's proposals; in Landon Carter's view they found them "too round about and too passive for people infringed in their common right."[35] Beverley's hopes declined even more when the First Continental Congress showed no more interest in reconciliation. Congress's action was all the more tragic for Beverley because he felt "fully persuaded that the ministry and nation . . . are cordially disposed to accommodate the matter." Britain, he argued, had made a meaningful gesture by proposing Lord North's plan of conciliation. Conceding the unpopularity of North's proposals, he characteristically declared, "I do not by any means approve it, but am sincerely concerned it was not made use of for the purpose of opening a negotiation."[36]

4

The failure of the colonies to seek reconciliation rendered meaningless Beverley's sole concrete suggestion. His halting retreat into isolation left a terminal moraine of warnings about the consequences of independence, but primarily he nursed personal grievances against men who had ostracized him. Acknowledging his ignorance of what colonial leaders were actually doing, he felt that his disregard of tactical considerations gave him a clearer vision of larger problems. "Take it from me," he told Fitzhugh, "though [I am] *no adept in politicks,* as my present character will plainly evince, . . . America can enjoy no solid or even tolerable advantages from an independence."[37] The colonies, he asserted, could only prosper in close commercial relationship with Britain; they needed British protection from European powers; they possessed neither the technical skills nor resources to wage war against Britain. The disunity of the colonies, their proliferation of political systems, religious groups, and ways of life all undermined their apparent unity. "It is true indeed that there seems to be a union of sorts at present, but . . . only in appearance. Ambition, resentment, and interest have united us for a moment." But inevitable disagreements about taxes, the autonomy of the states, the powers of the central government, and the conduct of foreign policy would surely tear apart any American union. In the face of these perils, negotiations with the British ministry seemed a mild ordeal. Regretting the unwillingness of the House of Burgesses to seek reconciliation, Beverley condemned the representatives for jeopardizing the safety of their constituents. Had the responsibility been his, Beverley declared, "I would scrupulously have kept the claims and grievances of the people in view, and would in an ingenuous and declaratory stile have laid them before the Crown." Nothing more complicated seemed necessary. "These [grievances] would have been attended to, and no exception could have been made to the propriety or legality of the petition."[38]

As his hopes for negotiation and restraint crumbled, Beverley could only ponder his own position. The hostility with which other planters regarded his neutrality and criticism of whig tactics caused him unrelenting pain. "I want only to vindicate myself in the estimate of my friends," he told Fitzhugh, "from the cruel suspicion of being unfriendly to my country." He encountered that suspicion in what seemed to him bizarre forms. Men suspected him of seeking special favors from Governor Dunmore, he complained, and even of aspiring to a position in the royal government. All he desired, he replied, was to be left alone to tend his plantations and enjoy the companionship of his family. That privacy was, for Beverley, his "constitutional liberty." Though resisting bitterness, he occasionally burst out in resentment before lapsing into despondency. "You seem surprised," he told Fitzhugh, "that I should conceive I have been ill-treated by my quondam friends. But I tell you I have been, and by some nearly allied to me—or mine." He wished his tormentors well in their political ambition but questioned whether they would find inner satisfaction. What hurt him was not their disagreement with his views, but their inability to separate personal regard from public differences. "It is astonishing," he complained, "that men cannot differ in political opinions without unhinging their former intimacies." In his complete withdrawal from the issues of the pre-Revolutionary debate, he could define his feelings about events only in terms of the damage men had done to his self-esteem. Tolerance and relaxed discussion had always been an essential feature of gentry society, he reflected. Men had an obligation to state their views candidly and temperately. In his limited participation in political discussion he believed he had always done so.

The apprehension he felt, but could not fully express, impelled him in July 1775 to state in conceptual terms his perception of what had happened to political discourse: "I do not esteem a man a jot the less for differing with me in opinion; 'til of late it was common to do so. But by some strange metamorphosis or other, this contrariety of opinions is denied." *"Some strange metamorphosis or other"*—this comment came close to expressing the essence of his view of the Revolution. Because he perceived no difference between ordinary discussion and intense political strife, he could not realize that for his contemporaries the pre-Revolutionary debate had passed the stage of a conversation between gentlemen. Driven by events he profoundly misunderstood, he tried to acquiesce gracefully. "I have found the torrent strong, and therefore shall not oppose it," he wrote, concluding his apologia to Fitzhugh. "The die is cast; I must await the event with melancholy concern." To the end he kept his fundamental commitment clearly in view. "I have always endeavored to avoid any side but that of reason and justice," he wrote in a perceptive summary of his conduct. "I have ever disliked the idea of being thought a party man."[39]

1. Bernard Bailyn, *The Ideological Origins of the American Revolution* (Cambridge, Mass., 1967), p. vi; on the theme of indecision and ambivalence during the pre-Revolutionary crisis, see Wallace Brown, *The King's Friends: The Composition and Motives of the American Loyalist Claimants* (Providence, R.I., 1966), pp. 251–52; William H. Nelson, *The American Tory* (Oxford, 1961), chap. vi; Alan Heimert, *Religion and the American Mind from the Great Awakening to the Revolution* (Cambridge, Mass., 1966), chap. viii; Leonard Woods Labaree, *Conservatism in Early American History* (New York, 1948), pp. 156–66; Sydney V. James, "The Impact of the American Revolution on Quakers' Ideas about Their Sect," *William and Mary Quarterly*, 3rd ser., 19 (1962): 360–82.
2. David D. Wallace, *The Life of Henry Laurens* (New York, 1915), pp. 207–12; cf. *The Works of John Witherspoon* (Edinburgh, 1805), vol. 7, pp. 103–04.
3. [Richard Wells] *A Few Political Reflections...* (Philadelphia, 1774), pp. 59–60, 26, and *The Middle Line...* (Philadelphia, 1775), p. 3.
4. *Proceedings of the Massachusetts Historical Society,* Second ser. (1885–1886), vol. 2, pp. 481–86.
5. William Smith, *Sermon on the Present Situation of American Affairs...* (Philadelphia, 1775), p. 19.
6. Robert M. Calhoon, ed., " 'A Sorrowful Spectator of These Tumultous Times': Robert Beverley Describes the Coming of the Revolution," *Virginia Magazine of History and Biography*, 73 (1965): 41–42.
7. Beverley to Edward Athawes, July 11, 1761, Robert Beverley Letterbook, 1761–1793, Library of Congress.
8. Beverley to Page, Nov. 10, 1761, ibid.
9. Beverley to Edward Athawes, March 3, [1762], ibid.; on Beverley's indebtedness and his comparatively successful efforts "eventually to surmount his financial difficulties," see Emory G. Evans, "Planter Indebtedness and the Coming of the Revolution in Virginia," *William and Mary Quarterly*, 3rd ser., 19 (1962): 521, and on his property holdings during the 1790s, see Jackson T. Main, "The One Hundred," ibid., 11 (1954): 369.
10. Charles Carter to Landon Carter, Jan. 4, 1763, Sabine Hall Collection, Alderman Library, University of Virginia.
11. Jack P. Greene, ed., *The Diary of Colonel Landon Carter of Sabine Hall, 1752–1778* (2 vols.; Charlottesville, Va., 1965), vol. 2, p. 704.
12. Beverley to Carter, Dec. 23, 1771, Sabine Hall Collection.

Part I: Ideas

13. Beverley to Carter, Aug. 28, 1774, Robert Beverley—Landon Carter Correspondence, typescript, Research Department, Colonial Williamsburg, Inc., p. 38.
14. Ibid., p. 43; on Landon Carter's relationships with his children, see Jack P. Greene's introduction to the *Diary of Landon Carter,* vol. 1, pp. 52–57.
15. Calhoon, ed., " 'A Sorrowful Spectator...,' " p. 46 n.9; Beverley to Carter, Oct. 9, 1765, Beverley—Carter Correspondence, pp. 9–10.
16. Beverley to Carter (fragment), Oct. 7, 1770, ibid., p. 21.
17. Beverley to Carter, Dec. 23, 1771, Sabine Hall Collection.
18. Calhoon, ed., " 'A Sorrowful Spectator...,' " p. 42.
19. Beverley to Samuel Athawes, [n.d. ca. June 1775], Beverley Letterbook.
20. Gordon S. Wood, "Rhetoric and Reality in the American Revolution," *William and Mary Quarterly,* 3rd ser., 23 (1966): 27–30.
21. Beverley to Samuel Athawes, [ca. June, 1775), Beverley Letterbook.
22. Beverley to William Fitzhugh, July 20, 1775, Calhoon, ed., " 'A Sorrowful Spectator...,' " pp. 45–46, 48; the significance of this letter is discussed on pp. 42–45, ibid.
23. *Ibid.,* pp. 47–48.
24. *Ibid.,* p. 48; on Virginia's reaction to the suspension of the New York Assembly, see *ibid.,* n. 11.
25. *Ibid.,* pp. 47, 48, 49, 53.
26. *Ibid.,* p. 50.
27. Beverley to John Backhouse, Aug. 10, 1775, Beverley Letterbook.
28. Beverley to ?, Sept. 6, 1774, ibid.
29. Beverley to Samuel Athawes, June 6, 1775, *ibid.*
30. Calhoon, ed., " 'A Sorrowful Spectator...,' " p. 50.
31. Greene, ed., *The Diary of Landon Carter,* vol. 2, pp. 933–34.
32. Calhoon, ed., " 'A Sorrowful Spectator...,' " p. 49; Beverley misunderstood the Burgesses' response to Botetourt, see n. 12, ibid.
33. Beverley to Carter, June 18 and Aug. 28, 1774, Beverley—Carter Correspondence, pp. 35–36, 38–43.
34. *Ibid.,* pp. 46–47.
35. Carter's marginal notation, *ibid.,* p. 48.
36. Calhoon, ed., " 'A Sorrowful Spectator...,' " p. 49.
37. *Ibid.,* p. 52.
38. *Ibid.,* p. 51.
39. *Ibid.,* pp. 53–55; on Beverley's experience after 1775, see ibid., p. 45 n.10. See also "American Nationalism and Other Loyalties in the Southern Colonies, 1763–1775," *Journal of Southern History,* 34 (1968): 50–75 and Robert M. Calhoon, review of William Eddis, *Letters from America,* Aubrey C. Land, ed., *Studies in Burke and his Time,* 13 (1971–72): 2168–2171.

Part II

ACTION

7

THE CHARACTER AND COHERENCE OF THE LOYALIST PRESS

I. "Subservient to the Intentions of Government": The Nature and Dilemma of the Loyalist Press

The loyalists' use of the press—like almost everything else they did—eludes precise definition. Strictly speaking, the term *loyalist press* refers to manifestly pro-British, anti-whig newspapers published during the crises of 1774 to 1776 and still more appropriately to newspapers published in British-held garrison towns from 1776 through 1783. These papers abounded with anonymous opinion essays which perpetuated a tradition of support of British authority and colonial subordination in the press during the entire pre-Revolutionary controversy. Both as a *journalistic enterprise* during the War for Independence and as a *polemical form* throughout the Revolutionary era, the loyalist press is a unique source of insight into the behavior, expectations, and anguish of the American loyalists.

One way to gauge the quality and thrust of pre-Revolutionary loyalist newspaper polemics is to survey the most celebrated of the series of essays appearing under the same pseudonyms. The "Dougliad" essays in the *New-York Gazette and Weekly Mercury* in 1770—written in response to Alexander McDougal's sensational broadside 'To the Betrayed Inhabitants of...New York'—were a full-scale indictment of licentiousness, turmoil, and the Cromwellian antecedents of the doings of the New York Sons of Liberty.[1] Two years earlier the same paper carried numerous installments of the "Whip for the American Whig" by Myles Cooper and other high Anglicans, a series that scourged colonial society for its hostility to Anglicanism

Part II: Action

and to constituted authority.[2] Another Anglican clergyman, Henry Caner, writing anonymously as "Chronus" in the *Massachusetts Gazette and Boston Weekly News-Letter* in 1771–72, set forth a comprehensive rationale for protecting colonial liberty by the "wise and prudent use of the privileges and advantages we enjoy."[3] In 1769 William Henry Drayton and William Wragg wrote a barrage of letters to the *South-Carolina Gazette* condemning the nonimportation movement—Drayton noting that its coercive machinery institutionalized popular opposition in a new and destabilizing way and Wragg denouncing coercion and intimidation as a gross violation of traditional political conscience among the South Carolina elite.[4] The famous "First Citizen"—"Antilon" exchange in the *Maryland Gazette* in 1773 between Charles Carroll and Daniel Dulany, though ostensibly concerned with the powers of the Maryland proprietary governor, grew into a dispute over the meaning of the British constitution, the sources of imperial authority, and the historical roots of colonial liberty.[5]

Surpassing all other loyalist newspaper polemicists was Jonathan Sewall, who published five series of essays between 1763 and 1775. Writing as "J" in the *Boston Evening-Post* in 1763, he replied to attacks on the Bernard administration by James Otis and Oxenbridge Thacher with an argument that, Carol Berkin explains, "espoused liberty, then redefined it in its most conservative form . . . ; endorsed the vigilance of the citizen against tyranny, but reversed the direction from which that tyranny threatened society." As "Philanthrop" in 1766–67 he used the same arguments to deflect the criticism heaped on Governor Bernard during the Stamp Act crisis, and under the same pseudonym in 1770–71 he refuted Samuel Adams's attempt to retry the Boston Massacre trials in the Boston press. As "Philalethes" in 1773 in the *Massachusetts Gazette and Boston Weekly News-Letter,* he sought to stem the torrent of abuse being heaped on Governor Hutchinson, and as "Phileirene" in 1775, he examined in detail the sources and impetus of the Revolutionary contagion.[6]

Finally, John Adams's and Daniel Leonard's climactic duel as "Novanglus" and "Massachusettensis" in the *Boston Gazette and Country Journal* and *Massachusetts Gazette and Boston Post-Boy and Advertiser* in 1774–75 raised what Bernard Mason calls "antithetical models of society," a tory model of "order and imperial stability" and a whig model in which the 'key ingredients' were "liberty and innovation."[7]

While these major series of anti-whig polemics made a thorough case for dutiful submission and restraint by the colonists, scores of individual anonymous essays elaborated on the loyalist argument in the pre-Revolutionary debate and reflected the range and seriousness of the impediments to a unified colonial opposition against British policy. Some of these articles appeared originally or were reprinted in newspapers closely identified with the

The Loyalist Press

whig position while most filled the columns of identifiably pro-British or "tory" papers: the *New-York Gazette and Weekly Mercury* and the two *Massachusetts Gazettes* already mentioned; the *Georgia Gazette,* the *South-Carolina and American General Gazette, Rivington's New-York Gazetteer,* the *Boston Evening-Post,* the *Boston Chronicle,* the Boston *Censor,* and the *New Hampshire Gazette.*[8]

Beginning with the seminal research of Stephen Botein, scholars now emphasize that colonial printers sought to perform a nonpolitical service of opening their columns to all shades of opinion, a role that became increasingly untenable during the early 1770s. As late as July 1774, James Rivington declared that "the printer of a newspaper ought to be neutral in all cases where his own press is employed" and publish all materials submitted to him, "whether of the Whig or Tory flavour." Rivington's perilous neutrality collapsed when a crowd of seventy-five horsemen under Isaac Sears vandalized his press on May 10, and wrecked it completely on November 23, 1775.[9] Hugh Gaine, printer of the *New-York Mercury,* was the classic example of a colonial printer driven against every professional instinct toward a partisan role in the Revolution. Throughout the pre-Revolutionary controversy he gave balanced, objective accounts of political upheaval and published anonymous essays on both sides that were decent and moderate in tone.[10]

Rivington's sympathies undoubtedly lay with the British while Gaine, like many loyalists from the middle colonies, felt equally torn between his sympathy for colonial rights and his aversion to rebellion and violence; the important point is that neither became a partisan of the British cause until the outbreak of war and royal occupation of New York City made neutrality impossible. For a short time in September and October 1776 Gaine tried to print a paper in Newark, New Jersey, in a territory controlled by the patriots while allowing Gen. William Howe's secretary, Ambrose Serle, to manage the *New-York Mercury.* Financial losses in Newark and patriot suspicion forced him to abandon this arrangement, take refuge in New York City, and make the *Mercury* into an avowedly loyalist newspaper.[11] Rivington, who had gone to England in early 1776, returned in September 1777 and resumed publication of his paper on October 4. In his second issue he candidly and accurately affirmed his willingness to make the *Gazette* "subservient to the intentions of government—the restoration of peace, order, and happiness through the continent—by recalling the infatuated multitude to the use of their reason and understanding and by convincing them how grossly they have been imposed upon by the misrepresentations and false glosses of their leaders in sedition and rebellion."[12]

In addition to *Rivington's Gazette* and Gaine's *New-York Mercury,* ten other loyalist newspapers appeared in towns occupied by the British between 1776 and 1783. These included the *Royal American Gazette* in New York City from

Part II: Action

1777 to 1783; the *Newport Gazette* in Rhode Island from 1777 to 1779; the *Pennsylvania Evening Post, Pennsylvania Ledger,* and *Royal Pennsylvania Gazette* in Philadelphia for varying parts of the British occupation of Philadelphia from October 1777 to May 1778; the *South-Carolina and American General Gazette, The Royal Gazette,* and the *Royal South-Carolina Gazette* during the British occupation of Charleston in 1780–82; the *Royal Georgia Gazette* in occupied Savannah from 1779–82; and the *East Florida Gazette* in St. Augustine in 1783–84.[13] The newspapers provided a necessary semblance of normality in towns under British military and administrative control. They spurred the economy by carrying advertisements and other information vital to merchants, artisans, and consumers; trumpeted British military successes; published the numerous official announcements for British commanders and civilian administrators; and provided a forum in which loyalists could lambast their patriot enemies, prod the British government to meet the needs of the King's friends, and explore the ramifications of their self-pitying and often paranoid view of recent history.[14]

The intrusion of Revolutionary politics into the workings of the press and the volatile public impact of political news and opinion in the newspapers together constitute a previously little-understood dimension of the political culture of Revolutionary America. Modern scholarship has explored the editing, coverage, management, and social role of loyalist newspapers.[15] Little systematic attention, however, has been paid to the intellectual and ideological content and character of the great mass of signed and anonymous opinion essays in the newspapers that opposed the Revolutionary movement and vindicated British authority over the colonies. This essay attempts such an appraisal.

2. "Disaffection, Petulance, Ingratitude, and Disloyalty": The Themes of Loyalist Polemical Journalism

In the sixteenth of his "Massachusettensis" letters, Daniel Leonard declared, with bitter sarcasm, "some idolaters have attributed to the congress the collected wisdom of the continent." It was an astute observation. The decision of the First Continental Congress to impose a trade boycott enforced by local committees, coupled with its resolution for a second Congress to assemble in May 1775, significantly altered the nature of the Congress. By setting these events in motion, the Congress shifted from a gathering of representatives of the colonial assemblies into an active guardian of American liberty and authoritative spokesman for American interests. Those functions required Congress to interpret the meaning of fast-moving events and respond with appropriate boldness and vigor to British actions. "The collected wisdom of the continent" exactly expressed

The Loyalist Press

Congress's new status, and Leonard's grasp of that political reality enhances the credibility and interpretive value of the remainder of the concluding paragraph in the sixteenth "Massachusettensis" letter. "It is as near the truth to say," he continued, "that every particle of disaffection, petulance, ingratitude, and disloyalty that for ten years past have been scattered through the continent, were united and consolidated in them [the Congress]."[16]

Disaffection, petulance, ingratitude, and *disloyalty* were terms that came easily to Leonard's pen. To the casual reader of tory diatribes against whig ideology and politics they are nearly synonymous words. At face value, certainly, they are overlapping terms which collectively describe several facets of colonial remonstrance and resistance. But when examined in the context of eighteenth-century usage, each word connotes values and beliefs that distinguish it from the others. *Disaffection* meant filling otherwise faithful subjects with discontent and described the understandable reaction of people to inconsistent, abusive government; it was therefore a process by which a people's natural affections and kindliness were eroded or subverted and replaced with malignant, persistent resentment against constituted authority. *Petulance* depicted a range of personality traits associated with immaturity: saucy, perverse, immodest, pert, insolent behavior. The word suggested too a more deeply engrained trait: wantonness—an undisciplined, animal quest for sensual gratification. In the hands of loyalist polemicists, petulance was an unwillingness, even refusal, to admit objective reality when it clashed with men's desires for domination over others and with their craving for freedom from all restraint. *Ingratitude* was an indisposition to acknowledge benefits received from a government, a patron, or a family. Gratitude implied the existence of interests that knitted groups of men together and provided a rational basis for social cooperation and political acquiescence. Identifying interests as useful, desirable, and beneficial social arrangements, the idea of ingratitude presupposed that men were capable of knowing whence their livelihood, security, and prosperity came and of knowing too that posing deeper questions about human nature and destiny was a dangerous, delusive, and futile activity to pursue. *Disloyalty* was the fatal, irreversible act of rebellion against legitimate authority, the inevitably violent exposure of the vicious animal appetites which, implanted in human nature, were barely restrained by the conventions and habits of civilization and the laws and authority of legally established institutions.[17]

Instead of being merely overlapping, redundant synonyms, Leonard's four terms of abuse conveyed distinct perceptions of politics, morality, and human nature. *Disaffection* was a malignant process; *petulance* a perverted reaction to the truth; *ingratitude* a denial of rational self-interest; and *disloyalty* an ugly and destructive action. Applying these broader meanings to the

Part II: Action

analysis of anti-whig, anti-Revolutionary, and pro-British opinion essays in the press of the Revolutionary era reveals something of the coherence of loyalist ideology. These terms were not rigorous, precise ideas in the loyalists' minds—indeed their cumulative adversities prevented them from ever developing a mature, stable system of thought—but they do provide a new and significant point of access into the interior of loyalist newspaper writing.

Most whigs found their disillusionment with Britain a painful experience and agreed that disaffection was a protracted process in which intellectual and ideological leadership played a critical role in weaning the populace from its accustomed allegiance to the British crown. In contrast to the loyalists, however, the whigs placed disaffection in the historical context of a struggle for political and religious liberty stretching from the eighteenth century back to the Middle Ages. Recent British encroachments on colonial liberty represented to them an aberration from that long historical movement—a tragic, benumbing reminder that even prominent, august institutions and statesmen were capricious and corruptible.[18] Disaffection arose, according to the loyalist press, from the central problem of social control in a free society. "Man is a social Animal . . . whose wants, whose natural powers of Reason, and whose capacity of improving those powers . . . demonstrate," wrote Jonathan Sewall in the first of his "Philanthrop" exchanges with Samuel Adams in 1771, "that he was made for social life." His reason, his need for companionship, and his ability to find safety in numbers dictated that man sacrifice "part of that unlimited freedom of action . . . to which he was born . . ." to obtain and enjoy "the more valuable blessings and benefits of *society.*" That realization of their own rationality and sociability implanted in human beings a moral obligation to "promote the general good" and a realization that "the public good and his own are so intimately connected and interwoven together that whatever is inconsistent with the *former* is equally incompatible with the *latter.*" For that reason, the preservation and maintenance of the public peace were a subject's "principle" responsibility and concern.[19]

Meeting the duty confronted the good citizen with every variety of political guile, aggression, and evil. As "dissentions and divisions" arose around him, the good citizen had to "endeavour, within his proper sphere, to keep up in the minds of all about him an inviolable respect for the *laws*" and "a rational submission to those in *authority.*" Expressed in these terms, obedience and acquiescence to authority required a high degree of self-consciousness and intellectuality. When individuals knew of error and abuse in government, they had a higher moral duty to restrain themselves from uttering harsh cricism lest they promote a general clamor, dishearten

The Loyalist Press

and discourage those entrusted with public office, and jeopardize "that *es-sential subordination* upon which the well being and happiness of the whole *absolutely depends.*"[20]

Disaffection therefore sprang from a single-minded tendency to see in particular political abuses evidence "that *all* in authority are traiterously combined in plotting the *slavery,* misery, and ruin of the society." The subject had a moral duty to assume the "*integrity of intention*" of public officials even when they exhibited their "*human fallibility.*" After all, public officials had to meet the most exacting tests of virtue over long periods of time, operate according to legal and administrative procedures, endure without complaint a constaint barrage of abuse, invective, and intimidation, and exhibit superior ability and blameless private conduct. They therefore deserved respect and deference from thoughtful, reflective subjects. "Arraigning, accusing, and condemning those in the most important stations," Sewall warned, would only "weaken the pillars of the state."[21]

Thus in 1771 Sewall reacted bitterly to the abuse heaped on himself and on acting governor Thomas Hutchinson following the Boston Massacre. By 1775 the cruel, judgmental outlook of the people had brought government to the verge of collapse and threatened to destroy the future stability of the colonial society. "If we look back upon the conduct of the Colonies for some years past, we may find many critical junctures where a prudent silence or a dutiful and rational remonstrance" would have exacted concessions from the British and cleared the atmosphere of rancor and crisis which harmed colonial society. Congress, Sewall complained, should therefore proceed with "extreme caution" so that everyone in the colonies would be "thoroughly convinced that we have truth, justice, reason, and equity for our foundation" before assaulting Parliament and the crown with hasty, ill-considered, patently erroneous grievances. Once again, he lamented, very few men had enough sophistication and toughness to perceive that tact, discretion, and patience were the foremost defenses for colonial liberty. "Such is the unhappy frailty of the human mind that we are in general less attentive to the calls of reason and prudence than the suggestions of passion, prejudice, and vicious habits."[22]

To counteract the infatuation that gripped the public mind, Daniel Leonard declared, involved telling people with painful bluntness that their conduct was dangerous and self-destructive. Was it unduly censorious to accuse the "leading Whigs" of deliberately misleading their unwary contemporaries? Leonard asked; "Whoever has been conversant with the history of man, must know that it abounds with such instances. The same game, and with the same success, has been played in all ages, and all countries." The "game" was to enflame—to politicize—the "bulk of the people" who had neither the "inclination or opportunity" to inform themselves about public

Part II: Action

life but who carried within themselves "a latent spark", of outrage and animal energy "capable of being kindled into a flame." The manipulation of that human weakness, Leonard insisted, "has always been the employment of the disaffected. They begin by reminding the people of the elevated rank they hold in the universe, as men; that all men by nature are equal; that kings are but the ministers of the people; that their authority is delegated to them by the people for their good, and they have a right to resume it, and place it in other hands, or keep it themselves whenever it is made use of to oppress them. . . . Thus the seeds of sedition are usually sown, and the people are led to sacrifice real liberty to licentiousness which gradually ripens into rebellion and civil war."[23]

The shameless dishonesty and diabolical cunning of the agitator therefore combined with the emotional immaturity and suggestability of his audience to create a powerful dynamic propelling society toward anarchy. "If you are so hurried along with the tide of general fanaticism which runs so strong at this day as to believe those *pretended* grievances, which are held up to the public view, to have any *real* foundation," Sewall declared, "you will perhaps think that nothing but a malignant party spirit . . . can stimulate me to thus arraign and condemn the proceedings of the Continental Congress." There was, he insisted, a legitimate human basis for his intransigence "when I see your fears alarmed, your tempers irritated, and passions inflamed, without any just cause, by men, the sole motives of whose conduct are envy, malice, or ambition, I think myself justifiable in attempting to expose the errors and defeat the inimical designs of such men."[24]

Once functioning in tandem, "the minds of the multitude" and their "crafty deceivers" communicated through language almost perfectly suited for conspiracy and sedition. Once men's "passions are engaged, . . . their reason is lulled into a perfectly stupid lethargy, and then mere sounds govern their judgments. The words king, parliament, ministers, governors, mandamus councillors, revenue, tea &c. carry the idea of slavery with them, while with as little color or reason the words congress, charter, patriots, delegates, charter councillors, independence, coffee, &c. carry with them all the powers of necromancy [i.e., magic] to conjure down the spirit of tyranny."[25] "Citizens," it appeared, "have been deluded by the cry of Liberty." Virtually mesmerized by such slogans, the mob committed numerous "violences" in the name of liberty and engaged in ritualistic and bizarre behavior—they marched around a field to a liberty pole, where some of their members harangued the rest, and then they elected committees to undertake the most trivial tasks.[26] "Are there not many among them whose case we may lament," wondered one supposedly bewildered observer, "who at some seasons appeared frantic, superstitious and in some degree idolators by their veneration for a tree and the number 92 . . . [and] their sacrifice

The Loyalist Press

on the annual solemnity or feast of dedication of the juice of lemons, wine &c. which, with the temper and behaviour of the votaries, appear to have some resemblance of the ancient Bacchanalia?"[27]

Disaffection, then, was like a poison infused into the populace to erode their reason, benevolence, and loyalty, and to evoke, instead, their passions, malignity, and licentiousness. Such baser instincts, which many loyalists believed lurked beneath the surface of mankind's rationality and kindliness, should be curbed by individual self-restraint and by the authority of the institutions of church and state. When, however, these barriers were broken down by unscrupulous intriguers who aroused the public by appeals to its passions, the less noble and more irrational side of human nature was exposed. The loyalist assumption that a small cabal of designing, crafty, and self-interested men had played upon weaknesses in human nature to bring out men's baser instincts and in this way to infuse disaffection into the populace was basic to their interpretation of the Revolution. Americans were rebelling, according to many loyalists, not because of concrete and well-founded grievances but because of the concerted designs of a well-organized and disaffected minority to subvert the authority of legally established institutions and undermine America's allegiance to the mother country.

For the loyalists petulance was an attribute of human depravity— conclusive evidence that most people were unfit for political responsibility; only subordination of subjects to their rulers and the maintenance of social hierarchy protected society from the perverse childishness of the disobedient and restive. Whig ideology, on the other hand, rested on a far more comprehensive inquiry into human nature. Only a people imbued with a sense of a social covenant and determined to regulate the exercise of power through constitutional means, whig ideology contended, could guard against the greed and aggression that were intrinsic to human nature.[28]

The loyalists' judgmental rhetoric betrayed their exasperation with the public's tolerance of disorder and disrespect for authority. "Wake up my friends," an anonymous loyalist exhorted his readers, "act like men, like free men, like reasonable creatures.... See and judge and act for yourselves." "Truth," he proclaimed, "delights in free enquiry"; therefore, he was appealing to the colonists to read and consider both the patriot and loyalist points of view.[29] Daniel Leonard also pleaded with his readers to "divest" themselves of "prejudice" and to "hear and weigh everything that is fairly adduced on either side of the question with equal attention and care."[30] Similar attempts to persuade the public to reflect dispassionately on both interpretations of the Anglo-American crisis were made by other loyalists. The Boston *Censor,* for instance, asserted that "truths" were arrived at by "compar[ing] discordant opinions,"[31] and an unknown New York loyalist

Part II: Action

proclaimed, "The ears of a genuine son of liberty are ever open to all doctrines; it is his glory to hear them, examine them, to adopt them if they are true, to confute them if they are false. . . ."[32] Yet loyalists themselves seemed to sense the futility of their endeavors to convince the public and their opponents of the need for an open and dispassionate discussion of Anglo-American issues.

The touchstone of patriot resistance, various loyalist writers declared, was its petulant refusal to listen to or tolerate criticism. A Massachusetts loyalist denounced the Worcester Resolves for advocating that loyal Americans refrain from subscribing to loyalist newspapers like the *Massachusetts Gazette* and likened the patriots to the Catholics who supposedly kept their parishioners in "total heathenish ignorance" so that they could be more easily controlled.[33]

Jonathan Sewall denounced the patriots as a "set of *enthusiastical* persons, who seem to think they have a right to tyrannize over their fellow creatures, and to threaten, insult and abuse everybody that cannot think and speak with them upon the state of our public affairs."[34] The perverse unwillingness of the patriots to tolerate other points of view was also condemned by Myles Cooper, who asked rhetorically, "Can they be friends to liberty, who will not allow any to think or speak differently from themselves, without danger? Will they compel the society to act according to their arbitrary decisions, and yet tell us we are free?"[35] Such intolerance and abusiveness, Daniel Leonard declared, was the product of "an illiberal, bigoted, arbitrary, malevolent disposition."[36] "Whoever contradicts a prevailing humour," explained the author of a prolonged reply to Dickinson's *Farmer's Letters*, "draws upon him the clamor of the multitude. The voice of a modest and impartial enquirer is often drowned in the popular cry. Wild enthusiastical rant, disconnected and unintelligible declamation which only serve to heat the world without instructing it, pass upon the world for truth and solid reasoning."[37]

The patriots' use of intimidation and coercion to silence those whose views were incompatible with their own, the loyalists alleged, opened the door to various excesses and naive ideas about the possibility of imposing virtue on a people. A taste of coercive power over their fellow men so intoxicated the people that they lost the sense of purpose and discrimination that had dignified the parliamentary leaders in their opposition during the early stages of the English civil war:

> Treating all men as mortal foes,
> Who dare their high behests oppose.
> Stark raving mad with party rage,
> With coward arms, those foes engage.
> . . . Dares the poor man impartial be,

The Loyalist Press

He's doomed to want and infamy. . .
Sees all he loves a sacrifice,
If he dares publish, ought—but lies.
. . . Alas, vain men, how blind, how weak;
Is this the liberty we seek?
Alas, by nobler motives led
A Hampden fell, a Sydney bled.[38]

As the loyalists tried to analyze the perverse, petulant, abusive tide of American behavior, they perceived a new kind of revolutionary justice operating according to its own rules and imposing its own exalted standards of public virtue. The patriots did not appreciate the impossibility of imposing a new morality on their fellow men because they were blinded to the monstrous evil of intimidation and coercion. "You vainly imagined to force. . . belief [in] the treasonable articles of your absurd creed," Sewall complained, "by extorted *confessions, acknowledgements, recantations,* and *submissions.*" How could the patriots be so gullible, Sewall demanded to know, as to place any credence in extorted, coerced conversions to their cause. Only "inebriated and intoxicated devotees of rapine and licentiousness" could be so deluded and irrational "as to suppose that any promises, declarations, and engagements thus extorted can be binding upon those unhappy victims to popular frenzy."[39] "Union," another loyalist argued, "can then only be right when the principles upon which it is founded are so." These principles involved "bring[ing] us over by argument and conviction not terror." "It is from such a temper alone that a permanent union can be formed."[40]

In addition to being associated with an obstinate and aggressive intolerance of dissenting views, petulance was related to the apparent churlishness and undisciplined character of the colonists. One of the most thoughtful considerations of the later manifestation of petualant behavior was the high-Anglican series "A Whip for the American Whig." Only a powerful, conservative church that was closely allied with the government, the "Whip" argued, could inculcate enough respect for authority and decorum in public affairs to prevent liberty from degenerating into licentiousness and to restrain the passionate enthusiasts from trampling on the rights of the reasonable, dutiful subjects. "Religion is so confessedly advantageous to society that every reasonable man must endeavor to advance it," Myles Cooper posited, if only from the selfish motive of "increasing the happiness of the community of which he is a member." Reason and self-interest might incline some people to practice "honesty and obedience of government," but, for most men, the "sallies of ambition" and "the unresisted desire of unlimited freedom" could only be inhibited by the prospect of "future rewards" for "virtue" and "punishment of vice." By training people in self-discipline and reinforcing continually men's moral duty to respect and obey legitimate

Part II: Action

authority, religious teaching established "that *order* and *harmony* so requisite to the just motion in the springs of every political system."[41]

Deeply imbued with enlightenment ideas about equilibrium among theoretical political orders, the "Whip" series saw the Church of England and the British Crown subtly using each other—the church receiving protection and sponsorship, the Crown enjoying a gentle, noncoercive way of influencing its subjects. "This prerogative [by which the King was head of the church] tends. . . to create a reverence and veneration for the prince as head of two bodies united, as defender of. . . religious as well as civil privileges: a reverence extremely well adapted to engage his subjects to a ready and cheerful obedience."[42]

The incessant campaign of vilification against the Anglican church—characterized by its "abusive" criticisms, "Slander," "Invective," and "Billingsgate"[43]— and the misrepresentation of its role as a handmaiden of authority, the "Whip" authors argued, undermined public respect for both religion and government. By persistently and abusively attacking the established Church of England, "The American Whig" was in fact "endeavouring to prejudice the cause of Christianity and to bring its ministers into disgrace."[44] Besides leveling a blow at Protestantism in casting "the most odius reflections on the Reformation,"[45] Livingston and Smith, by attacking the established church which was "so interwoven" with the constitution of the British state "that the one must be bent and torn to pieces with the other," were attempting to "inflame the passions of the populace and so root their prejudice that they become, in a great measure, invincible."[46]

Petulance was therefore a mixture of impatient irrationality and limited but dangerous cunning. The Tryon County magistrates and grand jurors, on March 16, 1775, denounced "the artifices used by violent and designing men to practise on the easy credulity of the good people."[47] "These inconsiderate people," complained Bellisarius, "have made themselves idols, viz. Liberty Trees, Newspapers, and Congresses, which by blindly worshipping, have so engrossed their minds, that they neglect their honest professions and spend all of their time" in "taverns where they talk politicks, get drunk, damn King, Ministers, and Taxes and vow they will follow any measures proposed to them by these demagogues, however, repugnant to religion, reason, and common sense."[48] To some loyalists, the impulse behind petulant opposition to all restraint was narrow self-interest: "smuggling merchants" who, "finding themselves too closely watched," conspired to subvert all British authority in America. Resistance was clearly directed by "unprincipled, factious, designing men whose interest it has been to keep alive the coals of sedition."[49] "Every measure of the cabal" against enforcement of the Tea Act "is an undoubted proof that not your liberties but their private interest is the object," declared "Popicola" in the *Norwich Packet:*

The Loyalist Press

"They have too richly experienced the fruits from a contraband trade...to relinquish them to others without a struggle. To Liberty they can pretend no friendship. Every Step they have hitherto taken has been introductive of the most fatal tyranny, a tyranny of so high a nature as not to permit a fellow citizen even to think differently from them without danger."[50] "O poor *degenerate* children!," lamented two New York loyalists. "Such destroyers of liberty itself are a disgrace to their mother, if she is the goddess of liberty. For doth not liberty herself allow every man to enjoy his own sentiments."[51]

Conniving, avaricious politicians fed upon each other's weaknesses. "A New York Freeholder" commended the Athenian statute drafted by Solon that imposed banishment or forfeiture of property on any citizen who stood aloof from a controversy that divided society into two fiercely antagonistic factions. "Designing, passionate, or selfish persons," this writer explained, "are generally the promoters of faction in every state whereas men of real merit and judgment are naturally averse to tumults and fly from the boisterous haunts of discord." "Temperate, discreet colonists," "America's Real Friend" lamented, "have been too indolent; whilst restless spirits [have]... led the inconsiderate into the deep gulphs of sedition, where they lost virtue, loyalty, and good manners."[52]

Petulance was most dangerous because it perverted natural communication between parent state and subordinate colonists. "Far from exciting our gratitude or satisfying our uneasiness and discontent," Isaac Wilkins declared in the New York Assembly, the repeal of the Stamp Act "has only emboldened us to make further encroachments upon [British] authority. We foolishly attribute this gentle conduct towards us to fear and to a consciousness of her inability to compel us to submission." Colonial antagonism and hostility to Britain, Wilkins complained, displaced normal relations with the colonists' "kind and indulgent mother...whose arms are open to receive all such of her children as will return to their duty." Only "detestable parricides" would stab a mother's "bosom" simply to gratify the desire of "Ungrateful brethren" in Boston. The only way to secure redress of grievances from a firm and loving parent was to argue the undue exercise of power, not the illegitimacy of superior authority.[53] To the Anglican rector Henry Caner, the American opposition to British measures was marked by a childlike peevishness. Some American liberties had been "infringed," he admitted, but "will it therefore follow that like froward children we should peevishly throw away the rest, because some things have been taken away?" Instead, he advised that the colonists adopt attitudes of "peace and submission, union and harmony" to prevent all blessings from being taken away."[54] Another observer castigated the unruly and licentious methods adopted by the patriots in the dispute with Britain when he asserted, "Sirs, is mobs, bullying, riots, treasons, rebellions &c. the only ef-

Part II: Action

fectual method for you to prosecute, to obtain his Majesty's and parliament's favour?"[55] Insolence and wantonness described the Continental Congress's approach to the Anglo-American dispute, according to an unknown loyalist who contended that instead of pursuing "wise and prudent" courses of action, the Congress adopted "rude, insolent and absurd resolves" and "wantonly" altered the "constitution."[56] The colonists made fools of themselves when they "gravely assert that [the British] people long famed for wisdom and love of liberty" would spend "a thousand years in compounding and rearing up a constitution out of the materials of the different simple forms of government" and in the end "select nothing but the tyrannical forms of each." Too much of the history of England had gone into the making of the constitution that the colonists now found oppressive and too much blood had been spilled in defending it against domestic and foreign tyrants for colonial diatribes to weaken British resolve to maintain parliamentary supremacy. "Arguing from the abuse" of parliamentary and royal power "rather than from the use" of those "things," the colonists would only forfeit any right to be taken seriously as commentators on British constitutionalism.[57]

To some loyalist writers, the Bostonians, who appeared to be spearheading the American opposition to Britain, epitomized the petulance characteristic of the patriots. Several loyalists criticized their intolerance and desires for domination over others. Peter Oliver in his "Address" to the Massachusetts militia depicted other Americans' attitudes toward Massachusetts as follows: "*the Massachusetts have a different interest from the rest of the Continent; they are a set of brave, hardy dogs; and are always encroaching upon their neighbours.*"[58] The Anglican authors of "A Whip for the American Whig" reminded their readers that it was the people of Massachusetts who hanged the "poor, harmless, inoffensive Quakers," while another defender of the Anglican church recounted the history of seventeenth-century Puritan bigotry.[59] The New England clergy, in the opinion of "Bellisarius," were "the instigators and abettors of every persecution and conspiracy."[60] A Quaker in Massachusetts itself shared the same view of the intolerance of his fellow colonists: "we tell thee friends we esteem George [III] a good sort of a Man ...he is willing every Man should worship God according to his Conscience... which the town of Boston is not."[61] The "insidious" actions of the First Continental Congress, which were comparable to those of the "Spanish Inquisition," were, in the eyes of one loyalist, "borrowed from the seditious Bostonians."[62] The wantonness and self-righteousness associated with the Massachusetts capital was suggested by a group of New York freeholders who spoke of the "rebellious Saints at Boston."[63] A Massachusetts loyalist satirized the insolent and immodest behavior of the Bostonians by contriving a conversation in which a "high Patriotic Bostonian" was made to say

The Loyalist Press

"do not we in Boston live at the fountainhead of political knowledge and are we not to be believed?" In light of such patriot self-perceptions, the author concluded that it was dangerous to speak unless one were unalterably opposed to Britain and that the liberty of the press was for patriots only.[64] In describing the endeavors of the "cunning" and "zealous" patriots in the late 1760s to arouse the passions of the multitude, "Z.T." of Massachusetts paused "to consider the part acted by the town of Boston." "Their spirited resolves and instructions, polemical writings and...practices, and their undue influence and example must have had some effect," he reasoned. "Did not the inhabitants of that town on all occasions keep up such a perpetual din to people from the country about politics, that they were even confounded with the clamour of it?," he began. "They so abounded with politicians, or the echoes of them," he continued, "that in all companies, the poor countryman must hear them display their oratory or vociferations, whether they would or not." Besides being assertive and rabble rousing, the Bostonians were cunning and intolerant: "if any one did offer to oppose them in their extravagant flights and invectives...he might depend upon being ill treated; and called a d——g sl——ve, t——ry, or f——l; and it was also very difficult for a countryman to find where he might set in quiet to drink something...for there are those who are more ready to stir up sedition or slander than to stir a bowl of punch; by which practices the weaker sort are misled, and the less credulous abused."[65]

Petulance, associated with insolent, pert, and undisciplined behavior, a childish unwillingness to consider seriously the reasoned arguments of critics, and an aggressive intolerance of dissenting views, was regarded as being a fatal weakness of the patriots. It led them, according to loyalists, to ignore the best long-term interests of the colonies—a reconciliation with the mother country—which required mature, prudent, discreet, and dutiful representations of colonial grievances to a supposedly just mother country, and to persevere in the belligerent, irresponsible, and shortsighted courses of action that were aggravating the dispute with Britain.[66] And to many loyalists, it was this kind of insolent, provocative, and uncompromising behavior on the part of the patriots that was largely responsible for the crisis in Anglo-American relations. After discussing at length the high-handed, unrestrained and intolerant patriot methods, "Z.T." stated "that it may be justly concluded that such proceedings were greatly instrumental to our present distresses."[67] Henry Caner also believed that if "our affairs...are not so eligible now it is manifestly owing to the improper conduct of our officious patriots...."[68] The Boston Port Bill, in the opinion of a "New York Freeholder," was the result of American "provocation."[69] Daniel Leonard was distressed at the measures adopted by the Continental Congress, which he felt would "irritate and enrage the inhabitants of the two countries,

Part II: Action

against each other, beyond a possibility of reconciliation"; however, the tone of the resolves could be explained to some extent by the fact that "some of the most influential of the members were the very persons that had been the *wilful* cause of the evils they were expected to remedy."[70] And a group of loyalists in White Plains, New York, declared, "our disapprobation of many hot and furious proceedings against the measures taken by the mother country, as, in our opinion, they will rather tend to ruin this once happy continent, than remove grievances."[71]

Moreover, the patriots' attempts to intimidate or coerce those who held opposing views convinced many loyalists that, while mouthing shibboleths about liberty, the patriots were in fact infringing the most basic civil freedoms of Americans. This conviction led several loyalist writers to conclude that the most substantive threat to their freedom emanated not from Britain but from the patriot congresses, committees, and mobs in their midst. As early as November 1773, Myles Cooper advised his readers that "while we are watchful against external attacks upon our freedom, let us be on our guard, lest we become enslaved by...tyrants within"[72] "Take heed," another loyalist warned, "that while the words tyranny and oppression are bandied about, and fixed on Britain, you are not unawares enthralled at home."[73] After denouncing the tyrannical implications of the First Continental Congress's Association, one loyalist declared, "I shall not dare to think or act, but I shall be in danger of being held up as an enemy to my country....Am I to be a slave? I will then be a slave to a King and a Parliament."[74]

The charge of ingratitude touched a sensitive nerve in whig consciousness. The Revolutionary generation had become increasingly enmeshed in its dependence on British consumer goods, capital, and credit. The price of this economic Anglicization, Marc Egnal and Joseph A. Ernst argue persuasively, was periodic liquidity crises and the erosion of colonial mercantile independence in the marketplace.[75] Against this background of provincialism and uncertainty, many colonists groped toward a reassessment of the benefits they enjoyed as subjects of the empire. Loyalist writers to the press, in contrast, boldly seized the issue of colonial self-interest in imperialism and made it their own. Ingratitude for the benefits of the empire weakened the fabric of colonial subordination, the loyalist press argued, because men ignored their own best interests, misunderstood the reciprocal benefits that colonists and the British nation received from the imperial connection, and lacked the patience and sophistication to engineer a reconciliation of the imperial controversy which would preserve American liberty without destroying the empire. Concerned with economic interests, with the preservation of stability and harmony in society, and a pragmatic approach in dealings with imperial authority, the denunciation of patriot ingratitude was grounded in reason and experience.

"It is impossible to review the advantages we derive from our connection with Great Britain," "A Philadelphian" declared, "without wishing it to be perpetual. We are formed by her laws and religion: we are clothed by her manufacturers and protected by her fleets and armies. Her kings are the umpires of our disputes, and the center of our union. In a word, the Island of Britain is the fortress in which we are sheltered from the machinations of all the powers of Europe." Here was the classic loyalist view of the nature of the empire which portrayed Britain as a dynamic culture from which law, religion, military security, and political authority flowed irresistibly to weaker, far-flung colonial societies. The colonists, this writer maintained, were instinctively anxious and insecure about their own ability to survive in a world of powerful assertive European nations. It was therefore axiomatic that a "review" of imperial benefits would strengthen people's identification with the empire: "no wonder... we look forward with horror to those conclusions which must attend ([for] ages hence) our separation from that country."[76]

The stabilizing effect of the British tie was emphasized by Isaac Wilkins, who argued, "Shall we not derive strength, protection and stability from that oak around which we have so long twined ourselves and under the shadow of whose branches, we have so long flourished in security"; it is "our interest" and "our duty" to "cultivate the closest and most intimate union with her [Britain]."[77] Other loyalists stressed the security and freedom guaranteed to the colonists by the British constitution. To Henry Caner, the English constitution was "most perfect," most "favourable to Liberty," and a constitution under which "the subject enjoys more liberty, is more secure in his property, and in the enjoyment of every valuable blessing and Privilege than the subject of any other nation under Heaven." Similarly, a group of loyalist Associators joined together "to declare our firm and indissoluble attachment to our most gracious Sovereign George the third... and with grateful hearts to acknowledge that we are indebted to his paternal care for the preservation of our lives and fortunes."[78] In the opinion of another loyalist, the unity, harmony, and vitality of the various colonies depended on the maintenance of the British tie. "The superintendence and mediation of Great Britain seems to be necessary to balance... the different interests of the several plantations and colonies, and to direct, command and govern the operations and powers of *each* for the benefit and defence of *All*." Furthermore, he contended, "protected by her navy and armies, we shall rise with fresh vigour and strength, and see her free and well balanced constitution gradually communicated to us. In a state of separation, on the contrary, ages may pass, and rivers of blood be shed before any regular form of government could be adopted and fixed on a firm basis."[79] An important factor in colonial economic growth and prosperity, declared "Rusticus," was Britain's "readiness to increase our industry and protect us from foreign injuries. . . . Surely some returns of gratitude, such as become a free and liberal people are justly due for favours received."[80]

Though mutual interest and obligation knit the empire together, the relationship of the colonies to their parent state depended upon British restraint in the use of imperial authority and colonial passivity in responding to British measures. "Eugenio" felt unable to conceive of the empire in terms other than those of "a parent and her children. . . . I look upon it as the duty of Great Britain," he declared, "to give her colonies that countenance and protection to which as children they are certaintly entitled, . . . not only defense of person and property against our common enemies abroad, but [also] the preservation of our essential rights and liberties." He counted on "mutual forebearance" to compensate for "any little appearances of severity on one side or petulancy on the other." The need for such familial goodwill was imperative: "I can easily foresee that unnumbered calamities must burst upon these American colonies unless present difficulties between them and the parent land be speedily adjusted." If the British abridged colonial rights, then colonial self-interest required an added measure of toleration and acquiescence; conversely, the British needed to allow their headstrong children a healthy latitude in coping with the requirements of imperial policy.[81]

The colonists' ingratitude—their unwillingness to recognize the past, present, and future benefits derived from the imperial tie—led them, according to loyalists, to countenance a rebellion that was totally unnatural. The adjective *unnatural*, used frequently by loyalists to describe the Revolution, reflected their belief that the colonies and Britain were naturally tied to each other by the bonds of culture, history, and mutual interest. Severing such a beneficial and deeply rooted link was contrary to the dictates of both reason and colonial self-interest. Because of the "infatuated blindness"[82] of the colonists to their "true interest" and their ingratitude for past British aid and benevolence to the colonies, the patriots could assert what appeared to loyalists to be totally inconsistent with reason and history: that Britain was no longer the mother who "nourished, protected and established us," but had become a tyrant.[83] That such a perception of Britain was totally irreconcilable with common sense and history was asserted forcefully by Daniel Leonard: "Are we to take up arms and make war against our parent, lest that parent, contrary to the experience of a century and a half, contrary to her own genius, inclination, affection and interest, should treat us or our posterity as bastards, and not as sons, and instead of protecting, should enslave us."[84]

The Loyalist Press

The debate in Philadelphia in the spring of 1776 over the alternatives of independence and reconciliation matched the infectious radicalism of Thomas Paine's *Common Sense* against Provost William Smith's deft, adroit advocacy of delay, caution, and patience as bulwarks of colonial liberty. "I am bold to declare and hope yet to make it evident to every honest man," Smith asserted, "that the true interest of America lies in reconciliation with Great Britain upon constitutional principles, and...upon no other terms." Smith's bold pronouncement was at once aggressive and flexible. Inclusion in the empire was not merely a negative restraint, he explained, it was also a source of insight, capability, and strategy for the colonists. "We [have] considered our connection with Great Britain as our chief happiness" because under it "we flourished, grew rich and populous.... Let us then act the part of skillful physicians and wisely adapt the remedy to the evil."[85]

Smith realized that there was a broad coalition of moderates in Pennsylvania who feared the social disruption that would accompany independence and civil war. The Pennsylvania social order—with its numerous ethnic and religious factions and its divided political elite—was more than any other colony susceptible to this argument. "The world has already seen numberless instances of fine-spun political theories which, like the quackeries of mountebank doctors, are to cure all the political evils to which human nature is liable," Smith observed. Sweeping programs of political purification, he went on, invariably ran afoul of a "thousand little passions and interests" which protected people from the arbitrary whims of ambitious rulers and agitators. Independence won through armed rebellion, he warned, would produce "every convulsion attendant upon revolutions and innovations in government untimely attempted or finally defeated: the loss of trade for want of protection, the consequent decay of husbandry, bloodshed and desolation,...an exchange of the easy and flourishing condition of farmers and merchants for a life at best of hardy poverty as soldiers or hunters." Smith saw the society and economy of the middle colonies as rich, expansive, and rewarding while the political system governing the province was brittle, inexperienced, and vulnerable. While "agriculture and commerce have hiterto been the happy employments by which these middle colonies have risen in wealth and importance," all of these attainments could be lost if the British ceased protecting the colonies from the grasping designs of other European powers. Even a successful revolt against the mother country would leave the Americans discredited in the eyes of mankind as a "faithless people," and an abortive rebellion would disrupt the fragile infrastructure of trade, credit, and the honoring of civil obligations. "To see America reduced to such a situation may be the choice of adventurers who have nothing to lose or of men exalted by the present confusions into lucrative offices which they can hold no longer than the continuation of the public calami-

Part II: Action

ties," Smith declared. It was not only the bloodshed and dislocation of a civil war that alarmed him, but the emergence into leadership positions of new men hungry for recognition and impatient with the pace of advancement under imperial rule. Surely the "great and valuable people in *America,* who by honest industry have acquired a competency and have experienced a happy life," would do everything in their power to avoid an abrupt shift in leadership and power.[86]

The trouble with this conservative calculation, Smith acknowledged, was that "the people generally judge aright [only] when the whole truth is plainly laid before them, but through inattention in some and fondness for novelty in others" only "one side" in the imperial controversy was receiving wide circulation and appreciation. Politicians abused the privilege of addressing a public audience when, like the advocates of independence, "they exaggerate or conceal facts, . . . state but one side of a question, . . . warp the judgment [of their audience] by partial representation, . . . give railing for reason, invectives for arguments, and . . . urge the people into hasty resolutions by addressing [men's] passions rather than [their] sober reason."[87] Reconciliation, therefore, required a calm, dispassionate citizenry capable of hearing all of the arguments on both sides of the imperial dispute and secure enough to resist being stampeded into precipitous action. Smith conceded that independence could be legitimately declared if the whole community became "convinced by better arguments than declamations and abuse of things venerable and ancient that future connection with *Great Britain* is neither possible nor safe."[88] For all practical purposes, he argued, the colonists had already declared de facto independence by preparing to resist British coercion and by asserting broad claims of colonial liberty. "It is our duty to continue this resistance till Great Britain is convinced (as she must soon be) of her fatal policy and open her arms to reconciliation." Resolute but not offensive, united and eschewing factional agitation, the colonists, Smith argued, could secure redress without resorting to violence or rebellion. "Upon such a footing we may again be happy. Our husbandmen, our mechanicks, our artificers will flourish. Our language, our laws, our manners being the same as those of the nation with which we are again to be connected." It was an appealing formula. Political calm would restore a flourishing economy; an easing of imperial tensions would enable British culture to continue to serve as a stabilizing force in the diverse society of the middle colonies. Having shown firmness and patience in dealing with British encroachments, the imperial "connection will become more natural and we shall more easily guard against foreign innovations." "*Pennsylvania,*" Smith concluded, making his point unmistakably clear, "has much to lose in this contest and much to hope from a proper settlement of it."[89]

Loyalist writers stressed that colonial ingratitude was a self-inflicted

The Loyalist Press

wound that deprived the Americans of the leadership of some of their most courageous and unselfish fellow citizens. "Does not that man deserve to be heard with candour," asked "A Philadelphian," "who desires not to counteract the general sentiments of his countrymen but thinks it a duty incumbent upon him to endeavor to guard against an evil which may have a tendency to destroy the hope of every virtuous patriot—a hope of our united efforts may be a means to a redress of grievances [and] that the lasting and happy union may be restored between the Mother Country and her Colonies?" By identifying liberty and happiness with the maintenance of political calm and unity, the loyalists were able to depict ingratitude as a cast of mind into which people slipped when they tired of the burden of supporting a common public consensus—a middle position enjoying the widest possible support. The emotional gratification of fracturing that consensus by abusing individuals was, lamentably, very strong.[90] "Such is the violence of our disputing parties," wrote "A Moderate Man," that "whoever differs from either is immediately stigmatized as a *whig* or a *tory*, . . . terms of disgrace according as they are applied by these parties to each other." Many of those who suffer such vituperation "are really pursuing that which appears to them for the interest of the community." What was remarkable about this persecution of the innocent moderates, "A Moderate Man" explained, was a new self-consciousness and sense of political purpose which the experience instilled into the personalities of apolitical novices: "to moderate these party heats, to draw that zeal into a channel where it would really be serviceable, is the duty of every member of the community," he concluded; only when "mutual forbearance, amity, and love" replace "hard words" can "any society" become "quiet and happy."[91]

To execute this kind of political therapy, urged "A Farmer" in the *Pennsylvania Packet*, "let us equally shun the benumbing stillness of *overweening sloth* and the feverish activity of ill-formed zeal which busies itself in maintaining little, mean, and narrow opinions."[92] The most self-conscious newspaper advocacy of a fresh mental outlook in the pursuit of reconciliation appeared in a series of essays by Richard Wells in the *Packet* in the summer of 1774. "The more I consider the importance of the present controversy," he declared, "the more I am convinced of the need of wisdom in our councils. . . . Reason must command our forces. . . . The sparkling ideas of a warm imagination are too apt to soar into the regions of danger and, without providing a proper retreat, involve the bold adventurer in unthought of perplexities." Resisting parliamentary violations of the colonists' constitutional rights, Wells insisted, required rigorous self-control and disciplined use of imagination. "*I contend with a zeal which convinces me that I am right* that we must not pass by the present temper of the times" for a time of crisis was precisely the moment when a high sense of responsibility could offset men's rashness and

Part II: Action

mindless aggression. "Our passions cannot always remain upon the stretch; [soon] we shall gently relax from the severity of strict right and heedlessly and gradually slide down the hill of [mere negative] opposition [allowing] our rulers [to] become tyrants and from a country of happy freemen, we shall degenerate into a land of abject slaves."[93]

Pleading for a cautious, deliberate response to British encroachments, Wells advocated a circuitous strategy in which the Americans would ask the king to instruct his governors to recommend to the assemblies the gathering of a continental congress to draft *"an American Bill of Rights."* Colonial negotiators could then carry this document to London and bargain for British approval of a "legal and firm contract." Such a process would recognize that the empire was an amalgam of many activities, motives, and purposes: " 'tis offensive [and] defensive, connected [and] independent, a mixture of rivalry and friendship, a greater [entity] subordinate to the lesser, and yet all bound together by one interest and affection." By conceiving of the empire as a source of vast material benefits to the colonists, the advocates of reconciliation pointed within the social order itself for insights and wisdom to guide their fellow citizens in confrontation with British power.[94]

Confronted with an apparently brutish and immoral British regime, the whigs looked deeply into their collective selves as the final crises of 1774–76 crashed around them. Externally, they assumed a posture of defiant disobedience. As they prepared for defensive, hopefully peaceful, resistance to the Coercive Acts, they discovered their ability to decentralize resistance through local committees of inspection and correspondence and also how to entrust direction of the common cause to a continental congress. Surprised and emboldened by these discoveries, the leaders of resistance scarcely realized how much they had accelerated the pace of events leading toward independence and war.[95] A few years earlier, a unified movement for national independence would have been inconceivable; to the loyalists watching, the spectacle was incomprehensible and outrageous.

Overt, deliberate, violent disobedience to constituted authority, the loyalist polemicists declared, was rebellion—the ultimate outrage against God and society. "Rebellion is the most atrocious offence that can be perpetrated by man," exhorted Daniel Leonard; "it dissolves the social band, annihilates the security resulting from law and government; introduces fraud, violence, rapine, murder, sacrilege and the long trail of evils, that riot uncontrouled in a state of nature."[96] In one of the most cogent and informative loyalist newspaper polemics, "Plain English" in February 1775 depicted the threshold of rebellion in a listing of twenty-nine specific acts of aggression against "people, who from a sense of their duty to the King and a reverence for his laws, have behaved quietly and peaceably." "Barbarous

The Loyalist Press

cruelties, insults, and indignities, . . . disgraceful even for savages to have committed," composed his profile of "lawless mobs and riots." "Plain English" perceived clearly that the abuse and intimidation of known allies of the Crown and of all officials who refused to renounce the legitimacy of the Coercive Acts radically changed the framework of politics in Massachusetts. The assertion of the will of the people and the physical power that large numbers of people could exert created a new atmosphere of fear and terror in the province. "Last August a mob in Berkshire forced the justices of the court of common pleas from their seats and shut up the court house," the enumeration began; "they also drove David Ingersoll, Esq. from his house and damaged the same. . . . Col. [Thomas] Gilbert of Freetown, a firm friend to government, in August last, being at Dartmouth, was attacked at midnight by a mob of about an hundred but by his bravery [and] with the assistance of the family where he lodged, they were beat off." "Mr. [Jonathan] Sewall, his Majesty's attorney general for this province was obliged to repair to Boston for refuge; his elegant house at Cambridge was attacked by a mob, his windows broke, but they were beat off by the gallant behaviour and bravery of some of the young gentlemen of his family."

Rebellion, "Plain English" sensed, was more than the seizure of power through physical coercion and violence. Random, spontaneous acts of aggression created an aura of their own—unintended and unanticipated by the perpetrators of such conduct—which corroded the structure of civility and acquiescence to authority that were essential to civil government. Daniel Leonard was not only forced to evacuate his fine house in Taunton, but also compelled to watch as the mob fired bullets into the empty structure as a ghoulish gesture of their determination to destroy every vestige of support for the Crown. Vandals cut hair from the mane and tail of Timothy Ruggle's fine horse. At Worcester a crowd of 5,000 required thirty judges, sheriffs, and lawyers to walk bareheaded between two columns of armed men and then signify their compliance with the closing of the courts in defiance of the Coercive Acts. It was the mobs' insistence on symbolic victories that revealed to "Plain English" their design of destroying the symbols of authority and self-respect held by men of accomplishment and social standing in the community. "Daniel Dunbar of Halifax, an ensign of militia there," this account explained, "had his [regimental] colours demanded by the mob, some of the selectmen being the chief actors; he refused; they broke into his house, took him out, forced him upon a rail and was held on it by his hands and legs and tossed up with violence." When Dunbar "resisted" being put "on the rail, they seized him by his private parts to drag him on it, then beat him and after keeping him two or three hours in such abuses, he was forced to give his colours up to save his life."[97]

In the extreme form of rebellion, political disobedience was a mania compounded from the guilt and desperation of evil leaders. "Your officers, my countrymen!," Peter Oliver appealed to Massachusetts militiamen in January 1776, "have taken great pains to sooth and flatter you, that you may not quit your posts and forsake *them* until they have accomplished their ambitious and desperate schemes. Your leaders know that they have plunged themselves into the bowels of the most wanton and unnatural rebellion that ever existed; they think that by engaging large numbers to partake in their guilt that they shall appear formidable, and that by so numerous an appearance the hand of justice will not dare to arrest them." That desperate gamble, that willingness to plunge society into chaos without any consideration of the consequences, generated powerful destructive energies. In what would be a preview of his full-scale history of the Revolution, Oliver narrated the "origin and progress of the publick disorders which . . . terminated in a most unnatural and ungrateful rebellion." By systematically engaging in smuggling, a group of merchants had accustomed themselves to "defrauding King," "injuring and publickly ruining" their fellow subjects, and "by degrees" abandoning every pretense to virtue and responsibility. In the pursuit of illegal gain, the smugglers enlisted as an ally James Otis, Jr., who through oratory and radicalism "swore he would set the province in a flame if he died in the attempt." But the flame that Otis ignited and fanned, because it originated in compulsive ambition and vindictiveness, was the "sort of flame that consumes not only a man's property but also [his] understanding." To offset the "popular commotions" aroused by an attack on the authority of Parliament, Otis felt "it was necessary to enlist a *black regiment*" of clergymen to cast an aura of religiosity on these turbulent and vicious actions. What had started as an opposition to the acts of trade became a torrent of perverted moral outrage: "the press roared out its libels; the sacred desk . . . sounded the trumpet of sedition and rebellion. . . . Libertinism, riot, and robbery soon became the effects of this sort of public spirit; houses were plundered and demolished; persons were beat, abused, tarred and feathered; courts of justice were insulted; the pillars ⁻of justice were destroyed; and no way to escape the torrent of savage barbarity but by paying obeisance to the sovereign mandates of a mob." In this macabre setting, the drama could lead only to death and desolation. "Garretts were crowded with patriots; mechanicks and lawyers, porters and clerygmen huddled promiscuously into them; their decisions were oracular, and from thence poured out their midnight reveries: . . . to form an independent empire" in which "all the friends of licentiousness were to be reimbursed out of the estates of the friends to government."[98]

Rebelliousness, the loyalists concluded, was therefore an irreversible contagion sustained by the desperation of its fomenters and the fear and ignorance of its growing circle of adherents. Once they employed violence and

The Loyalist Press

deceit, the patriots could not hope to control and regulate the behavior of their own supporters; the most ambitious and most cowardly among them would always succumb to the temptation to commit fresh outrages. The career of Nathanael Greene, "A British American" in Charleston wrote in May 1781, illustrated perfectly the way in which "political phrenzy" elevated the most "infamous" men to positions of profit and power. Greene's avarice had been whetted by speculation in Rhode Island paper currency; his ambition ignited when he inveigled his way into Washington's favor early in the war. His early attachment to the dignified and upright Washington was further evidence of his unscrupulous behavior. Washington, at the outset of the war, was known to have doubts about the wisdom of independence. Greene must have known that Washington's heart was not wholly committed to the patriot cause and must have planned to consign "Washington to oblivion" and take his place. "Did you indeed expect Washington would resign?," "British American" demanded. "Is it possible ambition had so totally obliterated humanity that"—unlike Washington—"you could look forward to the redoubled calamities of war and ruin of your country without emotion? Recent experience answers you could....The deliberate murders committed in cold blood, under your influence and direction in the Carolinas in the space of two months, exceed the number ever committed in any one war recorded in the history of Europe....Entrusted with a separate command,...your vanity has been partly gratified,...and the peaceable inhabitants of America now feel, what they might have long expected, from such a commander as you are."[99]

Disobedience and rebellion, the loyalist press maintained, dissolved the delicate network of social relationships that held human aggression under control and enabled people to live in peace and security. By drawing large numbers of people into lawless behavior and by creating large geographical areas where no law or constituted authority functioned, warfare accelerated and magnified this process of social disintegration and moral abandon. Among the most vivid documents illustrating these conditions and expressing this point of view was the narrative of Levi Smith, a South Carolina loyalist militia officer, which told of his capture and imprisonment by the patriots in the South Carolina backcountry during May and June 1781. Disobedience and rebellion generated rampant falsehood, Smith complained; "our enemies have been indefatigable in propagating and screaming accounts of every circumstance by which they feel themselves aggrieved or improperly treated by our government" while "a uniform silence prevails on our side under the hardest usage,...although we have had by far the greatest reason to complain." Loyalist prisoners of the patriots, Smith testified, had received "the most cruel treatment" from their captors, and these "shocking" atrocities should be made known to the whole world. Skeptical readers of his narrative, Smith suggested, could consult numerous loyalist refugees and British soldiers—several identified by name—who had been eyewitnesses to the outrages he had seen.

Smith's story was a grisly one. Upon capture he had been stripped to his undershirt and forced to run for a mile ahead of his mounted captors. When he collapsed, the patriot soldiers beat him with the flat edges of their swords. Once confined in Francis Marion's camp, he arranged to be exchanged for Samuel Cooper, a patriot held by Lord Rawdon. Cooper's brother, William, one of Smith's captors, initiated the exchange. For the next few days he was treated leniently, even allowed to go fishing with a single guard and visit his wife and children while awaiting the prisoner exchange to be completed. Then on the afternoon of May 14, the patriots captured a British outpost and confined their new loyalist and British prisoners, along with Smith, in a mill house. The American commander, Col. Francis Lee, then ordered the hanging of a young loyalist militia officer named Fulker who was accused of turning a sick woman from her house and thereby causing her death. Next the Americans condemned two loyalist militiamen to death. For carrying intelligence to the British army, Priv. John Jackson "was hurried off, stripped, and tied up [by the neck] about dark, and left hanging all night. . . while Fulker's body, which had been cut down to make room for him, lay naked under the gallows." The following day a militiaman named Hugh Maskelly, charged with various forms of collaboration with the British, was led off to the gallows with "only an old dirty shirt tied round him," executed "without the slightest trial or hearing." To his horror, Smith discovered that he was next on Francis Lee's execution list. Demanding to know the charges against him, Smith was charged with having had a part in the burning of the tavern of a Mrs. McCord, whom Smith knew as "a person of notorious disaffection to the British cause." Protesting he had known nothing of the burning until two hours after it occurred, Smith convinced several Continental officers standing nearby that he deserved a trial. Nevertheless, "I was now made ready for execution. The old dirty hunting shirt was taken from Maskelly's body and wrapped around mine." Fearing that Rawdon would retaliate by executing his brother, Samuel, William Cooper got a message to General Marion who arrived at the improvised gallows in time to save Smith's life.

Greene then ordered Smith put in irons. While waiting further disposition of their cases, the loyalist captives in Greene's camp underwent a further ordeal. John McCord, the son of the woman whose tavern had been burned by the patriots, arrived in the camp with a group of loyalist prisoners in chains. These prisoners brought harrowing rumors. A few days earlier, their reports contended, McCord had taken fourteen loyalist militiamen prisoner and handcuffed them in seven pairs. Marching these prisoners to Greene's headquarters and fearful of being overtaken by pursuing patriots, McCord had ordered two of his subordinates to shoot the prisoners in cold blood. "All...died except one Joseph Cooper....The person who was handcuffed with him was named Conrad Millar and was shot first. The murderer...loaded his piece again" and "with great deliberation took sight at Cooper, who moved his head on one side when he perceived him drawing the trigger....The bullet passed through the right side of his neck and he fell; upon which one of the guard run his sword through his neck to make sure of dispatching him and observed he had never seen a son of a bitch bleed so much in his life." Miraculously, Cooper did not die from these wounds. He dragged his dead companion and himself under a shade tree. The next day, the "stench" of Millar's body attracted the attention of two women in the neighborhood. They returned with a knife, cut off Millar's arm below the elbow, and moved Cooper to a house where his handcuff could be broken off and his wounds treated. (Some of these details Smith learned later when both he and Cooper were safely in Charleston.) News of this atrocity filled Greene's camp and so terrorized many loyalists that, fearful of the same fate, they enlisted in the rebel cause to escape captivity. Smith, however, refused to renounce his British allegiance. By this time Greene was in possession of captured documents showing that, prior to his capture, Smith had provided the British with military intelligence. "He asked me if I did not deserve death, as I was American born. I told him that the province had been conquered and that I had, of course, become a British subject." Apparently taking account of Smith's previous mistreatment, Greene paroled him to a nearby plantation to regain his health, and Smith—with some moral qualms—took the chance to escape and, still clad in Hugh Maskelly's bloody shirt, found safety with Lord Rawdon's force which was marching to relieve Fort Ninety Six.[100]

Rebellion, in these gruesome terms, was the natural, predictable outgrowth of all of the political opportunism, social degeneracy, and perverted communalism that had precipitated the upheaval. It fused all of these symptoms into a single fatal malady. The process of disaffection climaxed in a state of rebellion where the whole network of social relations and the traditional authority of institutions of church and state, which restrained passions and inculcated morality, were undermined to unleash the thinly veiled depravity of mankind. Released from the restraints of law and morality and aroused by a cabal of cunning and aggressive intriguers, the passions of the populace knew no bounds. Atrocities took place, often without the knowledge of the Revolutionary leaders themselves, which were unimaginable in a civilized community. For Daniel Leonard this descent into barbarity was what rebellion meant: "a state of war, of all against all...[where] might overcomes right; [and] innocence itself has no security."[101] America had

Part II: Action

been led down the fatal road to rebellion, in the opinion of the loyalist press, by a minority of crafty and aggressive patriots who displayed an incomprehensible ignorance of the best long-term interests of the colonies and an obstinate refusal to take account of the reasoned appeals of critics. They had plunged the colonies into an irrational, unjustifiable, and self-destructive war against a mother country whose benevolence, protection, and aid to the colonies, and whose commitment to constitutional liberty, should have evoked Americans' gratitude rather than their disloyalty. Calm, dispassionate colonists who tried desperately to warn their fellow Americans of the dangerous route that they were embarking upon were, loyalist writers contended, intimidated, coerced, and silenced by patriots who would brook no opposition. As was often the case, Daniel Leonard summarized succinctly the loyalist view of the Revolution when he proclaimed, "the annals of the world have not yet been deformed with a single instance of so unnatural, so causeless, so wanton, so wicked a rebellion."[102]

3. "To Make Blind Eyes Blinder and the Deceived People [to] Imagine Vain Things": The Ultimate Moral Indictment of the Revolution

The corpus of loyalist essays in the press of the Revolutionary era depicts the psychic turmoil wrought by a radical change in the political culture. As old patterns of acquiescence collapsed, as new standards of political morality came to dominate public affairs, and as the pace and tempo of events accelerated, the loyalists' sense of identity, probity, and composure came under severe stress. Internalizing a political culture that was rapidly disappearing and assigning themselves a new role as agents of virtue and reason in a world gone mad, the writers of the loyalist press illustrate the intimate connection between the human spirit and the larger culture of values, expectations, and behavioral norms within which people live. Convinced that the dominant culture of their society no longer motivated people to adopt proper conduct, they sought to "revitalize" it—to make it satisfying and coherent once again. They tried to understand the plight of a strife-ridden and war-torn political order by rethinking and recasting their own deepest yearnings and aspirations in a manner that would harmonize once again their inner and outer worlds.[103]

Simply recognizing the disparity between their own perception of the truth and the motivations and impulses of the patriots liberated the loyalist writers from uncertainty and apprehension. An open letter to "Peyton Randolph" by "Grotius" in January 1775 gained momentum and accusatory power as it identified the tension: "how then, sir, could you thus attempt to make blind eyes blinder, to make the mad Americans rage, and the deceived people imagine vain things. How could you thus set yourselves and take counsel against the Lord's anointed—stimulating the inhabitants of this continent to wage war with their parents and rebel against their lawful sovereign after declaring yourselves his most *loyal subjects* and avowing an *affection and regard for your fellow-subjects?*" "Grotius's" dialectic between morality and disobedience was so taut and highly charged that his argument fairly leaped from assumption to prescription: "surely you could not suppose" that the Continental Association was "a healing measure, tending to an accommodation of our unhappy differences. You must know your preamble was calculated to blind the reason and enflame the passions of Americans, and your association an open act of hostility which could not fail to sharpen the resentments of an affronted, powerful nation, jealous of their rights and tender of their honour."

It was this insensitivity to the known and natural predispositions of British national sentiment that represented for "Grotius" the clearest evidence that the patriots were ignoring the most obvious moral and political realities: "Englishmen, Sir, can never submit to [the] despotism" of illegal committeemen; "an Englishman cannot tamely look on and see bread snatched by ruffians from his children's mouths—it is too much for human nature to bear—it will drive men to desperation, and must surely be productive of confusion and bloodshed." By the grossness and barbarity of their behavior, "Grotius" explained, the patriots would goad humane British rulers to unleash the severe retribution at the hand of a long-suffering, almost infinitely patient, parent finally driven to impose discipline. "It is strange indeed," he concluded increduously "that wise men should hit upon treason and rebellion as a means of *pacifying* an *offended sovereign;* upon *violence* and *robbery* as the preservatives of *civil liberty.*" Reason and elementary political judgment indicated that just the opposite was true; "how much more certainly would the tendency of a gentle, peaceable, orderly conduct have been to obtain these desirable ends."[104]

By adopting a system of moral absolutism, the loyalist press maintained, the patriots dehumanized the British—forgetting the human feelings that ingratitude and rebellion aroused in the minds and hearts of British rulers. When the New York Constitutional Convention, in early 1777, castigated Britain for its coercion and abuse of colonial Americans who had a long record of loyalty and service to the empire, "Integer," in Gaine's *New-York Mercury,* seized the polemical initiative. Incredulously, he quoted the convention's characterization of "the inhabitants of Britain" as a "nation and people bound to us by the strongest ties; a people by whose side we have fought and bled; whose power we have contributed to raise, who owe much of their wealth to our industry, and whose grandeur has been augmented by our exertions." "Gentle reader," retorted "Integer," "here is a great deal of matter

Part II: Action

in a few words.... 'Bound to us by the strongest ties'; I suppose the Convention meant by saying this to give us a proof of their great strength in having burst those ties asunder.... 'Whose power we have contributed to raise'; that is, Great Britain had no power till after she had drained herself of people in order to strengthen us, that we might strengthen her." By making their own ego the center of their political culture, "Integer" explained, the New York patriots had "totally inverted...the order of things" in claiming that the British had reduced them to being *"miserable slaves."* "All of us know," "Integer" scornfully declared, "what wretches, what Israelites in bondage, we have hiterto been till our good representatives...undertook our deliverance. Nobody could possess his farm or dispose of his merchandise; nobody lived in peace or security. Nobody could even say that he had life or property before we were under the direction of our Congresses, Conventions, and watchful committees."[105]

Imbibing unnatural and untried doctrines about their obligations as subjects, the loyalists contended, the patriots became victims of their own desperation. "It was the universal and professed maxim" at the outbreak of hostilities with Britain, wrote the Reverend J. J. Zubly under the pseudonym "Helvetius" in the *Royal Georgia Gazette* in 1780, that *"if we succeed we will be called a revolution and deemed a rebellion if we miscarry."* This "neck or nothing" frame of mind anesthetized the patriots from the pain of anticipating the "ruin and destruction...coming on apace." "Helvetius" had even heard South Carolina patriots say, "we must not look to the consequences," as though the very possibility of defeat and punishment, seriously considered, would be enough to unnerve the radicals. "Upon no other principle than the prospect of success, and that success would abolish the criminality of the means," he concluded, "would men that have any regard for their lives engage in any desperate action." The rebellion not only ignored the truth and gloried in violence, injustice, and irresponsibility, it necessarily converted truth into falsehood and good into evil: "upon this plan...men must place perjury in the room of a lawful oath, to murder must be no crime; rapine and violence hold the place of equity and justice, nor can any design be too dark or any action too villainous for men that expect to succeed in wickedness." By this circular morality, the Revolution became a self-justifying endeavor in which "success will sanctify...all the measures made use of to obtain it."[106]

Bound together by their desperate flight from reality, by an abandonment of traditional moral norms, and by the perversion of the truth, the revolutionaries had plunged their society into a moral and social morass. "Before the interruption of regal government [in South Carolina], plenty, affluence, and increasing prosperity seemed to combine to render the people happy, while poverty, wretchedness, and ruin characterize the era of democratick

The Loyalist Press

oppression," wrote "Drusus" in the *South-Carolina and American General Gazette* early in British reoccupation of the province. Yet pacification and submission to British authority was not yet complete. "Can any man be so absurd as to imagine that the inhabitants of this country were subjects to Congress?" If Congress could not provide protection and military security for the people living under British occupation, how could it claim allegiance?, "Drusus" demanded. In theoretical terms, no confederation even existed until the Articles of Confederation were ratified. In practical terms, the disintegration of the insurrectionary administration in South Carolina was ample evidence of Congress's artificiality and illegitimacy. "If...this MIGHTY STATE [i.e., South Carolina from 1775 to 1780] in possession of *legislative authority*" and an *"executive"* inflicting "vengeance and confiscation against the refractory and, exercizing arbitrary and despotick power in violation of every principle of the constitution, could not prevent its DISSOLUTION, can it be reasonably supposed... that Congress, aided by a few republican enthusiasts in this province will be able to reestablish its independency and participation in the union?"[107]

In their quest for a coherent understanding of the Revolution—for a reasonable way of dealing with capricious, illogical events—the writers of the loyalist press commented astutely on revolutionary behavior. They noted, as we have seen, the symbiotic union of moderation and radicalism in whig rhetoric: a defense of the existing social order that magnified to fantastic dimensions the evil potential of British policy and heightened the moral drama of colonial opposition. The resulting tension within American society was excruciating, and the loyalists noted the release of guilt and desperation into every political transaction. Aware that this emotional energy needed to be channeled and conserved, some patriot leaders advocated Spartan discipline, and others struggled to construct and operate constitutional government. Unable to appreciate those corrective, self-denying measures by the revolutionaries, some of the most thoughtful and knowledgeable loyalist polemicists believed that they alone lived in a world of discipline and constraint. "There are bounds to all human power," "Helvetius" declared in the *Royal Georgia Gazette;* "the doctrine of nonresistance has long and deservedly been exploded, but its opposite, like some powerful and dangerous medicine, ought to be handled with the utmost caution, lest it become a dangerous weapon in the hands of a madman." The history of modern Europe, explained Zubly—who chose the name "Helvetius" because he was a Swiss emigrant—showed that civility and maturity were the mark of people who did not resist every injustice or jealously guard every scrap of power. "The Swiss never revolted," and ever since the height of the Roman Empire they "pleaded, petitioned, and appealed" against imperial encroachments but "suffered" with grim dignity

Part II: Action

rather than "taking up arms or revolting." The Spanish Netherlands, "Helvetius" continued, did revolt against Phillip II, goaded to violence by the Duke of Alva's barbarous suppression of the Dutch Protestants; in marked contrast with the American revolutionaries who casually printed millions of dollars of worthless currency and boasted of their national greatness, the Dutch were tenacious, humble, and soft-spoken. Even courage and genuine patriotism, "Helvetius" concluded with a final example, did not guarantee success to a people fighting for their freedom. The Corsicans had fought bravely for more than forty years against their Genoese overlords only to have "the French, like true politicians, after weakening both parties at last make a conquest of it for themselves"—inflicting cruel atrocities on the Corsican patriots. The lesson of history was clear: "intestine commotions and civil wars are productive of such infinite mischiefs that humanity shudders at their approach, and very great evils and just complaints grow foul and unworthy of the resentment they might otherwise deliver, where the evils produced by an intestine war for redress are thrown into the opposite scale of the balance."[108]

"Helvetius" skillfully arranged a series of quotations from Emmerich de Vattel's treatise on international law. This humane and rational commentary on the limitations of military power as an agent of change placed extremely narrow limits on the meaning of a just war. Vattel observed that while legitimate national interests were at stake in many wars, the passions and aggressiveness of particular rulers were more intimate causes of conflict. He underscored—in the passages "Helvetius" quoted—the futility of war as a means of achieving social change; war itself settled nothing, it only compelled a defeated national to submit to negotiation. If peace settlements depended on "exact and punctual" compliance by all parties, no war would ever end short of the utter desolation and annihilation of the losing side. Because warfare itself spawned so much incidental injustice, a war was never an instrument of justice. The civilized way to end a war, Vattel insisted, was for both sides to strike an imperfect bargain and "extinguish differences by the most equitable" feasible arrangements. On the basis of these terms, the concessions proposed by the Carlisle Commission in 1778 conceded virtually every American claim short of independence. "Is it a just and lawful plea against generous offers of peace," he demanded, "that they cannot be accepted because those to whom they were made" are allied to France? Is fear of insulting an opportunistic ally a valid reason to perpetuate a dreadful war?

Ultimately, the unity of the moral order—which the Revolution had so savagely torn—depended not on history or philosophy but on God's final judgment. Looking forward to that vindication, "Helvetius" defined the Revolution in much of its complexity: "The penalty due to obstinate rebel-

The Loyalist Press

lion in this life is a trifle not to be mentioned with what you must expect when all of the ghosts of the slain, every drop of innocent blood you spilt, every act of violence you concurred in or committed, all the confederates of your crime whom you have forced or seduced, every injured widow's groan and every orphan's tear whom you have ruined, the spoils of the honest and innocent whom you have robbed, every friendly warning which you rejected, will at once arise in judgment against you and render you as compleatly miserable as you have rendered yourselves distinguishedly wicked."[109] No single sentence in all of the loyalist press dealt so comprehensively with the nature and impact of the Revolution. In a single spacious and ominous image, Zubly juxtaposed the innocence, agony, spiritual and physical isolation, virtue, and brutalization of the loyalists with the destructive force and inner nature of revolution: the self-justifying use of violence, the way coercion expanded outward until it overwhelmed even the weak and helpless, and the patriots' determination to pay any price—moral or material—to insure the permanence of their new regime.

The loyalist press did not enunciate a fully developed alternative ideology or a coherent political code, nor did it refute very cleverly the novel and untested features of patriot constitutionalism and mission. But it did articulate a profound sense of moral estrangement from the values that the revolutionaries claimed for themselves and that permeated their republicanism. Loyalist pamphleteers, Leslie F. S. Upton argued, failed to confront the colonists with "the conventional wisdom" of Georgian political orthodoxy.[110] Writers to the loyalist press operated at the more elemental level of moral self-vindication. They internalized their perceptions of upheaval and vented the anguish they felt as innocent victims of a cruel and unnatural rebellion.

1. Patricia U. Bonomi, *A Factious People: Politics and Society in Colonial New York* (New York, 1971), pp. 270–71; *New-York Gazette and Weekly Mercury,* Apr. 9–June 25, 1770, hereafter cited as *New-York Mercury.*
2. Robert M. Calhoon, *The Loyalists in Revolutionary America, 1760–1781* (New York, 1973), pp. 255–56; see also "Poplicola," *Rivington's New-York Gazetteer,* Nov. 18, Dec. 2 and 23, 1773 (for the various titles of this newspaper, see Timothy M., Barnes, "Loyalist Newspapers of the American Revolution: A Bibliography," *Proceedings of the American Antiquarian Society* 83 [1974]: 227), hereafter cited as *Rivington's Gazetteer* for the years 1773–75 and *Rivington's Gazette* thereafter.
3. Catherine B. Mayo, ed., "Additions to...Hutchinson's History of Massachusetts Bay," *Proceedings of the American Antiquarian Society* 59 (1949): 42; "Chronus," *Massachusetts Gazette and Boston Weekly News-Letter,* Jan. 23, 1772, hereafter cited as *Boston Weekly News-Letter.*
4. Robert M. Weir, ed., *The Letters of Freeman, Etc.: Essays on the Nonimportation Movement in South Carolina Collected by William Henry Drayton* (Columbia, S.C., 1977), pp.

142

Part II: Action

53–57, 86–95, essays by Drayton and Wragg from the *South-Carolina Gazette* dated Oct. 26 and Nov. 16, 1769.

5. Peter S. Onuf, ed., *Maryland and the Empire, 1773: The Antilon-First Citizen Letters* (Baltimore, 1974), pp. 3–39.

6. For a convenient listing of Sewall's letters to the press except for the "Phileirene" letters and an analysis of his ideas, see Ann Gorman Condon, "Marching to a Different Drummer: The Political Philosophy of the American Loyalists," in Esmond Wright, ed., *Red, White, and True Blue: The Loyalists in the Revolution* (New York, 1976), pp. 1–18 and 175–77 and Carol Berkin, *Jonathan Sewall: Odyssey of an American Loyalist* (New York, 1974), pp. 31–34, 37–43, 87–89, 97–100 and "Jonathan Sewall: One Tory's Conception of the Press," paper read at the St. Augustine Conference on American Loyalism, St. Augustine, Fla., Feb. 8, 1975.

7. Bernard Mason, ed., *The American Colonial Crisis: The Daniel Leonard-John Adams Letters to the Press, 1774–1775* (New York, 1972), pp. ix–xix.

8. Stephen Botein, " 'Meer Mechanics' and an Open Press: The Business and Political Strategies of Colonial American Printers," *Perspectives in American History* 9 (1975): 215–17; Timothy M. Barnes, "The Loyalist Press in the American Revolution, 1765–1781," Ph.D. diss., University of New Mexico, 1970, chaps. 1–8; Janice Potter, *The Liberty We Seek: Loyalist Ideology in Colonial New York and Massachusetts* (Cambridge, Mass., 1983); Larry R. Gerlach, *Prologue to Independence: New Jersey in the Coming of the American Revolution* (New Brunswick, N.J., 1976), pp. 236–39, 335–36; S. F. Roach, "The *Georgia Gazette* and the Stamp Act: A Reconsideration" and C. Ashley Ellefson, "The Stamp Act in Georgia," *Georgia Historical Quarterly* 55 (1971): 471–91 and 46 (1962): 1–19; and John E. Alden, "John Mein: Scourge of Patriots," *Publications of the Colonial Society of Massachusetts* 34 (1937–42): 571–99, and Sidney Kobre, *The Development of the Colonial Newspaper* (Pittsburgh, 1944), p. 148. For loyalist essays printed in newspapers closely identified with the whig position, see for example "Pacificus," *Pennsylvania Chronicle,* July 25, 1768, "A Barbadian," ibid., Aug. 1 and 8, 1768, "Machiavel," ibid., Aug. 15, 22, and 29, 1768, "Country Farmer," ibid., Aug. 22, 1768; "Anticentinel," *Pennsylvania Journal,* June 16, and Sept. 29, 1768, "Anatomist," ibid., Sept. 8, 25, and 29, and Oct. 13, 1768.

9. Botein, " 'Meer Mechanics,' and an Open Press," pp. 217–19, and Leroy Hewlett, "James Rivington: Tory Printer," in David Kaser, ed., *Books in America's Past* (Charlottesville, 1966), pp. 172–76.

10. Ann Y. Zimmer, "Hugh Gaine, Loyalist Printer," paper read at the St. Augustine Conference on American Loyalism.

11. Ibid. and Barnes, "Loyalist Newspapers...a Bibliography," pp. 225–26.

12. *Rivington's Gazette,* Oct. 11, 1777; quoted in William F. Steirer, "Losers in the War of Words: The Loyalist Press in the American Revolution," paper read at the St. Augustine Conference on American Loyalism; Botein, " 'Meer Mechanics' and an Open Press," pp. 217–19.

13. Steirer, "Losers in the War of Words"; Ralph Adams Brown, "The *Newport Gazette:* A Tory News Sheet," *Rhode Island History* 13 (1954–55): 11–21, 97–108 and "The *Pennsylvania Ledger:* Tory News Sheet," *Pennsylvania History* 9 (1942): 161–75.

14. Timothy M. Barnes, "Occupational Allegiance and Political Neutralism: Loyalist Printers during the Revolutionary War," paper read at the Pacific Coast Branch of the American Historical Association, Aug. 13, 1977; John M. Coleman, "Joseph Galloway and the British Occupation of Philadelphia," *Pennsylvania History* 30 (1963): 289–94; George S. McCowen, *The British Occupation of Charleston, 1780–1782* (Columbia, S.C., 1972), pp. 24–42.

The Loyalist Press

15. The participants in the session on "The Loyalist Press" at the St. Augustine Conference on American Loyalism, Feb. 6–8, 1975, generously assisted the authors of this paper. Carol Berkin, William Stierer, Anne Y. Zimmer gave us copies of their papers and Lucas discussed his findings with us in conversations and correspondence. Timothy M. Barnes, a commentator at the conference, placed at our disposal his extensive collection of photocopies of the loyalist press and answered innumerable questions.

16. *Massachusetts Gazette, and the Boston Post-Boy and Advertiser,* Mar. 27, 1775, hereafter cited as *Boston Post-Boy Advertiser;* for the prescience of Leonard's observation on the First Continental Congress see Daviod Ammerman, *In the Common Cause: American Response to the Coercive Acts of 1774* (Charlottesville, 1974), chaps. 6 and 8.

17. See "disaffection," "petulance," "ingratitude," and "disloyalty" in *Dr. Johnson's Dictionary* and the *Oxford English Dictionary.*

18. The classic analysis of disaffection from the whig point of view was John Adams, "Dissertation on the Canon and the Feudal Law" (1765), *The Works of John Adams* (Boston, 1851), 3: 447–64.

19. *Boston Evening-Post,* Jan. 14, 1771.

20. Ibid.

21. Ibid.; see also "A Suffolk Yeoman," *Boston Weekly News-Letter,* Dec. 29, 1774; "Philo Patria," ibid., Dec. 22, 1774; "C.," ibid., Feb. 16, 1775; "Mercator," *Rivington's Gazetteer,* Aug. 11, 1774; "Major Benjamin Floyd and a great number of others," ibid., Apr. 6, 1775; "An Answer to the Declaration of the General Congress," *Pennsylvania Evening Post,* Mar. 25, 1778.

22. *Boston Weekly News-Letter,* Apr. 6, 1775; for an exhaustive historical argument that the 1692 Charter did not fetter in any way the authority of the crown in Massachusetts, see "A.Z.," ibid., Mar. 2, 1775, and also the major pro-administration arguments in the controversy over the removal of the General Court from Boston by "Verus," "Aequitas," and "Chronus," in ibid., May 16, July 18, 1771 and Jan. 2, 1772.

23. *Boston Post-Boy Advertiser,* Dec. 26, 1774.

24. *Boston Weekly News-Letter,* Mar. 30, 1775; see also "A.B.C.," *Boston Evening-Post,* Sept. 20, 1773; "Protector Oliver," *Rivington's Gazetteer,* Feb. 9, 1775.

25. "Plain Heart," *Boston Weekly News-Letter,* Feb. 16, 1775.

26. "Anti-Licentiousness," *Rivington's Gazetteer,* Apr. 20, 1775.

27. "Z.T.," *Boston Evening-Post,* May 15, 1769.

28. Bernard Bailyn, *The Ideological Origins of the American Revolution* (Cambridge, Mass., 1967), pp. 55–60.

29. "Plain Heart," *Boston Weekly News-Letter,* Mar. 2, Feb. 16, 1775.

30. *Boston Post-Boy Advertiser,* Dec. 12, 1774, Feb. 20, 1775.

31. [Boston] *Censor,* Nov. 30, 1771.

32. "T.W.," *Rivington's Gazetteer,* Dec. 15, 1774; see also "Conciliator," *Boston Post-Boy Advertiser,* Feb. 6–13, 1775; "A Farmer," *Rivington's Gazetteer,* Dec. 2, 1773.

33. "Plain Heart," *Boston Weekly News-Letter,* Mar. 2, 1775; "A Card," *Rivington's Gazetteer,* Mar. 9, 1775, called the Revolutionaries "Protestant Jesuits"; see also "Yeoman," *Boston Weekly News-Letter,* Dec. 10, 1772.

34. "Phileirene," ibid., Feb. 9, 1775.

35. "Poplicola," *Rivington's Gazetteer,* Dec. 2, 1773.

36. *Boston Post-Boy Advertiser,* Feb. 20, 1775.

37. "Letters...which contain a compleat Answer to the Farmer's," *Boston Evening-Post,* Feb. 6, 1769.

38. *Rivington's Gazetteer,* Dec. 8, 1774.

Part II: Action

39. *Boston Weekly News-Letter,* Jan. 12, 1775.
40. "Agrippa," *Rivington's Gazetteer,* Mar. 30, 1775.
41. "A Whip for the American Whig," No. 22, *New-York Mercury,* Sept. 5, 1768.
42. Ibid., No. 32, Nov. 14, 1768.
43. Ibid., No. 2, Apr. 11, 1768.
44. Ibid., No. 19, Aug. 15, 1768.
45. Ibid., No. 14, July 4, 1768.
46. Ibid., No. 21, Aug. 29, 1768.
47. *Rivington's Gazetteer,* Apr. 6, 1775.
48. Ibid., Mar. 9, 1775.
49. "Phileirene," Mar. 2, 1775, and Jan. 12, 1775, *Boston Weekly News-Letter,* see also [Samuel Seabury], "The Congress Canvassed," *Salem Gazette,* Jan. 13, 1775.
50. *Norwich Packet,* Nov. 25–Dec. 2, 1773.
51. John Grou and John Peters in *Rivington's Gazetteer,* Sept. 2, 1774; see also "An Answer to the Declaration," *Pennsylvania Evening Post,* Feb. 24, 1778.
52. "A New York Freeholder," *New-York Mercury,* Oct. 10, 1774; "America's Real Friend," *Rivington's Gazetteer,* Feb. 16, 1775.
53. Ibid., Apr. 6, 1775.
54. "Chronus," *Boston Post-Boy Advertiser,* Dec. 2, 1771.
55. "John Herbert," *Boston Evening-Post,* Mar. 13, 1769.
56. "A Freeholder of Essex and a Real Lover of Liberty," *Rivington's Gazetteer,* Jan. 5, 1775.
57. "Cato," "To the People of Pennsylvania, VII," *Pennsylvania Gazette,* Apr. 10, 1776; see also "An Answer to the Declaration," *Pennsylvania Evening Post,* Feb. 17, 1778.
58. [Peter Oliver], "An Address to the Soldiers of Massachusetts Bay who are now in Arms against the Laws of their Country," *Boston Weekly News-Letter,* Jan. 11, 1776.
59. *New-York Mercury,* Apr. 25, 1768; see also "Anatomist III," *New-York Journal,* Oct. 13, 1768, and "A Dissenter," *Boston Evening-Post,* January 11, 1773.
60. "Bellisarius," *Rivington's Gazetteer,* Mar. 9, 1775.
61. "A Letter from a Quaker," *Boston Evening-Post,* Jan. 25, 1773.
62. "America's Real Friend," *Rivington's Gazetteer,* Feb. 16, 1775.
63. "Major Benjamin Floyd and a great number of others," ibid., Apr. 6, 1775.
64. "Dialogue Between a high Patriotic Bostonian and a plain honest country-man," *Boston Weekly News-Letter,* Jan. 14, 1773.
65. "Z.T.," *Boston Evening-Post,* May 15, 1769.
66. "Juba," *Rivington's Gazetteer*, Sept. 2, 1774.
67. "Z.T.," *Boston Evening Post,* May 15, 1769.
68. "Chronus," *Boston Post-Boy Advertiser,* Jan. 6, 1772.
69. "A New York Freeholder," *New-York Mercury,* Sept. 26, 1774.
70. *Boston Post-Boy Advertiser,* Mar. 27, 1775.
71. "Subscribers, Freeholders, and Inhabitants of White Plains in the County of Westchester," *Rivington's Gazetteer,* Jan. 12, 1775; see also "A Freeholder of Essex and a Real Lover of Liberty," ibid., Jan. 5, 1775.
72. "Poplicola," ibid., Nov. 18, 1773.
73. "Philo-Libertas," ibid., Oct. 18, 1774.
74. "A Freeholder of Essex and a Real Lover of Liberty," ibid., Jan. 5, 1775; see also "Declaration of the Grand Jury and Magistrates of Tryon County," ibid., Apr. 6, 1775; "Anti-Licentiousness," ibid., Apr. 20, 1775; "Phileirene," *Boston Weekly News-Letter,* Jan. 12, 1775; "X.," ibid., June 16, 1774.

75. Marc Egnal and Joseph A. Ernst, "An Economic Interpretation of the American Revolution," *William and Mary Quarterly*, 3d ser. 29 (1972): 3–32.
76. *Pennsylvania Gazette*, May 18, 1774.
77. Isaac Wilkins, "Speech to the New York General Assembly," *Rivington's Gazetteer*, Apr. 6, 1775; see also [Joseph Galloway], "A West County Farmer," *Pennsylvania Gazette*, June 16, 1768.
78. "Chronus," *Boston Post-Boy Advertiser*, Dec. 2, 1771; "Form of an Association in Cortlandt's Manor," *Rivington's Gazetteer*, Feb. 16, 1775; see also "Philanthrop," *Boston Evening-Post*, Jan. 14, 1771; "A New York Freeholder," *New-York Mercury*, Sept. 12, 1774.
79. "Extract of a Letter from London," *Rivington's Gazetteer*, Feb. 16, 1775.
80. "Rusticus," *Pennsylvania Packet*, Jan. 2, 1775; see also "Rusticus," *New-York Mercury*, Jan. 16, 1775; "An Account between Great Britain and her Colonies," ibid., June 6, 1774; "Phileirene," *Boston Weekly News-Letter*, Jan. 26, 1775; "Mr. Cruger's Speech in Answer to Lord North," *Rivington's Gazetteer*, July 13, 1775.
81. *Pennsylvania Ledger*, Jan. 28, 1775; see also "Masschusettensis," *Boston Post-Boy Advertiser*, Jan. 2, 1775; "Phileirene," *Boston Weekly News-Letter*, Jan. 26, 1775; "Isaac Wilkins' Speech," *Rivington's Gazetteer*, Apr. 6, 1775; "Form of an Association in Cortlandt's Manor," ibid., Feb. 16, 1775.
82. "Phileirene," *Boston Weekly News-Letter*, Jan. 26, 1775.
83. "Isaac Wilkins' Speech," *Rivington's Gazetteer*, Apr. 6, 1775.
84. "Massachusettensis," *Boston Post-Boy Advertiser*, Mar. 20, 1775.
85. "Cato," "Letter to the People of Pa., II," *Pennsylvania Gazette*, Mar. 13, 1776.
86. "Rationalis," ibid., Feb. 28, 1776.
87. "Cato," "To the People...VIII," ibid., Apr. 24, 1776.
88. "Cato," "To the People...III," ibid., Mar. 20, 1776.
89. "Cato," "To the People...IV," ibid., Mar. 27, 1776; on Smith's use of the press, see Don R. Byrnes, "The Pre-Revolutionary Career of Provost William Smith, 1751–1778," Ph.D. diss., Tulane University, 1969; on Smith's emphasis on social pluralism and instability in Pennsylvania, see Stephen Lucas, "Between Protest and Revolution: The Ideology of Reconciliation and the Popular Debate over Independence," paper read at the St. Augustine Conference on American Loyalism, and *Portents of Rebellion: Rhetoric and Revolution in Philadelphia, 1765–76* (Philadelphia, 1976), chap. 7.
90. *Pennysylvania Gazette*, Sept. 7, 1774.
91. *Boston Weekly News-Letter*, Feb. 2, 1775.
92. *Pennsylvania Packet*, Feb. 27, 1775.
93. Ibid., June 22, 1774; see also "Anti-Tormentor," ibid., Nov. 21, 1774.
94. Ibid., July 20, 1774; see also "Amor Patriae," *Boston Weekly News-Letter*, Jan. 19, 1769; "A Plan of Reconciliation," *Rivington's Gazetteer*, Nov. 2, 1775; "Isaac Wilkins' Speech," ibid., Apr. 6, 1775.
95. Pauline Maier, *From Resistance to Revolution: Colonial Radicals and the Development of American Opposition to Britain, 1765–1776* (New York, 1972), chap. 9 treats the interior of these tactics and perceptions while Ammerman, *In the Common Cause*, examines their external thrust and impact.
96. *Boston Post-Boy Advertiser*, Feb. 6, 1775; see also "Chaubullagungamuggensis," *Rivington's Gazetteer*, Sept. 22, 1774 ("I cannot but consider the present opposition to Parliament as resistance of lawful authority and the beginning of a rebellion") and "Tranquillus," *Pennsylvania Gazette*, Sept. 7, 1774.
97. *Boston Weekly News-Letter*, Feb. 23, 1775; *Rivington's Gazetteer*, Mar. 9, 1775.
98. *Boston Weekly News-Letter*, Jan. 11, 1776.

Part II: Action

99. [South Carolina] *Royal Gazette,* May 30–June 2, 1781; see also "Drusus," *South-Carolina and American General Gazette,* Aug. 2, 9, 1780 and in [S.C.] *Royal Gazette,* May 2–5, 1781.

100. [S.C.] *Royal Gazette,* Apr. 13–17, 1782.

101. *Boston Post-Boy Advertiser,* Feb. 6, 1775.

102. Ibid., Mar. 20, 1775.

103. See Anthony F. C. Wallace, "Revitalization Movements," *American Anthropologist* 58 (1956): 264–81; Clifford Geertz, "Thick Description: Toward an Interpretive Theory of Culture," in *The Interpretation of Cultures: Selected Essays* (New York, 1973), chap. 1; Peter Berger and Stanley Pullberg, "Reification and the Sociological Critique of Consciousness," *History and Theory* 4 (1965): 196–211; and George Grant, *Lament for a Nation: The Defeat of Canadian Nationalism* (Toronto, 1965).

104. *Boston Post-Boy Advertiser,* Jan. 30, 1775; for a similar diagnosis of British sensibilities see "Scotus Americanus," *South-Carolina Royal Gazette,* June 8, 1780 and "Planter," ibid., Dec. 19, 1780.

105. *New-York Mercury,* Mar. 3, 1777.

106. *Royal Georgia Gazette,* July 27, 1780; "Helvetius" was the Reverend J. J. Zubly, a Presbyterian clergyman who frequently referred to his Swiss origins and whose diary (Georgia Historical Society, Savannah) bore an acrostic which spelled "Helvetius." Zubly was a classic case of a "whig-loyalist" who vigorously defended colonial liberty before 1775 and reluctantly became a loyalist in 1776; see Calhoon, *Loyalists in Revolutionary America,* pp. 180–82 and Bailyn, *Ideological Origins,* pp. 169, 181–82, and 217.

107. *South-Carolina and American General Gazette,* July 20, Aug. 2, 1780.

108. *Royal Georgia Gazette,* Aug. 3, 1780; see also "An Address to the People of this Country by an American Loyalist," *South-Carolina Royal Gazette,* Dec. 25, 1780.

109. *Royal Georgia Gazette,* Sept. 28, 1780; see also ibid., July 27, Aug. 31, Sept. 7, and Oct. 12, 1780; to appreciate Zubly's skillful use of Vattel, cf. James Turner Johnson, *Ideology, Reason, and the Limitation of War: Religious and Secular Concepts, 1200–1740* (Princeton, 1975), pp. 240–53.

110. Leslie F. S. Upton, "The Dilemma of the Loyalist Pamphleteers," *Studies in Burke and His Time* 18 (1977): 71–84.

8

CIVIL, REVOLUTIONARY, OR PARTISAN:

The Loyalists and the Nature of the War for Independence

The loyalists are a perplexing element in the history of the War for Independence. Piers Mackesy considers loyalist writings and documents about the war to be "a nightmare world" of fantasy, contradiction, and venom.[1] The loyalists were, nonetheless, the most immediate victims of the war and among the closest eye witnesses of the struggle, so they cannot be ignored.[2] The loyalists were, to be sure, not an identifiable segment of the population during the war. In the more sparsely settled parts of the middle and southern colonies much of the population was inclined to acquiesce to whatever regime could maintain order and security. In this context, John Shy suggests, the British and patriots were competing for the allegiance and respect of a sizable, uncommitted segment of the population which was loyalist, neutral, inoffensive, or disaffected, depending on an observer's immediate perspective. John Shy has called on historians to think of the war as a "process which entangled large numbers of people for a long period of time in experiences of remarkable intensity."[3] To do so for the loyalists—to define the loyalists' military role, to appreciate their perception of military reality, and to assess their weight as military assets and liabilities—requires that we examine the ways in which the war worked upon, and interacted with, American society, British and American political systems, and the personalities of the participants. Seeking to place loyalists in a broad social context, historians have used the terms civil, partisan, and revolutionary to define the kinds of social conflicts which generated and fueled the War for Independence.[4] Civil war implies two conventional armies arising within the same populace; partisan war refers to the resort to decentralized, guerilla

147

fighting by at least one side; and revolutionary wars are grand upheavals against existing institutions.

This paper will show how useful these terms can be in examining the factual record of loyalist military activity, especially in the first half of the war. However, another concept, "internal war," must be used if one is to see the later stages of the war through loyalist eyes and to understand the psychological impact which the war had on those loyalists who brooded over the military dilemma confronting them and the British.

From Lexington and Concord in April 1775, to the British occupation of New York City and much of New Jersey in the autumn and winter of 1776, and onward into the Howe and Burgoyne offensives of 1777, the advent of war in America was a ragged, chaotic affair. No simple formula can account for the nearly 10,000 loyalists who bore arms during the first half of the war.[5] There were roughly five categories of impulses that drew loyalists to arms. In the first place, some loyalists in arms simply represented Britain's natural assets in America (recently arrived British emigrants, those tied by interest to the British army in New York City or in Albany, or to the Indian Superintendents); second, other loyalists entered the fray in moments of rage, confusion, or fear; third, still others believed themselves to be strategically situated to unleash terrible vengeance on the rebels and acted from a combination of calculation and impulse; fourth, others responded to the need for organized pacification and reconciliation by supporters of the Crown; and fifth, a few groups of armed loyalists were agrarian radicals in conflict with aristocratic patriot elites. Clearly these categories overlap, dissolve into one another, and describe shifting behavior in different circumstances. In light of recent scholarship these are the principal dynamics of loyalist military involvement; we must, therefore, first examine the way in which each of these factors surfaced and interacted with one another.

During the critical early months of the Revolution in 1775 and 1776, British officials and loyalist leaders conceptualized boldly about the role which the loyal populace should play in quelling rebellion. At no other time during the war did initiatives in support of British authority occur so freely and spontaneously. While General Thomas Gage did not place a high priority on exploiting weaknesses in whig control of American territory, he responded positively to every opportunity for preliminary implementation of coordinated, widespread counterrevolutionary activity. He instructed John Stuart and Guy Johnson, Indian superintendents for the southern and northern tribes respectively, to place friendly Indian tribes in a posture of readiness to support British military efforts. He permitted Lieutenant Colonel Allen McLean, who on his own initiative had secured authorization to recruit recent Scottish immigrants, to operate from a base in Boston and to send covert agents to New York and the Carolinas. In North Carolina Gov-

The Nature of the War for Independence

ernor Josiah Martin, a former British officer, generated widespread opposition within the province to the work of the whig leaders. Then he planned a rising of loyalist partisans in the backcountry in early 1776 which would march to Wilmington to rendezvous with British regulars. Independent of Martin's appeals for a quick invasion of North Carolina, the ministry decided that such a move would be an effective means to checkmate the contagion. In May 1775, Gage dispatched part of the regiment at St. Augustine in East Florida to Virginia in order to assist Governor Dunmore in suppressing rebellion. These troops, plus a handful of Virginia loyalists and runaway slaves, occupied the towns of Gosport and Norfolk where from September 1775, until forced to evacuate in January 1776, Dunmore jeopardized the final transit of power in Virginia. At Dunmore's suggestion John Connolly, British governor at Fort Pitt, journeyed to Boston to present to Gage a plan for a massive tory uprising in the upper Ohio valley and around Fort Detroit. Gage alerted General Guy Carleton in Canada and Guy Johnson in the Mohawk Valley to coordinate their movements with Connolly's.[6]

None of these risky, imaginative schemes functioned as their planners intended. Connolly was arrested on his way from Boston to Fort Pitt. The North Carolina loyalists arose prematurely, before the arrival of British troops was yet imminent, and were defeated decisively at the Battle of Moore's Creek. In spite of John Stuart's best efforts to manipulate events on the southern frontier, the Cherokees in the summer of 1776 sought to capitalize on the opportunity posed by the start of hostilities to drive white settlers from their lands. The Indians went to war before the arrival of British troops could divert patriot militia from a campaign of extermination.

Carleton, for his part, took firm charge of British dealings with the Iroquois during the summer and autumn of 1775. He vetoed Guy Johnson's plan for immediate Indian reprisals against rebel militia around Fort Ticonderoga; probably played a role in the dismissal of Daniel Claus, longtime Indian Superintendent for Quebec; and appointed Colonel John Butler, an aggressive, blustering, western New York landowner, to be acting Indian Superintendent when Guy Johnson, Claus, and Mohawk leader Joseph Brant sailed for England to lobby for a more substantial role in quelling the rebellion. Carleton's fear that premature Indian uprising would jeopardize Quebec's defense was sensible, but that admirable caution was offset by his inability to conduct Indian diplomacy. His jealousy of Claus and Johnson and his reliance on the heavy-handed John Butler deprived the British of a capacity to negotiate effectively with the Iroquois in late 1775. This was the very time when American representatives successfully were luring elements of the Iroquois confederacy into neutrality. Butler's jealousy of Brant and his refusal to treat Mohawk loyalists as equals

Part II: Action

significantly reduced British power. In July and August of 1777, when Indians and white loyalists made up half of Barry St. Leger's force that was besieging Fort Stanwix (in conjunction with Burgoyne's movement into the upper Hudson Valley), the Indians were so underfed, poorly supplied, and unsupervised that the 500 Seneca and Mohawk warriors in the offensive added little strength to the British strike force. When the siege on Fort Stanwix failed, retreating Indians plundered and assaulted their British and white loyalist compatriots.[7] The failure of these initiatives and preliminary maneuvers made them look clumsy and bizarre. Certainly they point up the truth that irregular warfare is at best only a supplement to, and not a substitute for, conventional military operations. But these British efforts also indicated a willingness to see the armed rebellion as a geo-political process and to experiment with appropriate ways of dealing with an unprecedented military challenge. Even these military setbacks did not stifle irrepressible loyalist activity in the backcountry.

The divisions in American society which Martin, Connolly, McLean, Carleton, Dunmore and numerous obscure loyal subjects sought to exploit in 1775 represented some of Britain's natural assets at the outset of the war. The events of 1775–1776 demonstrated how rapidly those assets could be expended. The early months of the war also revealed how quickly new sources of instability within Revolutionary society tended to develop under the pressures of war and how difficult it was for either the British or the loyalists to respond with the right degree of speed and sensitivity to these opportunities.

Vermont provides a vivid example. Loyalist strength there fluctuated erratically. The allies of the Crown in the New Hampshire Grants region, New York land speculators, were driven from the region in 1775 by the insurgent movement led by Ethan and Ira Allen. Amid chaotic conditions in 1776, especially the absence of an institutional structure of committees, courts, and militia which could manage the suppression of disaffection, mobs harried and threatened some prominent Yankee settlers who had economic or political ties to the departed New York speculators. To the victims who tried to remain inoffensive these attacks seemed capricious and spontaneous. In fright, anger, or confusion some fled to Canada and many enlisted in loyalist regiments, particularly the Queen's Loyal Rangers under the command of John Peters. When Burgoyne's invasion passed through Castleton, Vermont, in July 1777, local loyalists recruited 400 local residents to help clear a road for the British force. After Saratoga, however, Vermont's prosecution of the leaders of this treasonable conduct was strikingly mild and confiscated property was resold to patriot members of the same families of convicted loyalists. The strongest political drive in the region, the desire for autonomy from New York, precluded internal bloodletting. Later

The Nature of the War for Independence

in the war the Allens' abortive negotiations with the British for a separate peace cast them into alliance with the large minority of covert loyalists in the state.[8]

The mere presence of large numbers of persons disaffected from the Revolution reflected and aggravated social instability which inhibited either side from exploiting its best opportunities. New Jersey was the classic case of Britain's inability to translate military predominance into political advantage. The Revolutionary regime disintegrated in that province as the British occupied New Jersey after the seizure of New York City in the autumn and early winter of 1776. Nearly 2,500 New Jersey volunteers drawn from a pool of some 13,000 loyalist sympathizers provided ample manpower to pacify a conquered province, and the advent of war snapped the already attenuated lines of community between the two factions of Dutch Reformed inhabitants, one reluctantly favoring independence and the other cautiously opposing it. Yet even in this promising setting pacification proved impossible. Plundering by Hessian and British troops and numerous acts of personal vengeance and cruelty by armed loyalists mocked British pretentions to be protecting the King's friends in the middle colonies. Even after the British were forced to retreat to isolated beachheads at Amboy and New Brunswick, turmoil in New Jersey at first presented the British command in New York City with the opportunity to make inroads and then pulled the miragelike advantages away. The community of Jersey exiles in New York City continually undermined the British commanders by their penchant for unauthorized terrorist activities.[9]

Garrison towns like New York City gave the British secure bases and havens for loyalist refugees. Garrison towns also were unstable, abnormal communities filled with violent, rootless men. St. Augustine in East Florida and Pensacola in West Florida were refuges for more than 15,000 loyalists driven from the southern colonies. In order to organize these bloated wartime communities the British distributed lavish new land grants and assured refugees that British rule in the Floridas would be perpetual. In East Florida large numbers enlisted into a loyalist provincial corps, the East Florida Rangers, which became a pawn in a vicious power struggle between Colonel Alexander Prevost and Governor Patrick Tonyn. Tonyn appointed the irrepressible South Carolina backcountry partisan, Thomas Brown, commander of the Rangers. First used to patrol the border between East Florida and Georgia, the Rangers increasingly carried out raids into Georgia to steal cattle and slaves.

Ambitious to recapture Georgia on his own initiative and constantly fearful that rebel militia and regulars would swoop down on St. Augustine, Tonyn expected Prevost to function as a subordinate. Tonyn also tried to undercut Indian Superintendent John Stuart's careful management of the

Creeks and Choctaws. The impetuous governor expected Stuart to arrange massive Indian support for the reconquest of Georgia and for the periodic reinforcement of St. Augustine. He could not comprehend Stuart's view that Indian support was a precious commodity that required careful bargaining and prudent use. For his part, Thomas Brown knew that there were thousands of potential loyalists still living in the Georgia and South Carolina backcountry and in pockets of the lowcountry as well. With Tonyn's support he committed the Rangers to a dangerous role as spearhead of the reconquest of the backcountry. Tonyn's and Brown's efforts to instill energy, purpose, and zeal into the loyalist exile community in East Florida were just the sort of energetic civil-military policy so badly lacking elsewhere in America in 1776–77, but these efforts came at a high price. Incursions into Georgia, attempts to use Indians as shock troops, and the resort to savage, irregular warfare awakened the disspirited and chaotic Revolutionary governments of South Carolina and Georgia to the magnitude of the threat which the war posed for their society.[10]

The most thorough and competent effort to pacify Revolutionary America and to reinstitute British authority was, of course, Joseph Galloway's administration as Superintendent of Police and of Exports and Imports in occupied Philadelphia from his appointment in December 1777, until British evacuation the following June. Galloway successfully expanded a subordinate job in the military bureaucracy into that of a powerful administrative overseer of British policy in the city. Since his flight to refuge in New York City in December 1776, Galloway had labored to persuade Howe to move against Philadelphia. He even arranged for pilots familiar with the Delaware River to rendezvous with the British attack force. He was upset to learn that one of these men was caught and summarily hanged when Howe decided on the less risky and longer Chesapeake route to southeastern Pennsylvania.

Disdainful of Howe's languid movement into the city, Galloway assumed the role of civilian overlord of the region as soon as British troops landed at Head of Elk. He appointed a large staff of assistants and undertook systematic collection of intelligence, certification of loyalists, exposure of suspected rebel sympathizers, acquisition of food, establishment of hospital administration, and the issuance of regulations on curfews, garbage collection, tavern licenses, relief for the poor, and other local government functions. At his own expense he organized two companies of loyalist refugees and directed a number of guerilla agents and spies who exhibited great discipline and loyalty. Reestablishing civil government in all but name was for Galloway one essential precondition for reconciliation; the other was constitutional reform along the lines of his 1774 Plan of Union.[11]

Bitterly disappointed by Howe's failure to move aggressively, Galloway in

The Nature of the War for Independence

1779 was the star witness in a Parliamentary inquiry into Howe's conduct of the war. His ludicrous assertion that 80 percent of the population was loyal to the Crown has tended to discredit his assessment of the war. Actually Howe and Galloway shared many of the same assumptions about the nature of the war and of the requirements for pacification. Howe believed that the mass of the population would begin to adhere to the Crown as soon as they saw the Continental Army forced to retreat from centers of population and unable to resist the steady, methodical occupation of territory by British regulars. Galloway predicted that if the loyalist majority of the population was given an opportunity to support pacification, they would respond in large numbers, provided that they were cajoled, coaxed, and assured of safety and security. Howe's and Galloway's views on the disposition of loyalist strength and mechanics of pacification differed in emphasis and tone, but not in substance. This may explain why the two men worked together reasonably well during the occupation of Philadelphia in spite of strong mutual antagonism. The real cause of conflict was Howe's disinclination to nourish Galloway's self-importance and the General's deeply bred aversion to zeal and personal singlemindedness.

That urbane quality of mind prevented Howe from sensing that the middle colonies contained many pockets of desperate men willing to risk their safety and security to vent their hostility toward the Revolutionary regime. In the Hudson Valley and on the eastern shore of Maryland these groups were populist rebels hostile to social hierarchy and anxious to disperse political power much more widely then prevailing whig oligarchs in New York and Maryland would tolerate.

In the Hudson Valley, where tenant unrest had smoldered for a decade, tenants on Livingston Manor, the baronial holdings of the great whig family of that name, seized the opportunity in 1775 to petition for redress of their own grievances. Some four hundred tenants took up arms for the King in 1776; the militia was riddled with disaffection. Finally in 1777 news of Burgoyne's offensive triggered a premature uprising which was crushed swiftly by militia loyal to Livingstons.[12] On Maryland's Eastern Shore the war accentuated sharp economic and social grievances in a region where the Revolutionary regime lacked the institutions and lines of direct political control and influence. Some slaves in the region responded to Lord Dunmore's appeal to blacks to abandon their masters; the first three slaves caught attempting to flee to the British were publicly hanged, decapitated, and quartered. White loyalists were more numerous and more difficult to handle. Local committees of observation and the state Council of Safety lacked the practical power or the political strength to impose severe penalties on avowed British sympathizers. Thirty-four percent of Eastern Shore residents indicted for political offenses during the Revolution were landless, and popular pressure forced judges and juries to deal mildly with them. The militia was paralyzed by demands that officers be locally elected instead of centrally appointed. In salt riots groups of armed men summarily appropriated scarce supplies of that commodity from wealthy whig merchants. In numerous instances whig officials were beaten, cursed, and otherwise abused with impunity.[13]

These isolated cases of violent, lower-class loyalist insurgency did not constitute a real threat to the success of the Revolution, but they manifested an important characteristic of the social order: the presence of a sizable minority of groups who, in William H. Nelson's apt phrase, "felt weak and threatened" and "had interests they felt needed protection from an American majority."[14] These included pacifist and pietist groups, Mohawk Valley Indian and white settlers alike who looked to the Indian Superintendent for the northern tribes for leadership and protection, and newcomers to the southern backcountry. The presence and attitudes of these groups did not mean that Britain could have won the war if she had only tapped this asset; it does mean that Britain's strongest resource could be mobilized only at a price which the Mother Country could not afford to pay—the dispatch of enough troops to occupy the large regions where fearful, insecure subjects of the Crown resided and thereby to overcome the sense of weakness which immobilized these defensive people. This confused ebb and flow of loyalist military initiatives helps to define more precisely the nature of the partisan, civil, and revolutionary aspects of the war. Partisan war is irregular war which often involves terror inflicted by informal bands of insurgents. Partisan war occurs when the military and political institutions of one or more of the contending sides have ceased to function in part of the contested territory of the war. A leadership vacuum is created to be filled by men uninhibited by prudence, humanity, or obedience to duly constituted superiors. Irregular war does not replace conventional main force combat, but it occurs on the periphery of conventional combat in areas where neither side can restore stable administration with the use of regular troops. Although it occurs on the periphery of conventional operations, irregular war is destabilizing in that it empowers a relatively small number of men to upset the balance of power previously established between the contending parties. Brant's and Butler's campaigns in the Mohawk and Wyoming valleys were exercises in partisan war. If the loyalist resistance movements in the North and South Carolina backcountry and the Connolly conspiracy in 1775 could have been supported promptly by British offensive operations, partisan war would have been much more widespread.

Civil wars are protracted hostilities between irreconcilably antagonistic segments of society within the same country who intend to exclude one another from political power and social advantage and to extirpate one an-

The Nature of the War for Independence

other's beliefs and principles. By several standards the War for Independence was a civil war. Nineteen thousand loyalists bore arms at one time or another. But civil war was often important as a potential, rather than as an actual, condition. When individual loyalists beseeched the British to concentrate force in a given region—the Delaware Valley, around the Chesapeake Bay, the Hudson Valley, the Ohio Valley, southeastern Pennsylvania—in order to release the energies of numerous loyalist inhabitants,[15] these self-appointed strategic advisors were really saying that civil war was an imminent possibility. Such a war, they reasoned, would be based upon rival loyal and rebel zones of control. It would occur as soon as the British took the necessary risks and expended sufficient manpower and resources to establish secure zones on the colonial map where loyalist and passive adherents to the Crown could reside.

A revolutionary war is the hardest to define because, strictly speaking, the term applies to a society in the midst of a radical redistribution of wealth and opportunity or to a society shifting abruptly from one life style to another—conditions which do not entirely obtain in the case of the American Revolution. The rejection of British authority and the advent of republican government aroused strong passions which approximated those of a revolutionary war. Moreover, the volatile mixture of civil and partisan war which occurred spasmodically during the War for Independence made that conflict potentially revolutionary because it raised the spectre of a descent into barbarism.[16]

From such a perspective the War for Independence was partisan on its periphery, civil only when Britain threatened to gain secure control over a large territorial area, and revolutionary in discontinuous moments when the prospect of American victory portended social changes which were terrifying to cohesive and self-conscious loyalist and neutralist constituencies. This provisional model[17] does not rigidly separate civil, partisan, and revolutionary warfare. Residents of the Mohawk Valley, for example, felt that they were involved in a continuous civil war,[18] but only the period of the St. Leger offensive conforms to a precise definition of civil war: two rival, conventional armies faced one another and Britain nearly gained regional dominance. Mohawk depredations against pro-American Oneida villages during this period, however, marked the threshold of partisan warfare by Mohawk warriors and by Butler's raiders against patriot white settlers and Indians alike.

That very kind of difficulty, however, has impelled political theorists like Harry Eckstein to develop the model of "internal war" to deal with the whole range of conflicts including social revolution, struggles for national liberation, wars of secession, and internal conflicts which accompany political modernization—"any resort to violence within a political order to

Part II: Action

change its constitution, rulers, or policies." Our understanding of such conflicts is incomplete, Harry Eckstein contends, because historians have focused on the specific "precipitants" of internal war and have neglected the "general disorientive social processes" which predisposed a society to slide into violent conflict. Internal war, moreover, becomes unavoidable only when the established government retains enough power to sustain itself in power long after it has ceased to command respect and acquiescence. In this way the concept of internal war encompasses both the "obstacle" thrown up by the old order and the mobilization of popular support needed to overcome those obstacles.[19] Loyalist writings about the last half of the War for Independence dealt with increasing urgency and cogency with the problem of internal war, with the sources of counterrevolutionary activity which lay hidden in the recesses of the social order.

These loyalist writings on the nature of the war may not be accurate objective accounts of military realists, but they reveal the harsh impact of the war on the human spirit and imagination, especially on people suddenly convinced that they were victims of both American cruelty and British incompetence. Conceiving of the war as an instrument of punishment was to recognize the immense complexity of the military dilemma facing the British and the loyalists. Colonel Robert Gray, South Carolina loyalist provincial officer, former whig, and backcountry native, recognized a yearning for order and fear of social disintegration in occupied South Carolina in the summer of 1780. "The conquest of the province was complete," he wrote; "the loyal...inhabitants,...one third" of the population "and...by no means the wealthiest, readily took up arms to maintain the British government and others enrolled themselves in the [loyalist] militia, partly because they believed the war to be at an end in the southern provinces and partly to ingratiate themselves with the conquerors. They fondly hoped they would enjoy a respite from the calamities of war and that the restoration of the King's government would restore to them the happiness they enjoyed before the war began. With these views [prevailing] on both sides, the Whigs and Tories seemed to vie with each other in giving proof of the sincerity of their submission" to British authority "and a most profound calm succeeded."

Far from being an advantage to the British, this state of stability was quicksand. Rebels who took an oath of submission returned to their farms and commerce in Charlestown revived. Caught up in this economic bustle, people were outraged by the British army's confiscation of horses, cattle and supplies. The sudden prominence of loyalists in the civil and military establishment afflicted former whig officials with "pangs of disappointed ambition." When notorious rebels were captured, "ignorant" British officers paroled them to their plantations and in a few days they broke parole and sought revenge on the loyalist militiamen who had assisted in their capture.

The Nature of the War for Independence

In this fluid situation, which oscillated unpredictably between benumbed submission and furious retaliation, the loyalist militia lost their cohesion as fighting units—"officers not able to inspire their followers with the confidence necessary for soldiers" and British regulars contemptuous "of a militia among a people differing so much in custom and manners from themselves." The destruction of Ferguson's loyalist force at Kings Mountain and the increasingly brutal treatment of loyalists captured in the South Carolina backcountry combined to shatter the tenuous control which the Crown enjoyed in the province. "The unfortunate Loyalist on the frontiers found the fury of the whole war let loose upon him. He was no longer safe to sleep in his house. He hid himself in the swamps." Because the British refused to impose execution on rebel insurgents captured by frontier loyalists, Gray believed, many loyalists were forced into collaboration with the rebels in order to be "safe to go to sleep without. . . having his throat cut before morning." Other loyalists simply resorted to the brutal guerilla tactics familiar to survivors of the Cherokee War—ambush, summary execution of helpless captives, decapitation of victims.[20] "In short, the whole province resembled a piece of patch work" in which "the inhabitants of every settlement. . . united in sentiment" took up "arms for the side it liked best" and made "continual inroads into one another's settlements."[21]

Both their keen perception of the strengths and weaknesses of the Revolutionary social order and their fixation upon the use of conventional and irregular violence to undermine that order induced the loyalists during the last half of the war to conceive of the conflict as an instrument of punishment, vengeance, and retribution and as a technique of social control. The Revolutionary social order, however, evaded punishment. Understandably frustrated and angered, the loyalists who dealt with the military situation became increasingly petulant and meddlesome. As a result their fundamental concern with the war as punishment has been neglected. Central to their viewpoint was the assumption that in 1778–1779 the Revolution was about to collapse and their belief that deft, purposeful British pressure could bring this process to fruition: "the rebel currency is tottering on the very brink of annihilation, if not allowed to recover; . . . the people in general are becoming indifferent if not averse" to a government which has brought them only distress and regimentation; "the enthusiasm which at first enabled the Americans without funds, arrangements, or visible resources to act with such success is now lost in disgust and disappointment. . . and in place of that general union and concert which then prevailed there now remains only a faction and a very limited and artificial army, neither of which are of the people." These were the conclusions which leading loyalist refugees in New York City asked Major Patrick Ferguson to convey to General Clinton in November 1779.[22] Taking seriously loyalist testimony about stress in Rev-

Part II: Action

olutionary society does not mean that pre-Revolutionary social antagonisms played a significant part in the causal pattern of the Revolution. Such testimony does suggest that the War for Independence was a sufficiently strong disruptive force to trigger or to exacerbate tensions in society which, while generally held in check, deeply alarmed Revolutionary leaders and impinged on the capacity of their political institutions to function effectively.[23]

The erosion of popular support for the Revolution and the artificial nature of the rebel regime, Ferguson told Clinton, provided the keys for a successful British prosecution of the war. Once the rebels realized that they could not drive the British from Georgia and once the fickle French fleet departed American waters, Britain would be free to undertake a campaign of retribution "distressing the countryside," seizing and punishing rebel leaders, and "living off of plunder." At this point Washington would have to do battle or suffer humiliating retreat, the currency would collapse, Congress would forfeit all capacity to punish deserters, and the people would "see no end of their fruitless sufferings." This scenario required Britain to employ "the only common, justifiable . . . modes of coercion, . . . destroying their resources," confiscating the property of anyone who impeded the suppression of the rebellion.

Joseph Galloway's trusted subordinate, Isaac Ogden, made much the same assessment a year earlier. "The rebellion hangs by a slender thread," he assured Galloway in November, 1778. The great majority of Americans "are heartily tired of the war and groan under the yoke of tyranny." John Butler's raids in the Mohawk and Wyoming valleys so disrupted the provisions trade that men were desperate for peace, and now Butler stood ready to support Clinton in a major offensive anywhere in the middle colonies. "In this situation what is necessary to crush the rebellion, . . . [is] only one vigorous campaign, properly conducted. I mean by . . . a man of *judgment, spirit,* and *enterprise.*"[24]

Ogden and Ferguson both acknowledged that the rebellion was an authentic social movement. This implied that Congress and the Army, initially at least, had been "of the people" and that "enthusiasm" had for a time taken the place of money, bureaucracy, and leadership. Until British actions dramatically demonstrated the futility of resistance to large segments of the populace, both men conceded, the movement would not die, and to this extent they were acknowledging its indigenous social roots. Ogden and Ferguson further seemed to sense that the rebellion's indigenous character provided the key to its suppression. By carrying the war to the whole society, by using plunder and destruction as psychological weapons, in short, by threatening to precipitate complete social chaos, Britain could convert disspirited rebels into desperate and disillusioned advocates of peace and submission. John Goodrich of Virginia proposed to Clinton a pincer

The Nature of the War for Independence

attack on Williamsburg, "the metropolis of infamy," from the James and York rivers. "I know the genesus of the Virginians," he explained; "an example of devastation would have a good effect, the minds of the people struck with a panic would expect the whole country to share the same fate. Offer rewards for bringing to justice the active rebels, let them be proportioned to their rank and consequence..., make proper examples, countenance and protect the inoffensive and honest farmers. This done, every rebel will suspect his neighbor, all confidence will cease, the guilty in crowds will retire to the back country without a possibility of removing provisions for their subsistence, hunger will make them desperate and open their eyes, they will fall on their destructive leaders, peace and submission, of course, must follow."[25]

Anticipating in November 1780, just such an imminent British invasion of Virginia, John Connolly explained to Clinton how the upper Ohio Valley could be reclaimed for the Crown by manipulating critical features in the social organization of the region.[26] The population which had burgeoned in the years 1767 and 1776, he reported, consisted of "adventurers allured by the prospect of an idle life" and former tenant farmers from the northern neck of Virginia "whose increase in children and desire to be independent" motivated them to become squatters in a frontier where "civil authority" was too weak to restrain their land grabbing conduct. Overnight the region changed from a "rude wilderness" into a "sociable and tolerably well cultivated settlement." In order to protect their own interest in western lands, Virginia Revolutionary leaders encouraged settlers in the region to join in the rebellion in 1775 and "royal authority" gave way "to a confused democracy." Predictably the rebel leaders in this unstable setting overplayed a strong hand by imposing harsh taxation and militia fines. Alienated by these measures "the great majority" of settlers, who are "valuable loyalists," "would be ready to shed their blood in support of the former constitution, yet, under their present embarrassments, their services are totally lost and we can expect nothing but their empty good wishes." With the loyalist majority entirely cowed, nothing stood in the way of rebel conquest of the Illinois territory. This would threaten Detroit and Niagara, cut off communications with Canada, and trigger new and more powerful raids down the Mississippi against West Florida.

Connolly emphasized the desperate quality of the situation because it contained the key to a miraculous British recovery in the west: "from the description given, your excellency will perceive that many of the people— dispersed over that extensive country—are unencumbered with families and their attendant cares, [or by ownership] of fixed property, accustomed to an erratic life, and ready for every adventure wearing the face of poverty. Abandoned to the influence of designing men, their constitutional courage and hardiness have been prostituted to the basest purposes and their arms opposed to their sovereign and their own proper interests. Policy requires that this unprovoked ill-humor should be turned from its present channel and directed to a proper object of resentment." By dramatically increasing the trade of the Ohio valley with Montreal and Detroit, Britain could give its loyal allies in the regions a compelling motive "to support that power from which they derived such striking benefits." Simultaneously, Britain should mobilize the Spanish-hating southern tribes for a massive assault on New Orleans. Once in control of the Ohio and Mississippi valleys Britain could invade western Pennsylvania and occupy Fort Pitt. All of this, Connolly admitted to Clinton, might seem an undertaking of "too considerable a magnitude," but he urged the general to trust him. "I feel myself so firmly convinced of the practicability of what I have advanced that I would stake my salvation upon a favorable outcome."

The loyalists' determination from 1778 through 1781 to use warfare in order to scourge and punish American society for its sins of ingratitude and disobedience was the same kind of curious mixture of political sagacity and moral absolutism which characterized whig ideology. The loyalist conception of military reality was a caricatured mirror image of the Spirit of '76.

1. Piers Mackesy, *The War for America, 1775–1783* (London, 1964), pp. 253, 511.
2. See, for example, Robert M. Calhoon, *The Loyalists in Revolutionary America, 1760–1781* (New York, 1973), chapters 6, 26.
3. John Shy, "The American Revolution: The Military Conflict as a Revolutionary War," in Stephen G. Kurtz and James H. Hutson, eds., *Essays on the American Revolution* (Chapel Hill, 1973), pp. 124, 139–40.
4. Sidney George Fisher, *Struggle for American Independence* (Philadelphia, 1908); Russell F. Weigley, *The Partisan War: The South Carolina Campaigns of 1780–1782* (Columbia, S.C., 1970); Shy, "The American Revolution...as a Revolutionary War."
5. On the numbers of loyalists in arms see Paul H. Smith, "The American Loyalists; Notes on their Organization and Numerical Strength," *William and Mary Quarterly,* 25 (April, 1968): 259–77.
6. Calhoon, *The Loyalists in Revolutionary America,* pp. 439–42, 462–64, 552–55.
7. Barbara Graymont, *The Iroquois and the American Revolution* (Syracuse, N.Y., 1972), chapters 5 and 6; James H. O'Donnell, III, *Southern Indians in the American Revolution* (Knoxville, 1973), chapter 2.
8. Hamilton V. Bail, ed., "A Letter to George Germain about Vermont," *Vermont History,* 34 (October, 1966): 226–34.
9. Paul H. Smith, "The New Jersey Loyalists and the British 'Provincial' Corps in the War for Independence," *New Jersey History,* 87 (Summer, 1969): 69–78; Ira Gruber, *The Howe Brothers and the American Revolution* (New York, 1972), pp. 146–54; Adrian C. Leiby, *The Revolutionary War in the Hackensack Valley: The Jersey Dutch and the Neutral Ground* (New Brunswick, N.Y., 1962).

The Nature of the War for Independence

10. See especially Tonyn to Germain, October 30, 1776, and Tonyn to Prevost, January 13, 1777, reprinted in Edgar L. Pennington, "East Florida in the American Revolution," *Florida Historical Quarterly,* 9 (1930): 29-31, 33-34 and Tonyn to Howe, February 24, 1778, Headquarters Papers of the British Army in North America, document no. 962, Colonial Williamsburg Microfilm, Williamsburg, Virginia.

11. John M. Coleman, "Joseph Galloway and the British Administration of Philadelphia," *Pennsylvania History,* 30 (July, 1963): 272-300; John E. Ferling, "Joseph Galloway's Military Advice: A Loyalist's View of the American Revolution," *Pennsylvania Magazine of History and Biography,* 98 (April, 1974): 171-88; for a very different role of loyalists in pacification, see the Minutes of the Board of Associated Loyalists, January to July, 1781, Henry Clinton Papers, William L. Clements Library, Ann Arbor, Michigan.

12. Staughton Lynd, *Class Conflict, Slavery, and the United States Constitution* (Indianapolis, 1967), pp. 68-77.

13. Ronald Hoffman, *A Spirit of Dissension: Economics, Politics, and the Revolution in Maryland* (Baltimore, 1973), pp. 184-95, 227-39.

14. William H. Nelson, *The American Tory* (Oxford, 1961), p. 91.

15. Several are described in George W. Kyte, "Some Plans for a Loyalist Stronghold in the Middle Colonies," *Pennsylvania History,* 16 (July, 1949): 177-90; other loyalist proposals in the Clinton Papers include George Chalmers to Clinton, September 12, 1778; Moses Kirkland to Clinton, October 13, 1778; Neil Jameison to Clinton, December 11, 1778; Christopher Sower narrative, December 13, 1778; West Jersey petitioners to Clinton, ca. 1778; George Chalmers to Clinton, July 26, 1779; Board of Associated Loyalists to Clinton, July 20, 1781; Harden Burnley to Clinton, September 17, 1781; Hector MacAlester to Clinton, n.d.

16. Richard Maxwell Brown, "The Violent Origins of South Carolina Extremism," in *Strain of Violence: Historical Studies of American Violence and Vigilantism* (New York, 1975), chapter 3; Graymont, *The Iroquois and the American Revolution,* chapter 7; Patrick J. Furlong, "Civilian-Military Conflict and the Restoration of the Royal Province of Georgia, 1778-1782," *Journal of Southern History,* 38 (August, 1972): 415-42.

17. For a variant of this model, see Calhoon, *The Loyalists in Revolutionary America,* 502-6.

18. David C. Skaggs suggested this difficulty to me.

19. Harry Eckstein, "On the Etiology of Internal Wars," *History and Theory,* 4 (1954-1955): 133-63.

20. Brown, *Strain of Violence,* pp. 75-81.

21. The entire foregoing paragraph is based on "Colonial Robert Gray's Observations of the War in the Carolinas," *South Carolina Historical and Genealogical Magazine,* 11 (July, 1910): 139-59; much the same view can be found in an anonymous letter to Lord Rawdon, n.d., ca. 1781, Clinton Papers.

22. Patrick Ferguson to Clinton, November 22, 1779, Clinton Papers; see also Ferguson to Clinton, November 25, 1779; "Cursory Observations on the Present Situation of the Refugees and the Means of Rendering them More Effectually Beneficial;" anonymous New York Loyalist to Tryon, November 1, 1775; and Samuel Hake to Clinton, n.d. and January 25, 1782, all in the Clinton Papers.

23. See Shy, "The American Revolution...as a Revolutionary War" and Jack P. Greene, "The Social Origins of the American Revolution: An Evaluation and an Interpretation." *Political Science Quarterly,* 88 (March, 1973), 1-22.

Part II: Action

24. Isaac Ogden to Joseph Galloway, November 22, 1778, Balch Collection, New York Public Library.
25. John Goodrich to Clinton, November 2, 1778, Clinton Papers.
26. John Connolly to Clinton, November 25, 1780, Clinton Papers; see also Connolly to Clinton, April 20, 1781, Clinton Papers.

9

THE FLORIDAS, THE WESTERN FRONTIER, AND VERMONT:
Thoughts on the Hinterland Loyalists

STUDY of the American Revolution has focused in recent years on the motivations and ideologies of participants in the struggle and on the organization of eighteenth-century American society. Both lines of inquiry have finally begun—belatedly and inadequately—to shape an understanding of the loyalists. Because we know that the pre-Revolutionary controversy was an intense, collective experience of self-appraisal for Americans, we can understand how it compelled defenders of British rule to renounce republicanism and why it persuaded them that imperial authority was a stabilizing factor in society and in their own lives. Furthermore, a growing body of research on loyalist groups and communities seems to confirm William H. Nelson's conjecture that the loyalist rank and file comprised cultural minorities who felt threatened by the rest of American society.[1]

These broad conclusions about the dynamics of the pre-Revolutionary debate and the structure of loyalist groupings during the War for Independence overlap but do not entirely coincide with another classification of loyalist motivation: an instinctive, unarticulated, but persistent expectation by loyalists living in the hinterland of Revolutionary America that British military, administrative, and diplomatic power ought to come to their protection and make the frontier the base for counterrevolutionary activity. There is little evidence of this sort of loyalist thought in traditional literary sources (pamphlets, correspondence, records of formal political activity); however, we can extrapolate evidence from the patterns of behavior of people in the hinterland, from concepts of empire which prevailed during the quarter century prior to the War for Independence, from notions of the nature of

Part II: Action

the empire held by British officials and loyalists on the frontier, and from recent scholarship on the actual level of British military, administrative, and
diplomatic capability during the War for Independence.

For many settlers, the hinterland of Revolutionary America—that is, East
and West Florida, the southern backcountry, the Ohio Valley, western New
York and the Mohawk Valley, and Vermont—was a setting where British
power and authority could be most readily exercised, indeed, that the British possessed a special talent for maximizing their assets and manipulating
events to their advantage in this vast crescent of territory. What no one realized at the time was that British capability in this hinterland of colonial
America was both expanding and retracting on the eve of the War for Independence. This flux in conditions deprived British adherents there of the
ability to predict events and make reliable estimates. The strenuous, and in
some ways highly sophisticated, efforts by loyalists and British officials on
the periphery of Revolutionary America to defeat the whigs were motivated
by a partial, inadequate comprehension of the flux in imperial capability.

The first and most important source of this confusion was the conduct of
the British army and civil officials in 1775–76. Gage instructed John Stuart,
British superintendent for Indian affairs in the South, and Guy Johnson,
his counterpart in the North, to guard against any rebel attempts to subvert
the loyalty of the Indians to the Crown. Neither Stuart nor Johnson saw any
value in precipitate Indian attacks on whig settlements, and both urged the
Indians to adopt a defensive posture until the deployment of British regulars in adjacent provinces. In North Carolina, Governor Josiah Martin encouraged the formation of a large loyalist force which would march to
Wilmington and there rendezvous with British regulars arriving by sea. In
Virginia, Governor Dunmore secured British regulars from St. Augustine,
invited slaves to escape and to take up arms under his banner, and, with a
handful of Virginia loyalists, temporarily threatened the security of the Revolutionary regime and delayed for several months the transit of power. From
Boston, Lieutenant Colonel Allen McLean, who had secured authority to
enlist loyalist soldiers, sent recruiting agents to New York and North Carolina. Gage himself authorized John Connolly, British governor at Fort Pitt,
to direct a loyalist uprising in the upper Ohio Valley and arranged with Guy
Carleton in Quebec and Guy Johnson in the Mohawk Valley to coordinate
their activities with Connolly's. Of course, none of these plans succeeded.
Connolly was arrested on his way back to Fort Pitt. The North Carolina rising occurred before British troops reached the mouth of the Cape Fear
River, and the North Carolina whigs were able to defeat the loyalists at the
Battle of Moore's Creek. Despite John Stuart's best efforts to manipulate
events, the Cherokees prematurely seized the opportunity to repel white settlers from their lands; they were defeated and their villages and crops de-

The Hinterland Loyalists

stroyed by Virginia and North and South Carolina militia. In failure, these initiatives look clumsy and bizarre, and certainly they suggest that irregular warfare is not a substitute for conventional military operations. But these early British efforts also indicated a British willingness to see the armed rebellion as a geopolitical process and to experiment in new ways of dealing with what was an unprecedented military challenge. And even these setbacks did not stifle irrepressible loyalist activity in the backcountry.[2]

As the war progressed, the most favorable laboratory for such experimentation was the Mohawk Valley in New York. There, Sir William Johnson, Indian Superintendent for the Northern Tribes, had won for the Iroquois over the preceding quarter century valuable territorial guarantees and protection from illegal white encroachment on Indian land, in return for military and political loyalty. When Johnson died in 1774, he left a magnificent network of alliances among elements of the Iroquois confederacy, local white settlers indebted to Johnson for loans and favors, wealthy western New York landowners like John Butler, and British officials in Quebec who were strategically located to oversee and direct counterrevolutionary efforts in the area and coordinate them with Burgoyne's projected invasion of New York. These interests loyal to the Crown were, in fact, a delicate network of relationships, ill designed to stand the severe stresses generated by the Revolution. Sir William's successor as Indian superintendent was his nephew, Guy Johnson, who in 1776 was trapped in New York City en route from a trip to England. Acting Superintendent Colonel John Butler was suspicious of the Johnsons and their close Mohawk alley, Joseph Brant. The maneuvering for advantage and leadership between Butler and Brant almost certainly prevented Brant from organizing in late 1776 and early 1777 a small, disciplined insurgent force of trusted Indian warriors and white loyalists to attack whig settlements in New York State and, in effect, to serve as the cutting edge for Burgoyne's invasion. Brutal Mohawk depredations against the pro-American Oneidas in the summer of 1777 shattered what was left of Iroquois unity. Burgoyne's defeat and the failure of Barry St. Leger's offensive into the Mohawk Valley in the summer of 1777 helped ignite a savage and debilitating civil war in the region, which did not materially affect the course of the war but which wrecked Iroquois society and mocked British pretensions to protect and defend its loyal subjects from the vengeance and violence of the rebels.[3]

Despite overwhelming political and military disasters, the loyalists in Vermont remained a potent and indestructible element during the Revolution. Most of the leadership for supporters of the Crown in the New Hampshire Grants (as the territory was called until 1777) were New York land speculators, who fled the region in 1775 when they lost control of the machinery of county government to insurgent Yankee settlers led by Ethan and Ira Allen.

Part II: Action

The instability of the Allens' insurgent regime, the precarious military security of the region in 1776 and 1777, and the immaturity and malleability of political institutions in Vermont all tended to influence inhabitants of the area to adopt supple political allegiances. Yankee settlers like Sylvanus Ewarts and Justus Sherwood filled the void in leadership just prior to Burgoyne's brief occupation of Castleton, Vermont, in July 1777. Ewarts recruited some 400 local residents to build a road for Burgoyne's force to use. The majority of these volunteers changed their allegiances with chameleonlike adaptability and led Burgoyne to assume that Colonel Frederick Baum, his Hessian subordinate, could expect a friendly reception when he led a foray into southern Vermont to seize a cache of rebel arms in August 1777. Instead, Baum stumbled into a defeat at the Battle of Bennington, in part because he believed that shirtsleeved insurgents approaching his rear must be local loyalists coming to his support.

While the Vermont loyalists evaporated as a military factor, they retained extensive influence in the state, and much of the property confiscated by the new state government in 1777 was resold at reasonable terms to close relatives of accused loyalists. When New York blocked Vermont's bid for recognition by the Continental Congress as an independent state, the Allens began the now famous "Haldimand negotiations" with the British to secure recognition of Vermont's independence in return for the state's repudiation of the American cause—a course of events which forced the Allens into alliance with covert loyalists in the state.[4]

Several factors weighed heavily in inducing the Vermont loyalists first to oppose the Allens and then to endure the vicissitudes of war while waiting for British authority to be reasserted. One was the seemingly capricious nature of local hostilities, which singled out some individual Yankee settlers with Yorker connections, labeling them tories and turning the rage of the community against them. Zadock Wright, John Peters, and Sylvanus Ewarts were all prominent Yankee settlers with close family ties to the Revolutionary leadership of Vermont. For reasons of both temperment and calculation, they tried to remain neutral in 1775–76, found themselves labeled tories by seemingly uncontrollable currents of opinion, and took up arms for the British from considerations of revenge, confusion, and desperation. More significantly, the strongest political force in the region was a desire for autonomy—a goal incompatible with internal bloodletting—so that the Allens maintained discreet alliances with covert loyalists and drew on this support during the Haldimand negotiations. At the core of this accommodation between the Allens and Vermont loyalists was the widespread expectation that Britain possessed sufficient leverage in Revolutionary America through its control of Quebec to checkmate rebel dominance in New England through prudent concessions to Vermont separatism.

The Hinterland Loyalists

Joshua Locke, Yankee loyalist from Vermont, wrote to Lord George Germain in 1781 explaining the special character of Vermont loyalism. In Vermont, as anywhere else, Locke assumed, the legal security of landed property was the most immediate obligation of government to the subject. When the Revolution began, the ownership of a large amount of land in "the Green mountains" was disputed by New York and New Hampshire claimants, and some Yankee settlers even took the law into their own hands. "But I never understood. . .that they ever disputed his majesty's prorogative to shift any part of his subjects from the jurisdiction of one province to another . . .the fee of the land onely is what they have been contending for." The Revolution vastly complicated—but did not fundamentally alter—that situation: "They declared themselves an independent state free from both king and Congress as they could obtain fee of their lands from neither." Locke noted that the kind of proclamation which General Henry Clinton had issued in South Carolina promising protection to persons who laid down their arms and took an oath of allegiance "strikes these people [loyalists in Vermont] with horror"; if New York should accept the same terms, the Crown might validate Yorker land claims in the region and thereby invalidate the claims of Yankee loyalists and neutralists in Vermont. "But if such a thing as granting to those people pardons confirming them in the title of their lands and forming them into a separate province could be settled" in England, the entire population could be induced to declare their loyalty to the King. Locke argued that landowners concerned about the legal security of their titles were "in the center" of the colonial social order: "I need not mention the advantage it would be to the British arms to have those people in favor of government." Moreover, if Britain neglected the Vermont loyalists, the region would become "a receptical for the sum of rebellion and a refuge for a numerous banditti" which would be most expensive to eradicate in the years after the Revolution—assuming it was suppressed by the British.[5] Locke's commentary was astute and not entirely inaccurate. Vermont, like other fringe areas of Revolutionary America, was particularly prone to violence and crime and especially fearful of the breakdown of law and order; the loyalists utilized this asset to the maximum in securing an accommodation with the Allen regime. At least some Vermont loyalists expected that Britain acting unilaterally could use this lever to swing the entire populace back to British allegiance.

East Florida, and in some respects West Florida as well, represented the nexus of command, that is, the location where leadership, civilian support, supply, manpower, relatively secure fortification, and proximity to theaters of conflict all coincided. The loyalists who fled to St. Augustine and Pensacola had good reason to expect the protection of a powerful military force. Lord Dunmore had secured reinforcements from St. Augustine in 1775.

Part II: Action

John Stuart, superintendent for Indian affairs in the South, transferred his headquarters to St. Augustine in 1775 and moved it again to Pensacola in 1777. In Governor Patrick Tonyn of East Florida and Governor Peter Chester of West Florida, the British had officials who were intent on galvanizing these elements of military power.

Tonyn empowered Thomas Brown, the irrepressible Georgia backcountry tory partisan, to enlist loyalist exiles into the East Florida Rangers, which operated initially as a defensive force along the East Florida–Georgia frontier. Together, Tonyn and Brown set about undercutting John Stuart's careful management of the Creeks and Cherokees. Impatient for a general Indian uprising to strengthen the province's security and undermine the Revolutionary regime in Georgia, Tonyn and Brown thought of Indian uprisings as a torrent of violent power which they could turn on at their discretion. The knowledgeable and experienced Stuart knew that Indian support was a finite, perishable resource; the Cherokee War of 1776, which Stuart had tried to prevent, had decimated the villages and crops of that tribe in the Carolinas. The Creeks feared similar whig reprisals and were increasingly leery, first of Tonyn's demand that they march in force to the defense of St. Augustine in the spring of 1778 and then of his appeal that they raise hundreds of warriors for the British invasion of Georgia in December 1778 and January 1779.[8] Tonyn further believed that bloody, irregular warfare along the Georgia–East Florida border would "distress...our deluded neighbors" and induce them "to return to their allegiance." By repeatedly sending raiding parties into Georgia to steal livestock, he provided the British garrision with fresh meat. "This, my lord, is not a very honorable method of making war," Tonyn wrote colonial Secretary George Germain, "but...it is the only one left for supplying this town and garrison with fresh provisions as the Georgians would not allow the cattle...to be drove hence. Besides, my lord, the love of plunder engages many daring fellows...to oppose the rebels...instead of joining with...them." "Regular troops," Tonyn added in a revealing aside, "are not well calculated for such moroding services."[7] Frederick George Mulcaster, wealthy East Florida landowner and surveyor-general, scoffed at Tonyn's faith in the combativeness of the populace. Of the 300 adult white males in the vicinity of St. Augustine, 200 were well-to-do government officials, merchants, or planters, while the remainder were overseers, cattlemen, fishermen, and "persons who live as they can....It is from this class of hunters &c. that recruits can be raised; ...as the price of workmanship is high, their wages support them too well to be easily tempted," but "some shift[ing]" for themselves "might be got." Money alone would not suffice, Mulcaster warned, but promises of land grants would bring East Florida pioneers to the King's standard: "the rage which these people have for that article might have some effect."[8]

The Hinterland Loyalists

Peter Chester in West Florida had fewer assets at his disposal. The province was vulnerable to rebel and Spanish attack. Although the population doubled during the War for Independence because Dartmouth had declared West Florida an asylum for loyalists driven from other colonies, the resulting influx of 2,000 to 2,500 people weakened as much as it strengthened royal administration. The young colony lacked an internal system of political and judicial institutions, kinship patterns, and traditions strong enough to bind its inhabitants into a community. Reckless land speculation along the Mississippi Valley had spread population into regions vulnerable to Spanish attack and had scattered the manpower resources of the province.[9] Maryland loyalist James Chalmers wrote Lord Rawdon that without "sugar to stimulate the avidity of planters or wheat to incite the industry of the inhabitants," West Florida was a languishing and dispirited province with "no vestiges of that youthful colonial ardor" which had sustained other newly established British colonies."[10] When the rebel James Willing led a daring raid down the Mississippi River into West Florida in 1778, for example, he extracted from settlers around Natchez a pledge to remain neutral in the war and to desist from aiding the British, and throughout the province news of the Willing raid caused panic and confusion. The exploitation of this fertile, plentiful territory with its strategic location for commerce had preempted the energies of the populace.[11] In spite of their lack of interest in the pre-Revolutionary controversy (apart form a mild remonstrance against the Stamp Act) and their ostensible support of the Crown in the war, the loyalist sentiments of the inhabitants were not particularly fervent. In West Florida, J. Barton Starr found official skepticism about the commitment of the populace to the British cause. "I find the inhabitants in general self-interested and without public spirit, whose minds are attached only to gain and their private concerns," declared General John Campbell. "In short, nothing can be had from them...but at an enormous extravagant price, and personal service on general principles of national defense is too generous and exalted for their conceptions." William Dunbar believed that half of the inhabitants secretly sympathized with the American cause and that, as a result, the others felt immobilized and fearful of making any zealous efforts in the support of British authority. Though the inhabitants fought bravely during the Spanish attack on Pensacola in 1781, that response to Spanish attack does not refute evidence of ambivalence and even indifference early in the war. Yet these liabilities of institutional immaturity, public apathy, and strategic insecurity were a hidden source of short-term advantage. If British West Florida was vulnerable to Spanish attack, Spanish Louisiana felt equally threatened by an expansionist British province. By mutually adroit diplomacy, Chester and Spanish Governor Bernardo de Gálvez tried to avoid conflict until Spanish entry into the war in 1779. Following the Willing raid, Chester moved vigorously and resourcefully to shore up the province's defenses and to instill a greater sense of urgency in the populace, but despite these efforts, the province fell to Spain in 1781.[12]

In the end, therefore, British strength and capability in the hinterland of Revolutionary America fell far short of the loyalists' ideal expectation of a vast, pervasive source of counterrevolutionary strength on which they would rely and to which they could contribute. The southern Indians, whom Stuart had so assiduously cultivated, were a highly perishable asset of negligible value by the time the reconquest of Georgia occurred. Iroquois effectiveness was negated by the internecine strife between the Brants and the Butlers and by the havoc wrought within the fabric of Iroquois life by the ravages of war. The Floridas did not significantly enhance the strength of the British invasion of the South prior to 1779–81. The promising start in the Haldimand negotiations did not checkmate rebel control of New England and adjacent New York State. The weaknesses and fragility of loyalists' expectations should not obscure the importance and intelligence of their position. It should prompt historians to treat loyalist ideas as an integral part of the larger history of ideas in the British Empire.

Loyalists' expectations about imperial vitality did not function as a self-conscious ingredient in their intellectual lives. If any terms characterize loyalist outlook during the War for Independence, they are *confusion, uncertainty, apprehension*. As Paul H. Smith wrote of many loyalists in arms, the Revolution was "too large an event for most persons to comprehend in its entirety" and it was therefore "perceived in terms of immediate, commonplace issues.... For many, the issue of their allegiance was never perceived as a matter upon which they might exercise some meaningful choice."[13] Loyalist expectations about the nature of the Empire were simply one element— albeit crucial and unique—in the milieu of doubt, confusion, and limited experience surrounding these people. Without endowing loyalist notions about the processes of empire with more formality than they deserve, it is nonetheless important to consider the ways in which hinterland loyalist expectations were a *system* of ideas, impressions, and beliefs, and the relationship of this intellectual experience to the larger ferment of thought occurring during the eighteenth century.

There are at least two obvious ways of going about this task. One is the sort of behavioral study of imperial institutions exemplified by Alison G. Olson and Richard M. Brown's edition of papers on Anglo-American politics—a vast undertaking beyond the scope of this paper. The other perspective is the study of the formal concepts of empire along the lines set forth by the late Richard Koebner and in the modification of Koebner recently suggested by John Shy and Jack P. Greene.[14] The Empire in the eighteenth century generated a large body of in-house treatises by men within or near the imperial bureaucracy, each seeking to define the genius of the empire, identify the sources of its vitality, and prescribe ways in which it could conduct men's energies into constructive channels. Franklin, Thomas Whately, Thomas Hutchinson, and William Smith, Jr., were only a few of the most important of those men who devoted a considerable share of their busy time during the 1760s and 1770s to this enterprise. While many of these theories and proposals had little immediate effect on policy, they all focused on those features of imperial administration which were in the greatest danger of malfunction, and sought to reconcile and bind together the traditional and the novel, the healthy and the sick, the routine and the unexpected elements of imperial development. It is no wonder that theories of empire were so rapidly consumed and supplanted. Franklin wanted British territory and institutions in America to be spacious enough to contain and encourage a population explosion; Pownall wanted mutual commercial prosperity to replace legal authority as the cement of empire; Knox and Whately wanted the undisciplined ways of colonial assemblies to give way to order, system, and direction from Whitehall; Hutchinson and Smith—in very different ways—sensed the psychic damage to American politics by the abrupt intrusion of royal authority into colonial life. Loyalist expectation of British vigor on the hinterland was a further stage in this search for a workable theory of empire.

The key to this concept was *predictability*. British conduct affecting the loyalists should be utterly predictable, and to insure against malfunctions of imperial policy and execution, loyalists should make their own needs and expectations painfully obvious. Self-consciousness and a literal view of political processes pervade two bodies of published sources familiar to students of Florida history: Joseph B. Lockey's documentary history of the transition in East Florida from British to Spanish rule, and *The Case of the Inhabitants of East-Florida. . . .*[15] These documents seem at first glance to have dubious value for the study of ideas. Written after British defeat and after news that the Floridas were to be returned to Spanish rule, they reflect the special pleading of men desperately, cravenly seeking favors from the Crown. Tirelessly, and tiresomely, they complain of the cruel fate visited on the East Florida loyalists by the fortunes of war and diplomacy. "The principle part of the original planters," Tonyn wrote to Secretary of State for Home Affairs Thomas Townshend in May 1783, "after having expended large sums of money began to feel themselves in comfortable circumstances. . . . They were happy in the full enjoyment of their native rights and privileges under his Majesty's auspices. . . . Amidst a general revolt" they "stood firm." Then came 12,000 loyalist exiles confident of royal protection. "This consideration . . . induced them liberally to lay out the wrecks of their fortunes in building Houses and forming Settlements . . . they were ambitious of this province ever remaining characterized for loyalty."[16] Yet these heavy-handed, melodramatic documents are the quintessential expression of the loyalist perception of political reality. East Florida loyalist spokesmen and Tonyn, who had a flair for translating their sentiments into the prose of official correspondence, did not invent new modes of expression, new assumptions about the nature of politics, and new rhetorical devices in 1783. These documents and characteristics of language represent an experience stretching back to 1775.

With ill-disguised attempts at subtlety and indirection, *The Case of the Inhabitants* argued deductively that as subjects they had during the course of the war no choice but "to hazard life, fortune, and all that is dear" in support of the Crown and to acquiesce willingly in the terms of peace including the cession of Florida; that, having lost all, their shattered lives could be restored in no other way than from the generosity of the British nation, and, therefore, Britain had no choice but to assume the cost of their resettlement and full compensation for the land, possessions, and slaves they had lost. The burden of responsibility for affirmative action was entirely on Britain; the East Florida loyalists had simply accepted their duty to fight against the American rebels and then to acquiesce in the peace settlement which returned Florida to Spain. They were nothing but pawns in a world where allegiance placed absolute obligations to obedience and acquiescence on subjects and where rulers axiomatically protected the interests of their faithful supporters. "To admit a contrary idea," the document declared, "would be to assert that Great Britain hath lost all public faith": that she punished the innocent, disregarded justice, and forfeited her reputation for "probity, justice, and good faith," and "untied the strongest bonds that unites civil society. . . . That language may suit our northern neighbors," it concluded pointedly, "but not the inhabitants of East Florida who have known Britain's "kindness and fostering hand." Belying the notion that allegiance required unquestioning acquiescence, it concluded, "and therefore we must now *as yet* complain."[17]

This helpless, immobile position provoked more than self-pity; it also prompted the East Florida loyalists to recall the whole range of emotions which had been brought forth by their experience and bad fortune. "Abandoned by that sovereign for whose cause we have sacrificed everything that is dear in life," a group of them wrote to the king of Spain in October 1784, "and deserted by that Country for which we fought and many of us freely bled," and "left to our fate bereft of our slaves by our inveterate Countrymen . . . We . . . are Reduced to the dreadful alternative of returning to our Homes, to receive insult worse than Death to Men of Spirit, or to run the hazard of being Murdered in Cold blood, to go to the inhospitable Regions of Nova Scotia, or take refuge on the Barren Rocks of the Bahamas where

The Hinterland Loyalists

poverty and wretchedness stares us in the face Or do we do what our Spirit cannot brook... renounce our Country."[18] This remarkable version of history depicted the empire as a place of opportunity and protection for venturesome men, where venturesomeness bred a "spirit" which made humiliation and a lack of options a galling fate. War had consumed economic opportunity and the terms of the peace had denied its replenishment. A certain naïveté and unconcern for political power permeated these remarks. Tonyn underscored this attitude: "I am confident," he wrote to Secretary of State Townshend, "that our gracious sovereign will make liberal allowances for human frailties and that you will represent in the most favorable light spirited men laboring under difficulties and misfortunes which a steady adherence to the duty they owe their King and Country has accumulated upon them." They are "unacquainted with the great engines by which government is upheld," and therefore "have been led to think of themselves as agrieved because [they are] unfortunate."[19] The antidote which Tonyn prescribed for this benumbed state of the "principle inhabitants" of the province, was a still more apolitical faith in royal beneficence: "nothing can give me greater pleasure than to find that you gentlemen—whom I have ever represented as well affected rather than [as] harbouring murmur and discontent in your present calamitous circumstances—[will] submit yourselves to the measures of government and rely upon the benignity of our sovereign, the justice of the nation, and the wisdom of His Majesty's ministers for a suitable provision to be made for you."[20] In April 1781, when the East Florida assembly renewed its contribution to the support of the empire, Speaker William Brown wrote in just such a tone of calculating innocence to Tonyn, "we hope the present smallness of our quota may not be considered as a measure of our loyalty to the most benificent prince in the world or our attachment to our bountiful mother country."[21]

But there were centrifugal forces at work in the province Tonyn acknowledged in a superbly analytical letter to General Guy Carleton, which wrought havoc with these civilized and gentlemanly British standards of conduct. Tonyn reported that he could not dismantle his administration until the treaty with Spain was finally ratified, and in the interim "an abandoned set of men" in the Georgia and East Florida back country had "committed several daring robberies and will certainly attempt to ravage this country and insult government in its feeble, disabled condition.... In this stage of impotence the settlements will be exposed and the Negroes plundered... and when His Majesty's daily bounties to the refugees cease ...they will become exceedingly clamorous and impatient, and the worst is to be expected from the lower sort. In addition to these evils, the licentious, disbanded soldiers who have discovered intentions of rapine and plunder are most to be dreaded." The logic of the situation was inescapable: "this

Part II: Action

ever loyal province, given up to accommodate the peace of the Empire, and the inhabitants thereby losing their pleasant abodes and property have, Sir, a just claim for every assistance and compensation which can be extended to them and indulgence in their choice of destinations to any part of His Majesty's Dominions."²² Only by adequate resettlement and compensation could the empire be true to its own best standards: a place where acquisitive, venturesome men could depend upon British reliability and predictability and receive, in addition to economic opportunity, just reward for risks and sacrifices in the service of the Crown.

1. See Robert M. Calhoon, *The Loyalists in Revolutionary America, 1760–1781* (New York, 1973), pp. 431–35, 502–6, 559–65.
2. Paul H. Smith, *Loyalists and Redcoats: A Study in British Revolutionary Policy* (Chapel Hill, N.C., 1964), chap. 2; Richard O. Curry, "Loyalism in Western Virginia," *West Virginia History* 14 (April 1953):265–74; James H. O'Donnell, *Southern Indians in the American Revolution* (Knoxville, Tenn., 1973), chap. 2; Robert L. Ganyard, "North Carolina during the American Revolution: The First Phase, 1774–1777" (Ph.D. diss., Duke University, 1962), pp. 120–48.
3. Barbara Graymont, *The Iroquois in the American Revolution* (Syracuse, N.Y., 1972), passim.
4. Chilton Williamson, *Vermont in Quandary, 1763–1825* (Montpelier, Vt., 1941), passim; Gwilym R. Roberts, "An Unknown Vermonter: Sylvanus Ewarts, Governor Chittenden's Tory Brother-in-Law," *Vermont History* 29 (April 1961): 92–102; Hamilton V. Bail, "Zadock Wright: That 'Devilish' Tory of Hartland," *Vermont History* 36 (Autumn 1968):186–203.
5. Hamilton V. Bail, "A Letter to Lord Germain about Vermont," *Vermont History* 34 (October 1966):226–34.
6. O'Donnell, *Southern Indians in the American Revolution,* pp. 32–34, 70; Gary D. Olson, "Thomas Brown, Loyalist Partisan, and the Revolutionary War in Georgia, 1777–1782," *Georgia Historical Quarterly* 54 (Spring–Summer 1970):1–19, 183–207.
7. Tonyn to Germain, October 18, 1776, quoted in Edgar L. Pennington, "Florida in the American Revolution, 1775–1778," *Florida Historical Quarterly* 9 (1930):29–31.
8. Mulcaster to Clinton, n.d. [ca. 1776], Henry Clinton Papers, William L. Clements Library, University of Michigan, Ann Arbor.
9. Cecil Johnson, "Expansion in West Florida," *Mississippi Valley Historical Review* 20 (March 1934):481–96.
10. Chalmers to Rawdon, May 21, 1779, Henry Clinton Papers.
11. Kathryn T. Abbey, "Peter Chester's Defense of the Mississippi after the Willing Raid," *Mississippi Valley Historical Review* 22 (June 1935):17–32.
12. J. Barton Starr, *Tories, Dons, and Rebels: The American Revolution in West Florida,* (Gainesville: University Presses of Florida, 1976), pp. 118, 147.
13. Smith, "The American Loyalists: Notes on their Organization and Numerical Strength," *William and Mary Quarterly* 25 (April 1968):259, 270.
14. Greene, "An Uneasy Connection: An Analysis of the Preconditions of the American Revolution," in *Essays on the American Revolution,* ed. Stephen G. Kurtz

The Hinterland Loyalists

and James H. Hutson (Chapel Hill, N.C., 1973), pp. 32–80; Shy, "Thomas Pownall, Henry Ellis, and the Spectrum of Possibilities, 1763–1775," in *Anglo-American Politics, 1675–1775,* ed. Olson and Brown (New Brunswick, N.J., 1970), pp. 155–86.

15. Lockey, ed., *East Florida, 1783–1785* (Berkeley, Calif., 1949); *The Case of the Inhabitants of East-Florida, with an Appendix Containing Papers by Which All the Facts Stated in the Case, Are Supported* (St. Augustine, 1784).
16. Lockey, *East Florida,* p. 97.
17. *The Case of the Inhabitants of East-Florida, with An Appendix,* p. 14.
18. Lockey, *East Florida,* pp. 301–3.
19. Ibid., pp. 96–9.
20. Ibid., p. 117.
21. *The Case of the Inhabitants of East-Florida, with An Appendix,* p. 29.
22. Lockey, *East Florida,* pp. 154–56.

Part III

PRACTICE

10

MORAL ALLEGIANCE:
John Witherspoon and Loyalist Recantation

When the Continental Congress returned to Philadelphia on July 7, 1778 following the British evacuation of the city, printer Benjamin Towne solicited several delegates for news and contributions to the *Philadelphia Evening Post*. One of the delegates, John Witherspoon of New Jersey, refused to cooperate unless Towne first publicly apologized for his collaboration with the British during General William Howe's occupation of Philadelphia. Out of either naïveté or servility, Towne asked Witherspoon to compose a suitable apology for him. Later, when Towne saw what Witherspoon had written, he realized what a blunder he had made in entrusting the rehabilitation of his public image to so didactic and judgmental a figure as the Scottish Presbyterian and academic. Towne refused to sign Witherspoon's statement without substantial deletions. Witherspoon thereupon circulated the document in manuscript around Philadelphia and it was published the following October in the Fishkill *New York Packet*.[1] Over the following weeks Witherspoon composed a wholly unsolicited recantation for another notorious loyalist printer, James Rivington. It was even more elaborate and demeaning than Towne's. These two bizarre documents[2] illustrate the nature of cultural and moral conflict in the Revolution; they reveal Witherspoon's elaborate behind-the-scenes leadership; and they provide important new insights into the development of patriot attitudes concerning allegiance, public morality, and the ethical underpinnings of republicanism.

Part III: Practice

1

Benjamin Towne was an emigrant from Lincolnshire, England, and a marginal figure in the Philadelphia printing community before the Revolution. In 1769 he had been employed by part-owner Joseph Galloway of the *Pennsylvania Chronicle* to serve as a watchdog over the paper's headstrong printer, William Goddard. Towne left this post a year later and worked irregularly as a coppersmith and journeyman printer until 1776, when he began printing the *Evening Post,* a paper which was generally nonpolitical but which occasionally carried pieces written by delegates to Congress. When the British occupied Philadelphia in September 1777, however, Towne's was the only newspaper that continued to appear, and it consistently supported British rule. A week before the British departed, in June 1778, Towne naively signaled his intention to support the American cause.[3]

As a confession of cowardice and civic irresponsibility, Witherspoon's "humble confession, declaration, recantation, and apology of BENJAMIN TOWNE" was a heavy-handed but powerful piece of satire. The pathetic admissions that Towne "never was, nor ever pretended to be a man of character, repute or dignity," and that he had become habituated to "meanness" and "scurrility" provided just the sort of titillation and groveling that Witherspoon needed to guarantee wide circulation and discussion of the confession. He wanted to underscore the way in which virtue could be utterly debased by prolonged subservience to the likes of Joseph Galloway. Incapable of purposeful and consistent civil conduct, Towne had degenerated into equivocation. Opportunistic neutrality and the shifting of loyalty, the apologia insisted, were respectable and understandable kinds of behavior. "[C]hanging sides is not any way surprising in a person answering the above description," Towne blandly contended. Did not Cato of Utica as well as "another senator of inferior note whose name I cannot recollect" commit suicide rather than adapt to the death of the Roman republic? Witherspoon here aimed an elaborate insult at Towne's supposedly skimpy knowledge of the classics; Cato of Utica did commit suicide rather than live under the tyranny of Caesar, but "another senator" could only be a reference to Statilius, an adherent of Cato, who announced his intention of following Cato's example but who was dissuaded by friends acting on Cato's instructions, and who later died in battle defending the republic.[4] Presumably, self-preservation was preferable to self-destruction. To be sure, Witherspoon had Towne concede, if an Adams or a Hancock had defected to the British, the patriots might understandably have punished his treachery severely. But "what occasion is there for the public to pour out all its wrath upon poor Towne?... why so much noise about a trifle?" After all, far more important Pennsylvanians—notably John Allen, Tench Coxe, and the Reverend

John Witherspoon and Loyalist Recantation

William Smith—had switched from opposition to support of the Crown during the Revolutionary crisis.[5]

Witherspoon's Towne flaunted stylish and superficial knowledge as the only protective garment available to a morally deficient individual with no deep roots in the civic values of his community. Witherspoon had Towne explain how

> the rational moralists of the last age used to tell us that there was an essential difference between virtue and vice....Now, with all due deference to these great men, I think I am as much a philosopher as to know that there are no circumstances of action more important than those of time and place. Therefore if any man pay no regard to the changes that may happen in these circumstances, there will be little virtue and still less *prudence* in his behaviour. ...[A]sk any plain Quaker in this city, what he would say to a man who should wear the same coat in summer as in winter in this climate? He would certainly say, "Friend, thy wisdom is not great."

This passage, which expressed Witherspoon's deep suspicion about learning not firmly grounded in personal virtue, revealed the inner logic of the Towne apologia: the buffeting of a loyalist by sensual impressions which he was unable to evaluate with normal discrimination, the perpetually whining tone when confronted with criticism, and the pathetic need to assume any available protective coloration, even that of an apolitical Quaker. So Towne pleaded that he "had no more regard for Gen[eral] Clinton, or even Mrs. Loring, or any other of the *chaste nymphs* that attended the Fête Champêtre, alias "Mischianza" of May 18, 1778.[6] Probably in consideration of these demeaning but revealing sentiments, Witherspoon included the more authentic remark: "I was neither Whig nor Tory, but a printer."

Witherspoon's "*Humble* Representation *and earnest* Supplication of James Rivington," written in late 1778, was another harsh parody of the dilemma faced by loyalist printers. Whereas Towne had inadvertently collaborated with Witherspoon in initiating his apology, there is no evidence that Rivington knew anything about the recantation Witherspoon attributed to him. Building on his experience with Towne, Witherspoon undoubtedly saw Rivington as a still more revealing example of loyalist printer amorality. Rivington was not originally a printer at all, but rather a bookseller in London. At the invitation of Governor William Tryon, Councillor William Smith, and others, he agreed to publish a newspaper of broad appeal which would offer, among other viewpoints, writings supportive of royal authority. Rivington was told that he could expect favors from the royal government if he would execute such a project.[7] Late in 1773 Rivington's *New-York Gazetteer* became the focus of attacks by those who demanded ideological conformity to the resistance movement. By the spring of 1775, increasingly shrill patriot criticism forced Rivington to sign an oath in support of the Continen-

Part III: Practice

tal Congress. The question of the printer's allegiance had become so important to the leading revolutionaries that his oath was acknowledged in Congress and even outside of that body as a recantation. This fact, however, did nothing to prevent a mob from destroying his print shop and forcing him to flee, eventually to London.[8] The attack on his newspaper was meant to chasten Rivington, but in London he was even more willing to put his press at anyone's disposal. Early in 1776 he urged the ministry to reestablish and subsidize his press in New York; the purpose would be to defend the ministry against critics at home and to attack the rebellion they supported in America.[9]

In the fall of 1777 Rivington returned to occupied New York with the title of "King's Printer" and began printing a newspaper that for the next six years would be unmatched in its assault upon the patriots and that would make him the object of their undying condemnation. However, it has never been recognized that Rivington's attack was being directed by William Tryon and William Smith. This oversight accounts for the myth that the *Royal Gazette* was an expression of Rivington's consistent and deep personal allegiance to toryism. As the King's printer, Rivington was the last person to be suspected of serving as a spy for Washington's secret service. Yet prompted by his own political indifference and disappointment at the unfulfilled promise of a royally subsidized press, Rivington in 1779 began to pass military intelligence to Washington's agents in New York.[10]

Oblivious of any of these complexities and nuances, Witherspoon again used florid, obsequious language to condemn loyalist motivation in a highly judgmental fashion and to expose the debilitating effect of loyalism on a person's character and self-respect. "Your petitioner has no desire at all, either to be roasted in Florida, or frozen to death in Canada, or Nova Scotia," Witherspoon had Rivington explain in a formal memorial; "having been a bankrupt in London, it is not impossible that he might be accommodated with a lodging in Newgate.... In this dreadful dilemma, he hath at last determined to apply to your High Mightinesses, and... to *lay himself at your feet,* which he assures you is the true modish phrase for respectful submission, according to the present etiquette of the court."

For all his superficial familiarity with the events of the Revolution, Rivington—as caricatured by Witherspoon—understood nothing of the spirit and values of the patriot cause. In order to ingratiate himself with patriot leaders who were "Presbyterians and Religionists," Witherspoon had Rivington take "pains to find out a scripture warrant of example for his present conduct... in the advice given" to Syrian King Benhadad humbling himself before the rulers of Israel in I Kings 20:31. Though Witherspoon allowed Rivington artificially plausible ground for arguing that he should not be punished by the victorious American regime, those very

John Witherspoon and Loyalist Recantation

claims affronted patriot concepts of political morality. Even if it were true that "a tory heart" possessed "a rancour of spirit and rottenness of heart, unattainable by any other class of men," Rivington could reassure the patriots that he was personally powerless and that, like Towne, he would write and circulate whatever views authorities told him to publish.

Witherspoon's Rivington went on to heap mortification upon himself by piteously explaining how impotent and defanged the adherents of the Crown had become by 1778. The "barbarity" with which loyalist officials abused American prisoners would surely behoove all former tories to observe the strictest good conduct toward the new American regime. Confessing that the loyalist press had shamefully slandered the patriots—"We never once made you *retreat*; seldom even to *fly* as a routed army; but to *run into the woods*; to *scamper away through the fields*; and to *take to your heels as usual*"—Witherspoon had Rivington indulge in language of unmanliness and cowardice. Rivington reminded the patriots of the public scourging they had received in British and in American garrison town newspapers: "You must remember the many sweet names given you in print in England and America,—Rebels—rascals—ragamuffins—tatterdemalions—scoundrels—black-guards—cowards and poltroons." Considering "what a miserable affair it must be for a man to be obliged to apply with humility and self-abasement to those whom he hath so treated," Rivington's apology concluded, many loyalist "refugees" and "friends of government" were immobilized by "fear and trembling" and the tory printer Hugh Gaine, "is so much affected, that some say he has lost, or will soon lose, his reason."

Fear of political retribution did not, however, prevent the recanting Rivington from being in "the very pink of courtesy, a genteel, portly, well-looking fellow." Though he was confessedly chastened, Rivington's assumption that his opponents would overlook past faults and indeed draw on his talents in the future revealed, in Witherspoon's portrayal, that Rivington had not truly undergone any inner reformation of attitudes. "I understand and possess the *bienséance,* the manner, the grace, so largely insisted upon by Lord Chesterfield," boasted the printer, betraying his misunderstanding of the nature of republicanism.[11] To maximize the effect of Rivington's inadvertent self-condemnation, Witherspoon made himself the butt of Rivington's smug remarks. "I have been informed," the "Supplication" explained,

> that a certain person, well known to your august body, has clearly demonstrated that virtue and severity of manners are necessary to those who would pull an old government down, which feat is now happily accomplished; but that luxury, dissipation, and a taste for pleasure, are equally necessary to keep up a government already settled. . .[N]ow that you have settled governments in all the states, you are looking out for proper persons to soften the

Part III: Practice

rigid virtue of the Americans, or as . . . Dr. Johnson would have said, to *somnify* them[12] . . . and lay them asleep. . . . I am proud to say, that there is not a man on this continent more able to serve you in this respect, than myself.

Precisely because he was, in Witherspoon's eyes, a stylish, transient, chameleonlike figure, Rivington could perform as a printer whatever services the shapers of opinion required of him. He could pander to their love of power and authority as readily as he had to British and loyalist interests.

In the "Recantation of Benjamin Towne" and the "Supplication of James Rivington," Witherspoon sought not only to pillory the moral bankruptcy of these two loyalist printers, but more importantly to teach his patriot contemporaries a lesson about their own republicanism. Out of the mouths of these two political trimmers came warnings about how easily human virtue could be perverted, how readily falsehood could circulate in a free society, and how plausibly scoundrels could speak in their own defense.

2

Witherspoon's fascination with ritual humiliation and his agitation in the face of evil were both rooted in painful experience with political conflict. For a quarter century prior to his emigration to the colonies, he had led Scottish evangelical Calvinists in an unsuccessful fight to wrest control from a moderate intellectual elite, determined to accommodate Presbyterianism to the Enlightenment. During these controversies, Witherspoon had twice published devastating satires of his opponents. In the colonies, however, he moderated this abrasive, combative style in order to preside over a consensus within American Presbyterianism.[13] Initially hesitant to participate in the pre-Revolutionary controversy, Witherspoon was appalled by American attachment to John Wilkes, who was, in his view, a mob leader who had opportunistically whipped up anti-Scottish hatred in his attack on the King. By the summer of 1774, however, Witherspoon was privately convinced that colonial protest was neither the result of Wilkesian "pride, resentment, . . . sedition,"[14] nor a desire to encourage Wilkes' vicious assault on the king's family. As a result, Witherspoon began open resistance by joining New Jersey's Somerset County Committee of Correspondence and by becoming a member of a colony wide convention to select delegates to the First Continental Congress. Although he was not selected as a New Jersey delegate, he went to Philadelphia to argue against compensating the East India Company.[15] In the following summer Witherspoon became the undisputed leader of New Jersey's independence movement, and in June 1776 he was elected to Congress.

During his first two years in Congress, Witherspoon's radical credentials

John Witherspoon and Loyalist Recantation

seemed confirmed by his opposition to any attempt at reconciliation, by his support of the alliance with France, and by the death of his own son at the battle of Germantown. Yet over the course of his six-year tenure in Congress, Witherspoon's colleagues assigned him to only three major committees out of the hundreds on which he served. His friend Benjamin Rush attributed his peripheral role to his being the only clergyman in Congress.[16] More significant, probably, was the fact that he was Scottish, a member of the minority that his New Jersey associate William Patterson called "the worst vermin under Heaven."[17] Anti-Scottish prejudice caught Witherspoon in such a maze of suspicions that his best efforts to secure a fair hearing for himself and other Scots seemed self-serving and hypocritical. His "Address to the Natives of Scotland Residing in America," published in July 1776, freely admitted that he felt "an attachment of country, . . ." to the land of his birth, but he insisted, only "as far as it is a virtuous or laudable principle." Many Scots, he explained, suffered from suspicion that they were less opposed to British encroachments than were colonists of English and Scots Irish stock, and he conceded that some Scots were "too much inclined" to acquiesce in British policy.[18]

His "Address" was, then, as much an explanation of Scottish political sensibilities as an attempt to change those views. Many Scots, he explained, had been justifiably offended by the American adulation of John Wilkes for appropriating the name *North Briton* and the symbolic number 45 for a scurrilous attack on George III. Sensitivity to Scottish feelings could make the colonial case stronger and more defensible. "If you want to establish a case for liberty," L. Gordon Tait writes, paraphrasing Witherspoon, "do not drag in examples of real or imagined injustice in Britain. . . . Leave Britain and Wilkes out of it." The advantage of this restraint, Witherspoon felt, lay in the fact that it allowed him to base his case for independence on American potentialities rather than on British misdeeds. America had a glorious and God-given destiny that was about to be realized; only "criminal inattention" could blind observers to the "singular interposition of providence . . . in behalf of the American colonies." The rare historical opportunity to create a new political order, coupled with the confidence of the people in their representatives, would motivate American leaders to choose and act wisely. "Too much Scoticism," snorted Ezra Stiles. "He wants to save his countrymen who have behaved most cruelly in the American conflict."[19]

Widespread loyalism and neutrality in New Jersey also prompted Witherspoon to contrast authentic allegiance with Rivington's gross disloyalty. Throughout the Revolution Witherspoon believed that the "great number of Tories in every state" was a more important danger to the Revolution "than the [military] force sent against us."[20] In New Jersey between 1776 and December 1778, when the Supplication was written, unusually

Part III: Practice

strong disloyalty was exhibited in the form of loyalism, neutrality, and allegiance-switching. Among the states, New Jersey ranked fourth in the percentage of active loyalists, and it would have placed higher had it not been for the British army's brutality against loyalists as well as patriots. Despite these indiscriminate atrocities the countries nearest New York and Philadelphia had a proportion of loyalists that probably went as high as one-third or even one-half. By the fall of 1776 Witherspoon and other New Jersey radicals faced a huge problem in maintaining affection for the Revolution. Six New Jersey Provincial Congressmen as well as Witherspoon's friend and colleague in Congress, Richard Stockton, had departed for the British lines. Furthermore, large numbers of those "of inferior rank" had defected.[21] In a fury, Witherspoon referred to such defectors as: "Hypocrite[s]..., Fools[s]..., Robber[s]..., Rogue[s]..., Blasphemer[s]..., Sycophant[s]..., and Liar[s]...,"[22] and would soon use the example of James Rivington to instruct others concerning a firm and proper allegiance.

This harsh condemnation of turncoats masked Witherspoon's apprehension and uncertainty over how to deal with the deteriorating political situation in New Jersey. He knew, for example, that Stockton's defection represented no overt change in loyalty. Both Witherspoon and Stockton had fled Princeton on November 29, 1776 just ahead of advancing British troops. Witherspoon and most other leading whigs had reached safety in Pennsylvania, but Stockton had inexplicably sought refuge in tory-infested Monmouth County, perhaps because Washington had just dispatched troops to keep order there. Stockton and his host John Cowenhoven were dragged from their beds and taken in freezing weather to New York City where Stockton was kept in a cold cell without food for twenty-four hours and then given only scant rations. Anxious for the safety of his family and exhausted by his ordeal, he had taken General William Howe's prescribed oath to cease participation in the rebellion and was released. A painful cancer which developed from a badly chapped lip in November 1778 and the destruction of his home and property, despite the fact that Howe's oath was obtained from him under duress, precluded Stockton's rejoining the American cause. He died from the cancer in 1780.[23]

Witherspoon was aware of these facts and he even ridiculed the charge that Stockton had pleaded to his captors that he was preparing to surrender to Howe at the time of his arrest.[24] Yet he included in the Rivington recantation a veiled but unmistakable attack on Stockton and on Governor William Livingston: "We have often heard of Hortensius the governor of N——J——a gentleman remarkable for severely handling those he calls traitors; and indeed has exalted some of them (*quanquam animus meminisse horret luctuque refugit*[25] [although my mind shudders to remember and has recoiled in grief]) to a high though dependent station." Here Witherspoon alluded to the first

John Witherspoon and Loyalist Recantation

election for governor under the 1776 New Jersey constitution. In the election, Stockton and Livingston at first tied in the voting and then Stockton was offered, but declined, the post of Chief Justice.[26] By savagely attacking the pitiable Stockton and by ridiculing Livingston's handling of the tory problem, Witherspoon could vent his rage at what he considered the real issue, the "secret enemies" of the Revolution in New Jersey, including loyalists and allegiance switchers as well as passive opponents of the patriot cause among the middle and lower classes of society.[27] Even the militia was "tinctured with Toryism" and could not be trusted. So Witherspoon agreed with Governor Livingston to the dispatch by Congress of a small group of Continental troops "to strike a Terror into the disaffected." These numerous equivocating enemies, who Witherspoon believed "more or less abound[ed] in every New Jersey county,"[28] did not disappear however.

So in late 1778, in Rivington's mock recantation, Witherspoon once again took up satire—that form he believed "most agreeable to the public"[29]—to attack the morality of those "chicken-hearted" creatures who failed to rally to the American cause "for no other reason, than that they might avoid fighting" altogether. Congressional military force had failed to deal with these overly prudent people. Now he hoped to humiliate and shame them, beginning with Rivington.

In the "Supplication," Witherspoon sought to vindicate fidelity to the principles of the Revolution. Here again the recantation of a well-known and widely hated loyalist provided an ideal device. Witherspoon had come to America on a mission. As Witherspoon was leaving Scotland, a fellow clergyman had reminded him of his wish to transport the "seat of truth and righteousness..." from the Old World, where it had been defeated, to America.[30] After his arrival Witherspoon had been disturbed by the "outrage and sedition" which accompanied colonial resistance. When he realized, however, that resistance in America offered the possibility of moral regeneration, he suddenly became a radical. By 1776 he was looking forward to the turmoil of a revolution as an opportunity for Americans "to shake off the encumbrances of sloth and self-indulgence," and to improve the "temper,...morals, national...manners and...public virtue" of their country. He urged "humility,...restraint, and moderation" as imperative for success. "The riotous and wasteful liver," he wrote, "whose craving appetites make him constantly needy, is and must be subject to many masters ...[b]ut the frugal and moderate person, who guides his affairs with discretion, is able to assist in public councils by a free and unbiased judgment...."[31] Witherspoon saw this moral republicanism in formation in 1776, and, like the Calvinist clergy elsewhere in America, he would make a crucial contribution to the idea. Virtue, he insisted, was the necessary ingredient for a successful republican revolution and an even greater need if a republic was

Part III: Practice

to stand permanently.[32] During the war Witherspoon's mission would take on forms as varied as the rehabilitation of Scottish prisoners,[33] the self-conscious wearing of clerical gowns in Congress,[34] various journeys to Princeton to reopen the College,[35] and intermittent attempts to improve male-female relations. His commitment to the process of moral education for America[36] would remain the same. The "Supplication" was part of this process of moral instruction.[37]

3

The character of Witherspoon's political thought and the degree of continuity and consistency between the Scottish and American phases of his career have been the subject of a long, poorly focused historical disagreement. According to a traditional viewpoint, Witherspoon's leadership of the orthodox wing of the Church of Scotland in the 1750s and 1760s and his opposition to the influence of Francis Hutcheson and other moral philosophers conditioned him to prize order and moderation in American politics.[38] More recent scholarship, however, has emphasized Witherspoon's combativeness and the political orientation of his religious thought. His so-called "moderate" foes in Scotland were closely allied with the aristocracy which, in 1712, had gained control of clerical appointments and continued to prefer genteel preaching leavened with Enlightenment rationalism. In Scotland, therefore, Witherspoon had attacked Enlightenment ideas as part of his larger struggle to reinstate congregational control of ministerial selection.[39] This effort at reform was not necessarily a democratic impulse but was rather part of a struggle between rival elites, the aristocracy and the ruling elders.

Witherspoon's political writings in 1774–1776, Fred J. Hood has observed, were "a blending of American experience, Common Sense philosophy, and Reformed theology" which made conscientious, pious resistance and revolutionary discipline into moral imperatives.[40] So complete was Witherspoon's acceptance in America of Common Sense realism, Mark A. Noll has recently argued, that he "set aside an Augustinian distrust of human nature" in favor of "a value-free science of ethics" in which science and reason would mutually substantiate Christian revelation. In drawing heavily, though with only fragmentary acknowledgment, on Francis Hutcheson, he utilized a writer deeply concerned with reconciling Enlightenment rationalism to Christian belief.[41]

Witherspoon's two loyalist recantations do not resolve the problem of how he reconciled his republicanism and his conservatism, but they both relied on Common Sense assumptions to argue that falsehood and vice were so

John Witherspoon and Loyalist Recantation

corrosive as to imperil society's slender resources of virtue and civic responsibility. So Witherspoon had Towne boast pathetically that sensual stimuli rather than consistent principle made him a chameleonlike political lackey. The "lies" he had printed for the British, he declared, were harmless precisely because they were so gross and absurd. The more craven and pathetic Towne could be shown to be—and the more drastic the loss of his public reputation due to his collaboration—the safer the people would be from the moral contamination spawned by shallow, opportunistic allegiance. Witherspoon's fascination with the details of loyalist immorality and his determination to explain Towne's and Rivington's behavior as a deviation from republican norms underscore Noll's suggestion that Witherspoon deemphasized human depravity as a theological concept and subordinated theology to moral philosophy. Towne and Rivington were not, according to the recantations, partakers of a common human infirmity so much as they were specific sources of moral contamination and products of exotic kinds of ethical vulnerability.

By concluding Towne's apology with the assertion that "I hope the public will consider that I have been a timorous man, or if you will a coward from my youth, so that I cannot fight—my belly is so big that I cannot run—and I am so great a lover of eating and drinking that I cannot starve," Witherspoon drove home the argument that the failure to cultivate an intrinsic moral sense left men prey to corruption, folly, and connivance with depostism. Similarly, he had Rivington predict that he would conform to the demands of victorious patriot opinion as readily as he had for the British: "A man that has run the gauntlet of creditors, duns, and bailiffs, for years in England, and has been cudgelled, kicked, and pissed upon in America, is in no danger of losing his reason . . . so long as there is the least prospect of saving his life."

Witherspoon had a good republican's understanding of a republic's fragility. And he was frantic in his efforts to weed out the "detestable selfishness" he saw in some leading revolutionaries. He feared that some of his congressional colleagues were "set upon nothing but making money."[42] Among the body of uninstructed Americans the possibility of a weak republican character could only be greater. The "Supplication of James Rivington" was written, therefore, to define for a popular audience the character necessary to the survival of the republic. Witherspoon believed that satirization of the widely known printer could encourage an appropriate public spirit.[43] Rivington's almost universal reputation as a traitor to the "liberties of this country" and a "vile ministerial hireling"[44] made him an ideal object lesson. Between 1774 and 1776 Committees of Correspondence from the middle colonies and New England had engaged in regular attacks on Rivington, more because of what he symbolized than the danger he

Part III: Practice

posed to resistance.[45] After 1776 the rise of "luxury, effeminancy, and the
. . . dissipated life" heightened Witherspoon's conviction that Rivington's
example was a public menace.[46] Witherspoon assumed that most of the
reading public knew how Rivington, before arriving in America, had gath-
ered a small fortune from an illegal printing scheme and then had quickly
gambled it away. Instead of liquidating his property to pay his creditors, he
had declared bankruptcy and fled. In America he was a sycophant who
again ruined himself while seeking to ingratiate himself with the provincial
aristocracy.[47] Witherspoon did not exaggerate Rivington's reputation
among contemporary printers and booksellers. They saw in his career a
thoroughly self-destructive pattern of behavior. In William Strahan's view,
he lacked "manliness and spirit," and in the face of a second financial ruin
he had married for money to maintain his pretensions to class. Furthermore, he was shallow, flippant, dissipated, arrogant, and so corrupt he was
"indulged beyond what a person of integrity could expect."[48]

To clinch his argument for Rivington's moral baseness and psychological
insecurity, Witherspoon drew on a vocabulary of degradation which he
knew intimately—that of anti-Scottish stereotypes. "I can assure your High
Mightinesses," he had Rivington implore, "that I am as great a coward as
King James the VI of Scotland, who never could see a naked sword without
trembling, having been, it is said, frightened in his mother's belly, when the
fierce barons of that country came in, and killed David Rizzio in her presence." Presenting Rivington as a person who would pander to any public
prejudice, Witherspoon also had his victim invoke the opinion of the
sixteenth-century Scottish historian George Buchanan, that "*Perfervidum est
Scotorum ingenium* [the Scot is by nature zealous]" to the point of unpredictable instability. These qualities, far from endowing Rivington with manliness, only reinforced his tendency to opportunism: "I hope . . . your
Honours will consider my sufferings as sufficient to atone for my offenses,
and allow me to continue in peace and quiet, and according to the North-
British proverb, to *sleep in a whole skin.*"[49]

The Towne-Rivington recantations Witherspoon wrote illuminate in unusually graphic detail the transactions which arose from conflicts of allegiance. As Stephen Botein observed in his brief treatment of the
controversy, "lack of principle" in Towne and Rivington invited public exposure and humiliation. The older professional standards of printers—
service, utility, and adaptability—abruptly became the public face of corruption and sinister motivation.[50] This transformation can be seen not only
in Witherspoon's contempt and denunciation but also in elements of the
older professional code which possibly survived Witherspoon's recasting of
loyalist arguments, as when he allowed Towne to plead, "it is pretended
[falsely] that I certainly did in my heart incline to the English, because I

John Witherspoon and Loyalist Recantation

printed much bigger lies and in greater number for them. . . . " The coercion which the Revolution inflicted on its internal foes, therefore, was often that of moral castigation. The embarrassing abundance of pain and pathetic, self-serving remonstrance in the recantations served to confirm the triumph of virtue over vice—what the Rivington document called "the dreadful motification, after our past puffing and vanity[51] of being under the dominion of the Congress."

Through the Towne and Rivington recantations, Witherspoon struggled to locate and vindicate the moral authority of the Revolution at a time when that authority had not yet become fully institutionalized nor hammered into fully recognized behavioral norms. Placing requirements of civic purity and righteous intention at the core of the authority of the Revolution, Witherspoon situated Towne and Rivington beyond the periphery of a morally defined political order. His territorial, exclusionary, and judgmental strictures were the kind of radicalism most congenial to his experience and intellect.

1. Isaiah Thomas, *The History of Printing in America* (Worcester, 1810), vol. 2, p. 74ff.
2. "The humble confession, declaration, recantation, and apology of BENJAMIN TOWNE, Printer in Philadelphia," *New York Packet* (Fishkill, N.Y.), 1 Oct. 1778, was printed later in *Miscellanies for Sentimentalists* (Philadelphia, 1778), appendix; in *Sermons to Ministers of State* (Philadelphia, 1783), pp. 76ff.; in Thomas, *History of Printing,* 2:453ff.; and in *The Works of the Rev. John Witherspoon* (Edinburgh, 1804–1805), 9:192ff. "The humble Representation and earnest Supplication of James Rivington, Printer and Bookseller in New York," *The United States Magazine: A Repository of History, Politics, and Literature* (Philadelphia), I (Jan. 1779), 34ff., later reprinted in Witherspoon, *Works,* 9:180–91 and in Thomas, *History of Printing,* 2:495ff. All quotations are from the earliest extant editions in the *New York Packet* and *United States Magazine* respectively. Witherspoon's "Supplication of . . . Rivington" carries the date Dec. 5, 1778, which we accept as authentic. Leroy Hewlett and Ashbel Green both misdated the Supplication to Nov. 1783, misconstruing internal evidence—references to Loyalists and imminent British evacuation which Witherspoon added to lend the document verisimilitude and which referred to the departure of 3,500 British troops bound for Savannah under Lt. Col. Archibald Campbell on Nov. 25, 1778. See Hewlett, "James Rivington, Loyalist Printer, Publisher, and Bookseller of the American Revolution:" A Biographical and Bibliographical Study, 1763-1783," Ph.D. diss., University of Michigan, 1958, 480, and Green, *The Life of the Revd. John Witherspoon, D.D., L.L.D., With a Brief Review of his Writings; and a Summary Estimate of his Character and Talents,* Henry L. Savage, ed. (Princeton, 1973), 190.
3. Robert Aitken, Waste Book, 229, Historical Society of Pennsylvania, Philadelphia; Dwight L. Teeter, "Benjamin Towne: The Precarious Career of a Persistent Printer," *Pennsylvania Magazine of History and Biography,* 89 (July 1965), 316–30.
4. Bernadotte Perrin, trans., *Plutarch's Lives,* Loeb Classical Library (New York, 1914–1926), 6:243; 8:395–411.

Part III: Practice

5. "Diary of James Allen, Esq., of Philadelphia, Counsellor-at-Law, 1770–1778," *Pennsylvania Magazine of History and Biography,* 9 (1885), 177.

6. On May 18, 1778 the British Arm in Philadelphia held an extravagant day-long celebration called the "Mischianza" as a farewell to General William Howe; Witherspoon called it a "Fête" to indicate that it was a vulgar unrepublican display.

7. Hewlett, "Rivington," 39ff.; Benjamin Booth to Henry Drinker, 28 Oct., 24 Nov. 1773; 4, 9, 13 July; 8 Aug.; 22 Oct. 1774; Henry Drinker to [?] Pigou & [Benjamin] Booth, 4, 9 Aug. 1774, Henry Drinker Papers, 1772–1786, ibid.; Peter Force, comp., *American Archives,* Ser. 4 (Washington, 1837–1853), 2:726.

8. Ibid., 2:836f., 899.

9. James Rivington to [George Germain], 6 Mar. 1776, Germain Papers, William L. Clements Library, University of Michigan.

10. James Rivington to Richard Cumberland, 23 Nov. 1778, Colonial Office Papers, 5/155:175f., Public Record Office, London; Catherine S. Crary, "The Tory and the Spy: the Double Life of James Rivington," *William and Mary Quarterly,* 3rd Ser., 16 (Jan. 1959), 61–72; Philip Ranlet, "James Rivington, Secret Agent," *Journal of Communication Inquiry,* 8 (Summer 1984), 21–30; Witherspoon assigned Rivington a different covert role by comparing him to Pandarus of Troy, whom the gods employed as an agent provcateur to sabotage a truce in the Trojan wars, *The Iliad,* Richard Lattimore, trans., (Chicago, 1951), book 4, lines 88–99.

11. See, *The Letters Written by the Earl of Chesterfield to his Son, Philip Stanhope . . .* (London, 1774) and James Boswell, *The Life of Samuel Johnson, D.D.* (London, 1872), 2:13.

12. The versions of the "Supplication" in Witherspoon's *Works* and Thomas' *History of Printing* substituted the words "in the lap of self-indulgence" following "asleep." In quoting Dr. Johnson, Witherspoon again subtly ridiculed Rivington's shallow literary knowledge; "somnify" does not appear in Johnson's Dictionary, in the concordance to his poetry, or in his two essays on sleep, *Idler,* No. 32 and *Adventurer,* No. 39; the *Oxford English Dictionary* entry on "somnify" does not cite a Johnson usage.

13. George A. Rich, "John Witherspoon: His Scottish Intellectual Background," D.S.S. diss., Syracuse University, 1964 and note 38 below.

14. Witherspoon, *Works,* 5:202f., 219f.; other Presbyterians could not make the move from Crown supporters to patriots; Jonathan Powell, "Presbyterian Loyalists: A 'Chain of Interest' in Philadelphia," *Journal of Presbyterian History,* 57 (Summer 1979), 135ff.

15. Varnum Collins, *President Witherspoon: A Biography* (Princeton, 1925), 1:160f.

16. Benjamin F. Stevens ed., *Facsimilies of Manuscripts in European Archives Relating to America, 1773–1783* (London, 1889–1895), 14:doc. 1399; Elias Boudinot, *Journal, or Historical Recollections of American Events during the Revolutionary War* (Philadelphia, 1894), 6.

17. William Patterson, *Glimpses of Colonial Society and the Life at Princeton College, 1766–1773, by One of the Class of 1763,* Weymer Jay Mills, ed. (Philadelphia, 1903), 48.

18. Witherspoon, *Works,* 5:218ff; Stiles remained sceptical, see Literary Diary of Ezra Stiles, 23 July 1777, Papers of Peter Force, Series 8-E, Box 67, Library of Congress, Washington, D.C.

19. L. Gordon Tait, "John Witherspoon and the Scottish Loyalists," *Journal of Presbyterian History,* 61 (Fall 1983), 305, 308.

20. Stevens, *Facsimiles,* 1:doc. 58.

John Witherspoon and Loyalist Recantation

21. Howe to Germain, 25 Mar. 1777, CO 5/177:64.

22. "Caspipina's Catechism," [n.d.], Papers of John Witherspoon, Library of Congress; Witherspoon to David Witherspoon, 17 Mar. 1777, Paul H. Smith, et al. eds., *Letters of Delegates to Congress, 1774–1789* (Washington, 1976–), 6:454ff.; see also John Covenhoven to Elias Boudinot, 30 Jan. 1778, Elias Boudinot Coll., Princeton University Library.

23. Alfred Bill Hoyt et al., *A House Called Morven: Its Role in American History* (Princeton, 1954, rev. 1978), 39–51.

24. Witherspoon to David Witherspoon, Mar. 17, 1777, Smith, ed., *Letters of Delegates,* 6:454ff.

25. H. Rushton Fairclough, trans., Virgil, *Aeneid,* Loeb Classical Library (Cambridge, 1916–18), 1:295.

26. Lucius Q.C. Elmer, *The Constitution and Government of the Province and State of New Jersey...* (Newark, 1872), 63.

27. "Witherspoon's Speech in Congress, [Sept. 5?], 1776, Smith, ed., *Letters of Delegates,* 5:112.

28. William Livingston to Witherspoon, May 7, 1777, C. E. Prince et al., eds., *The Papers of William Livingston* (Trenton, 1979), 1:322ff.

29. "The Druid" #1 [John Witherspoon]. *Pennsylvania Magazine, or American Monthly Museum* (May 1776), 206.

30. Thomas Randall to Witherspoon, 4 Mar. 1767, John Witherspoon Coll. Princeton University Library; for evidence that he considered his mission in America to be spiritual rather than political, see Witherspoon to [?], 10 July [1776?], Papers of John Witherspoon, Library of Congress.

31. Witherspoon, *Works,* 5:209, 214; Collins, *Witherspoon,* 1:140; "Druid #1" [Witherspoon], *Pennsylvania Magazine* (May 1776), 208.

32. Witherspoon, *Works,* 5:266; Stevens, *Facsimiles,* 51:doc. 487.

33. "Acknowledgment of Recept of four Prisoners of War," Aug. 25, 1779 in Board of War to Witherspoon, [n.d.], John Witherspoon Coll., Princeton University Library.

34. Green, *Witherspoon,* 161.

35. Witherspoon to the Rev. [?] Carmichael, Oct. 2, 1779 and to Jonathan Sargeant, Nov. 22, 1774, John Witherspoon Coll., Princeton University Library.

36. "X.Y." and "Epaminodas" [Witherspoon], *Pennsylvania Magazine* (April 1775), 150ff.; (May 1775), 197ff.; (June 1775), 262f.; (Sept. 1775), 408ff.; (Dec. 1775), 543ff., 557ff.; (Dec. 1776), 109ff.

37. "The Druid #1 [Witherspoon], ibid., (May 1776), 205ff.; (June 1776), 253ff.; (July 1776), 301ff.; Witherspoon, *Works,* 9:224–91.

38. Lyman H. Butterfield, *John Witherspoon Comes to America...* (Princeton, 1953), 12f.; Rich, "Witherspoon," chapter 5.

39. Mark A. Noll. "The Irony of the Enlightenment in Nineteenth-Century Religious Thought," *Journal of the Early Republic,* 5 (1985): 154–59; Roger J. Fechner, "The Godly and virtuous Republic of John Witherspoon," Hamilton Cravens, ed., *Ideas in America's Cultures...* (Ames, Ia., 1982), 9–21.

40. Fred J. Hood, *Reformed America...* (Tuscaloosa, Ala., 1980), 14; James L. McAllister "John Witherspoon: American Advocate of Academic Freedom," Stuart C. Henry, ed., *A Miscellany of American Christianity...* (Durham, N.C., 1963), 183–224; and James H. Smylie, "Madison and Witherspoon: Theological Roots of American Political Thought," *Princeton University Library Quarterly,* 22 (1961), 118–32.

41. Noll, "The Irony of the Enlightenment," 5; Norman S. Fiering, *Moral Philosophy*

Part III: Practice

at Harvard: A Discipline in transition (Chapel Hill, N.C., 1981), 198–206; Jack Scott, ed., *An Annotated Edition of Lectures on Moral Philosophy by John Witherspoon* (Newark, 1982), 27–43, 128ff., 165ff., 182ff.

42. Witherspoon to Benjamin Rush, 17 Nov. 1776, Smith ed., *Letters of Delegates,* 5:511.
43. Witherspoon, *Works,* 5:208f., 218; letter for the *Federal Gazette,* [n.d.], Papers of John Witherspoon, Library of Congress.
44. *Rivington's Gazette,* Mar. 2, 1775; *New York Journal,* Feb. 9 and 23, 1775.
45. *Rivington's Gazette,* Mar. 16, 1775; *New York Journal,* Feb. 9 and 23, 1775.
46. Witherspoon, *Works,* 5:269f.
47. Thomas, *History of Printing,* 2:111.
48. William Strahan to David Hall, June 21, 1760 and June 12, 1767, David Hall Papers, American Philosophical Society, Phila., Penna. and "Correspondence between William Strahan and David Hall, 1763–1777...," *PMHB,* 10 (1886), 327; see also Strahan to Hall, July 11, 1758; Mar. 24, 1759; Jan. 7, Feb. 13, 1760; Hall to Hamilton and Balfour, Dec. 22, 1760; Hall and Benjamin Franklin to Daniel Warner, Dec. 22, 1760, David Hall Papers; Rivington to William Alexander, Jan. 7, 1767, William Alexander Papers, New York Historical Society, New York City; *New York Journal,* Oct. 6, 1768.
49. George Buchanan (1506–1582) was author of *The History of Scotland* (London, 1690); we have not located the source of this quotation; the "North-British proverb" may be found in James Kelly, ed., *A Complete Collection of Scottish Proverbs...* (London, 1721), 220.
50. Stephen Botein, "Printers and the American Revolution," Bernard Bailyn and John B. Hench, eds., *The Press & the American Revolution* (Worcester, 1980), 46f.
51. The versions of the "Supplication" in Witherspoon's *Works* and Thomas' *History of Printing* substituted "vaunting."

11

THE REINTEGRATION OF THE LOYALISTS AND THE DISAFFECTED

1. A Decentralized Infrastructure

The reintegration of the loyalists and the disaffected began with one of the earliest and most authentically revolutionary actions by the patriots—the First Continental Congress's recommendation that local committees enforce the non-importation, non-exportation, and non-consumption provisions of the Continental Association and publicly discredit "as the enemies of American liberty" violators of its provisions.[1] The astounding result of this clause in the Continental Association was the creation of a network of more than 7,000 committeemen by the spring of 1775, a virtually indestructible infrastructure of local revolutionary leadership. "The success of the Whigs in tying so substantial a group of local leaders to the enforcement of the Association," David Ammerman rightly emphasizes, "was a psychological victory of the first magnitude."[2]

These bodies quickly concluded that it would be futile to try to catch violators of non-importation red-handed. Perhaps guided by the Manichaean language of Congress about "enemies" and "foes to the rights of British America," committees hit upon the dynamic tactic of collecting the names of potential or actual Crown supporters, summoning them for public interrogation, and thereby acting as protectors of the community as well as agents of resistance.

Exchanges between revolutionary committees and suspected tories were part of what Peter Shaw calls "the ritual language" of the American Revolution, and ritualization of these proceedings was nowhere clearer than in

195

the evolution of the loyalist recantation as documents dramatizing the bonds holding revolutionary communities together as well as tensions threatening to shatter community unity.[3] When six men in Marblehead, Massachusetts, apologized in May 1775 for signing a farewell address to Thomas Hutchinson a year earlier, each admitted that he had unintentionally jeopardized the safety of the town by signing the address, and then each declared that the hostility of the community was a cleansing force which could restore his public reputation and render him once again a fit participant in the affairs of the body politic.[4]

"As My comfort in life does so much depend on the regard and good will of those among whom I live," wrote Enoch Bartlett of Haverhill, Massachusetts, in September 1774, "I hereby give it Under my Hand that I will not buy or Sell Tea or Act in Any public office Contrary to the Minds of the people in General...and will yet hope that all My errors in Judgment or Conduct meet with their forgiveness and favour which I humbly ask."[5] Similarly, when David Wardrobe, a British schoolmaster in Virginia, apologized to the Westmoreland Committee of Inspection on November 29, 1774, for having written an indiscreet letter to a correspondent in Scotland about Virginia politics, he "implor[ed] the forgiveness of this country for so ungrateful a return made for the advantages I have received from it, and the bread I have earned in it, and hope, from this contrition for my offence,... to subsist among the people I greatly esteem."[6]

There was a difference in tone between recantations from New England which were apologies to the whole community and those in the Chesapeake, where a newcomer and outsider admitted his dependence on the sufferance and hospitality of the aristocracy. Recantations reflected local patterns of deference and social control and, in the midst of revolutionary turmoil, an elaborate etiquette of superiority and inferiority. The use of ritualized public language as a means of admitting errant loyalists into a republican polity indicated that the healing of political wounds was integral to the Revolution itself. The dramatization of political conflict, which Rhys Isaac has found at the core of the Revolution in Virginia, sprang directly from the manifold group antagonisms instigated and exacerbated by the Revolution.[7]

2. Moral Republicanism

John Witherspoon's ritual recantations for Benjamin Towne and James Rivington, described in a preceding chapter, were not authentic rituals of purgation and reintegration. but they did seek to educate a wide readership which enjoyed satire about the nature of republicanism, the fragile condition of republican virtue, and the ease with which scoundrels might sound plausible and innocent.[8] Witherspoon was deeply suspicious of learning that was not grounded in personal virtue. It was not that he believed that people were capable of goodness—though he moved surprisingly close to this repudiation of Calvinism—but that he especially despised those contaminated by dependence on British favor and habituated to servility. Such loyalists were, in Witherspoon's eyes, capable of insidious, chameleonlike mocking of republican virtues like sacrifice, duty, or the covenanted obligation to promote the common good. Witherspoon took special delight in exposing the intellectual emptiness of pro-British functionaries by having Towne and Rivington mouth parodies of Plutarch, Homer, and Samuel Johnson, which truly educated readers would recognize as shallow and obtuse. The superficiality and rhetorical excess of the Towne and Rivington recantations make them appear a minor episode in his career and a vacuous contribution to the discussion of reintegrating the loyalists and the disaffected. Witherspoon was the earliest patriot to deal extensively with the issue of reintegration. He not only produced an elaborate depiction of what Samuel Adams called a "Christian Sparta," he endowed moral castigation of loyalists, neutralists, and allegiance switchers with a kind of curative power. Like debased currency, condemnatory rhetoric was an asset the patriots possessed in abundance and could employ beneficially in the short term.

Loyalist reintegration arose as a political problem early in the war because of the existence of British garrison towns where people like Towne and Rivington—and their readers—could imbibe British corruption and arrogance. In Boston until March 1776, New York from September 1776 until November 1783, Newport from December 1776 until October 1779, Philadelphia from September 1777 until June 1778, Savannah from December 1778 until July 1782, Charlestown from May 1780 until December 1782, and Wilmington, North Carolina, from January to November 1781, loyalist exiles found refuge, British military and economic power acquired a concentrated base, and an unstable culture of violence, deprivation amid wealth, and martial law pervaded the conduct of the war. In those towns which returned to American control during the war, those who had collaborated with the British but had not departed had to come to terms with the patriots. Surrounding each of these towns was a no man's land where illicit trade, crime, and patriot-loyalist violence flourished. The British found administration of the garrison towns a vexing problem; indirectly, these towns nourished the Revolution by providing places to dispatch defiant loyalists. Even illicit trade, which drained resources needed by the Continental Army, provided a valuable injection of British spending into the fringes of patriot-held territory. The garrison towns, therefore, created a large body of defectors for patriot justice to process back into American society as well as a visible demonstration of British power, corruption, and vulnerability.[9]

Part III: Practice

3. Volitional Allegiance

The most important scholarly discovery about the reintegration of the loyalists and the disaffected is James H. Kettner's "idea of volitional allegiance" as a way of thinking about citizenship in Revolutionary America.[10] Simply stated, volitional allegiance was the notion that American citizenship should be a matter of "individual choice." This seemingly straightforward republican principle, however, was the product of a complex legal, political, and ethical situation—complexity central to the nature of the Revolution itself.

In the process of tracing the development of allegiance from *Calvin's Case* in 1608 to the Fifteenth Amendment in 1870, Kettner illuminates the conceptual problems peculiar to the study of allegiance. In Anglo-American tradition, he shows, concepts of allegiance have not taken the form of gradual accretions resulting from prolonged trial and error; rather, concepts of allegiance at any given time consisted of clusters of theory, practice, law, and tradition, which often coalesced suddenly under the pressure of events that thrust individuals and the state into new and ill-defined relationships. Very much like a Kuhnian paradigm, allegiance embodied contrasting and divergent elements complementary enough to meet the demands of specific situations and consequently fraught with potential internal stress—stress that became more pronounced as a particular definition of allegiance was applied to thorny political and legal cases.

Revolution and war disrupted the fragile web of suppositions undergirding obligation in British America. Drawing on traditional ideas, Revolutionary leaders insisted that George III had forfeited the allegiance of his colonial subjects and that their prior consent to British rule—expressed in the colonial charters—reserved ultimate constitutional authority to the whole body of the people as expressed by their representatives. But Anglo-America tradition provided little guidance in dealing with the question of individual allegiance in situations of revolution and civil war. Could state governments impose American allegiance on all their inhabitants? Did the ultimate success of American arms by 1783 entitle the new nation to the allegiance of all the people by right of conquest? Republican principles and practical realities dictated a negative answer to both questions. The sheer impracticality of prosecuting large numbers of loyalists for treason, the emerging conviction that in a civil war everyone should have a reasonable interval to decide which side to join, and the diplomatic need to strike a compromise between the sovereignty of the new nation and Britain's obligations to her loyalist supporters were all among the constitutent elements of the concept of volitional allegiance.

Reintegration of the Loyalists

Loyalists documented the formulation of volitional allegiance in two important instances. First, Peter Van Schaack privately expressed in the winter of 1775–1776 the view that "every individual has the right to choose the State of which he will become a member" when that person is caught up in the overthrow of an old government and formation of a new one. Van Schaack limited this right of personal choice to allegiance to the narrow interval between revolutionary overthrow and creation "for I admit that once a society *is* formed, the majority of its members undoubtedly conclude meaning to decide for the rest."[11] Chief Justice Thomas McKean of Pennsylvania took exactly the same position in 1781 when he ruled in the treason trial of Samuel Chapman that in Pennsylvania the interval of individual choice extended from May 14, 1776 (the date before Congress annulled the effect of the Penn charter) until February 11, 1777 (when the state enacted a treason statute making allegiance and protection reciprocal). At the time of Chapman's alleged offense of joining the British Legion in late December 1776, McKean ruled, "Pennsylvania was not a nation at war with another nation, but a country in a state of *civil war.*"[12]

The presence in Pennsylvania of a variety of large communities of religious pacifists both provoked the radicals to a program of coercion and served as a moderating buffer against revolutionary zeal. Mennonites were willing to sell farm produce to the Continental Army and to pay commutation fees in lieu of military service, but they refused to take the oath prescribed by law in 1777 because they would not abjure allegiance to a King who had done nothing to forfeit his claim to their obedience and because they had no reason to trust the new regime in Philadelphia. Moravian pacifism did not proscribe any bearing of arms, but regarded military service as sinful, if contrary to the conscience of the individual or performed under coercion. Schwenkfelders were the most apolitical and literalistic of the German pietist sects; one of their number, George Kriebel, told a judge that he could not take the oath of allegiance because the outcome of the war was still in doubt and therefore he did not yet know "upon what side God almighty would bestow the victory." The most visible pacifists and the most politically controversial were Quakers—a sect deeply split by the Revolution. Much of the traditional leadership of the Philadelphia Quaker merchant aristocracy refused on religious grounds "to join in any of the prevailing seditions and tumults," as one Quaker leader, Samuel R. Fisher, put it. Under Congressional pressure, Pennsylvania officials arrested more than forty prominent Philadelphia Quakers and sent them to detention in Winchester, Virginia, during the British occupation of Philadelphia. Beyond that harsh gesture, the discipline of the religious pacifists, the variety of the form of their noncompliance with Revolutionary dictates, and the weakness of coercive machinery all blunted punitive policies. Pluralism proved a powerful solvent of Revolutionary persecution.[13] Volition allegiance was the resulting equilibrium in this fluid situation.

A more complex and less studied setting for Revolutionary allegiance took shape in New York. Pressed to affirm allegiance to the Revolution in early 1777, Cadwallader Colden II told the New York Committee for Detecting and Defeating Conspiracies that "he conceived the former oath of allegiance which he had taken to the King of Great Britain to be binding upon him & professed a desire on being permitted to observe a state of neutrality." It took until the following October for the cumbersome machinery of revolutionary justice in New York to come to terms with this concept of allegiance. "No such state of neutrality can be known by the Council [of Safety]," Colden was told. Given time to reconsider his position, the stolid, apolitical son of New York's last royal lieutenant governor persevered in his claim to be "a faithful & true Subject to that State [New York] from which he receiv'd protection" and, while still bound by his allegiance to the king, he promised to be "a true and faithful Subject to the government of the Said State, So Long as it shall remain an independent State, and I reside therein."[14]

Colden's plight was emblematic of the situation of many loyalists and neutralists in New York. "The contest between Whigs and Tories is not what was most important about Revolutionary Queens [County]," Joseph S. Tiedemann concludes in a detailed study of early Revolutionary mobilization across the East River from Manhattan; "the truly significant reality was that a decisive majority remained neutral in the contest between Great Britain and her thirteen colonies." These neutralists were "traditional agricultural people, . . . more concerned with the soil, the weather, and the prospects for the next crop than with debating the merits of Britain's imperial administration." Whig and tory activists represented neither class nor generational constituencies; rather, they were a politicized minority already accustomed to elections, polemicism, public gatherings, and other forms of public display as ways of asserting virtue and denouncing vice.[15]

The keys to understanding most New York loyalists are a sensitivity to apolitical language and gesture and an intimate knowledge of the local history. The late Jonathan Clark brought both qualities to his study of loyalists and patriots in Poughkeepsie, New York. Clark tracked down personal and political data on nearly three-fourths of 329 male inhabitants of the town. He found 101 committed patriots and 61 staunch loyalists; the remaining 69 "pristine fence sitters" included 29 "occasional patriots" and 40 "occasional loyalists." The people in these four categories knew one another and to a large extent were intermarried. Clark's 69 "occasional" loyalists and patriots embodied the impulses and circumstances framing choices of alle-

Reintegration of the Loyalists

giance. One occasional loyalist, Peter Leroy, refused to sign the Association and had two sons fighting for the British, but under the influence of a patriot brother-in-law remained inactive in the struggle. Another, William Emmot, had agreed to take the oath of allegiance to the state and received, as a consequence, permission from Governor George Clinton to visit Long Island—behind enemy lines. That provoked a storm of protest from neighbors sceptical of Emmot's allegiance to the American cause. Known as a "sligh Designing fallow," Emmot took care to give no more offense and after the war emerged as a prosperous justice of the peace. In terms of wealth, both patriots and loyalists spanned the social scale in Poughkeepsie, but on the average patriots had more wealth in 1775 and even more of them were among the very well-to-do. Supporting the Revolution was a gamble, but those who had the most to lose feared British victory more than they did independence. Forty of the 69 "occasional" loyalists and patriots remained within the town and in possession of their property. "The resolution of the loyalist problem," Clark explains, "rested in the hands of men who, having made themselves noticeably large fish in a small pond, were as intent on saving their town as on saving their country. The destruction of their community, as they knew it, was not a price they would pay for victory."[16]

Finally, Michael Kammen's essay on "The American Revolution as a *Crise de Conscience:* The Case of New York," places the reintegration of the loyalists within a spacious intellectual framework, which included an ironic subsection on "The Meaning and Consequences of an Oath"—one of the first mechanisms used in New York to validate citizenship. New Yorkers knew that oaths were often meaningless, that people swore allegiance insincerely to save themselves from injury or legal punishment, and that in an atmosphere of upheaval unprincipled opportunism flourished. Why then were oaths widely employed? In the first place, Kammen argues, because they were means of rehabilitating the disaffected and the disloyal. An oath could serve as a written record of submission to the new state; its imposition was a stern warning to behave well in the future; and the language of oaths summarized past behavior, including lapses of allegiance, and therefore functioned as individualized prescriptions for conduct. An oath was a cheap, quick, uniform procedure that worked more often than it failed. Moreover, oaths gave individuals opportunities to verbalize and objectivize the hazards and pitfalls that entrapped the unprincipled and the naive in a revolutionary setting. As the Albany Committee of Safety discovered in late 1777, some people sided with Britain "thro' Fear, some thro' the persuasions of artful and designing Persons, others thro' the Allurements of Gain and the prospect of seeing their oppressed Country in the Hands of its base Invaders."[17] The clinical quality of such patriot diagnoses and loyalist admissions resembled what Gordon S. Wood has called "the Whig science of

Part III: Practice

politics"—the confident belief early in the Revolution that political behavior could be understood and handled by the careful discernment of virtue and corruption in the body politic. And the recognitioñ of the contingent character of affiliation and even allegiance implicit in these documents was part of a "new emphasis on piecemeal and the concrete in politics" which, according to Wood, soon replaced that body of classical principles.[18] In these terms, loyalist reintegration was part of the interface between whig assumptions and republican practice.

4. Military Triangularity

During the mid-1960s two quantitative estimates put the maximum number of loyalists at approximately 18 percent of the adult male population. Then in 1971 John Shy called attention to "the essential triangularity" of the War for Independence, that is, to the way British and American forces "contended less with each other than for support and control of the civilian population."[19] The triangularity hypothesis enables historians to make sense of a plethora of information about British frustration and American weakness. Despite the best efforts of conservative commanders on both sides, the war spilled off the formal battlefield and into the surrounding society in what the Rev. Samuel E. McCorkle called an "invasive" conflict. The politicizing and brutalizing of noncombatants hurt both sides but did far more damage to the British because it mocked their pretensions as protectors of the King's faithful subjects and guarantors of order in the colonies. The dual task of holding society together while conducting a socially divisive war, moreover, involved Revolutionary leaders in desperate experimentation, much of which ran counter to their basically conservative predilections. A sizeable body of recent scholarship on local conflict during the war bears on the problem of loyalist reintegration.[20]

In one of the best studies of the social dynamics of the war years, Ronald Hoffman discovered on the Eastern Shore of Maryland, especially in Dorchester County, a kind of tory populism among small farmers who defied the whig elite that had overthrown the Proprietary government in 1775.[21] Harold B. Hancock identified the same sort of loyalist defiance of a new state government in neighboring Sussex County, Delaware—for example, a bizarre episode in which a group of tory refugees descended on the home of constable Robert Appleton in Bombay Hook, Delaware, and ordered him to read a Methodist sermon, destroy legal papers pertaining to loyalists, and submit to being whipped by a black man.[22] The racial and religious references to the Appleton incident highlighted two intriguing features of Eastern Shore/Delaware tory insurgency. News of Dunmore's appeal to Virginia slaves to join him in suppressing rebellion in 1775 reached the ears

Reintegration of the Loyalists

of Eastern Shore blacks and may have prompted fearful Maryland officials into overreaction, which may have alerted yeoman farmers to the tenuous authority of the Revolutionary regime. As the war progressed, loyalist activity became increasingly identified with the influence of Methodist preachers who seemed intent, as they did in Virginia, on building a new kind of spiritual order among poor whites and some slaves and free blacks and were oblivious to the patriots' presumptions to serving a divine purpose.[23]

Everywhere loyalist deviance tested the discrimination and resiliency of patriot administration. Legislators, governors, and higher level judges were conscious of the practical difficulties of drawing and enforcing tight legal norms; ordinary citizens and local officials were aware of the dangers to their safety from failing to do so. Two recent studies examine this process, one in Connecticut and the other in North Carolina. In both states, a legal vacuum existed at a critical moment in the Revolution. In Connecticut it occurred in 1774–1776; David H. Villers argues that local committees played their role to the hilt, but when committee authority proved insufficient, as it often did, they relied on what Villers calls " 'Liberty' gangs," which waylaid and terrorized suspects, extracted confessions, destroyed property, and in one sensational case broke into a jail to release patriot rioters convicted of illegally burning personal goods belonging to a New London customs collector. State officials, though uneasy about such vigilante justice, found these methods a useful supplement to the tenuous authority of the state and cumbersome machinery of the courts.[24] Jeffrey J. Crow found the same tension between official and popular justice in North Carolina. Here the vacuum occurred in the summer of 1781, when the government was exhausted by Cornwallis's invasion of the state and suppression of the loyalists fell into the hands of individuals like Andrew Beard, "a person in the Practice of Shooting down peoples whom he is pleased to suppose disaffected to the...Government," in the words of Thomas Cabune, who nearly became one of Beard's victims. General Stephen Drayton saw events of this kind as part of a rough process of "convicting, reclaiming, or punishing of Tories" in which "our own imprudencies & irregular proceedings made more enemies than had ever become so from mere inclination."[25]

Both the Cabune and Drayton documents date from July 1781. Events in North Carolina during that summer provide a model for explaining regular and irregular warfare in the Revolution. Major James Craig occupied Wilmington in January 1781 and in July appointed David Fanning commander of loyalist militia, already operating under Fanning's leadership. Craig and Fanning had finally learned how to fight irregular war in America successfully. Fanning devised a new guerilla strategy based on what John S. Watterson calls "quickness, mobility, deception, and improvision." Fanning's raids concentrated on freeing tory prisoners, capturing the most no-

Part III: Practice

torious persecutors of the loyalists, operating widely in eastern North Carolina under cover of darkness, "plundering and destroying our stock of cattle and robbing our houses of everything they can get." Fanning's men were disciplined and violence was carefully targeted against key officials. Throughout Cumberland, Bladen, Anson, and Duplin counties, pockets of dispirited loyalists felt emboldened by Fanning's exploits. General Nathanael Greene and Governor Thomas Burke sensed almost immediately what was happening. The only safe remedy was to hunker down and wait for events outside North Carolina to shift advantage away from the British irregulars. The use of retaliatory terror against known or suspected loyalists only played into Craig's and Fanning's hands, enabling them to represent themselves as agents of justice for the oppressed and targets of barbarity.[26] The Fanning-Burke duel in North Carolina in the summer of 1781 therefore pitted for the first time in the war adversaries who thoroughly understood military triangularity.

In South Carolina, loyalist reintegration arose not only from patriot victory or from a stabilizing equipoise but from violence itself. The fierce civil war that convulsed South Carolina from late summer 1780 until the spring of 1782 played out memory of a previously learned experience with frontier lawlessness in the mid-1760s and harsh repression later in the decade by the South Carolina Regulators. The savagery employed by both whigs and tories in 1781 and 1782 frightened and shocked South Carolina patriot leaders. General William Moultrie did not exaggerate when he found, in early 1782, a shattered society of brutalized, frightened, impoverished people for whom "a dark melancholy gloom appears everywhere and the morals of the people are almost entirely extirpated." Even moderate, self-critical leaders like Aedanus Burke had felt an almost uncontrollable rage against the British and their loyalist lackeys in South Carolina.[27]

All of these examples of military triangularity involved either geographical conditions hampering the establishment of whig hegemony (as in Eastern Shore Maryland), or geopolitical fields of force giving Britain a competitive edge in dealing with the populace (as in areas adjacent to garrison towns in the middle states), or else the interplay of delicate social tensions making disaffection an understandable choice and reintegration a social and political imperative (as in South Carolina). One major variant remains: the state of Vermont, which lay beyond British or American control during the war and was for both sides an eagerly sought and finally elusive prize. Here military triangularity meant that the segment caught between Britain and America had the muscle to fight back. Within Vermont, patriots, loyalists, and, among both groups, Vermont separatists, were bound together by common ties and interests that would make reintegration of the disaffected a natural consequence of the creation of a state independent of both Congress and Crown.

Reintegration of the Loyalists

Peter S. Onuf places this story in the context of the jurisdictional territorial disputes of the Revolutionary era. Vermonters had to deal fundamentally with a problem that arose elsewhere in America only as an incidental feature of continental politics—the basis of statehood. The very existence of Vermont and the daily conduct of politics hinged on defining statehood in ways that would maintain cohesion within and cause the necessary degree of "havoc" in the affairs of grasping neighboring states. Vermont punished its loyalists, then quickly forgave all but the most egregious of them, nearly negotiated its way back under British protection, and finally won a kind of reintegration into the American nation for loyalists and separatists alike through admission as the fourteenth state.[28]

5. Cosmopolitans and Localists

The severity or lenity of the treatment of the loyalists at the conclusion of the Revolution has, for much of the twentieth century, been a test of the radicalism or moderation of the Revolution. That is not the only approach which can be taken to the postwar reintegration of the loyalists. Paul H. Smith's article on General Guy Carleton as British commander in New York in 1782–83 selects a different perspective. Carleton believed with good reason that even after Yorktown, British possession of the port of New York was an immense asset. He proposed to the ministry that Britain simply refuse to budge unless the Americans agreed to some symbolic acknowledgment of allegiance to the king. The Rockingham ministry rejected Carleton's suggestion, not because the idea was faulty but because the capacity to pursue British interests in North America had been temporarily unhinged by the fall of the North government.[29]

Out of such divergent contingencies as London's unwillingness to let Carleton test the discipline and cohesiveness of the New York state government in 1782–83 and Britain's continued hold on the city during those two years, the loyalists may have found the time and opportunity to make their way into republican society. Drawing on the sociology of conflict resolution, Joseph S. Tiedemann clusters those contingencies under four broad categories: withdrawal, imposition, compromise, and conversion. Using Queens County, New York, supposedly a tory stronghold, as a test case, he estimates that no more than 6 percent of the adult males in the county went into exile and that the imposition of terms on those who remained was a matter of mutual adjustment rather than arbitrary prescription. New York's harsh anti-tory legislation became in practice a kind of "psychic assurance" for the patriots "that their efforts had not been in vain" and haphazard enforcement an inducement to former loyalists to accept the new order.[30]

The legislative search for such solutions, Jackson Turner Main demonstrates in his massive roll call analysis of the Confederation period, brought

Part III: Practice

into the open and solidified two distinct orientations toward politics in the new republic, outlooks Main calls "localist" and "cosmopolitan." On roll call votes dealing with two major loyalist issues, 75 percent of localists favored confiscation against only 33 percent of the cosmopolitans; 61 percent of localists opposed readmission of returning loyalists as against 16 percent of cosmopolitans.[31]

In her dissertation "The Treaty and the Tories: The Ideological Reaction to the Return of the Loyalists, 1783–1787," Roberta Tansman Jacobs generally concurs with Main's profile of the supporters and opponents of loyalist reconciliation, although she suggests a strong surge of anti-loyalist sentiment and legislation in 1783–84, a sharply focused and influential nationalist response in 1784, and a dismantling of barriers to loyalist reintegration in 1785–86.[32]

David E. Maas's exhaustive study of loyalist reintegration in Massachusetts confirms Jacob's finding that localist hostility toward returning and remaining loyalists in 1783 was short-lived.[33] Of 1,423 adult male loyalists in Massachusetts (2 percent of the population), Maas has identified 627 who remained in the state and 233 who returned. Approximately a quarter of physicians, whose occupational skills were in short supply, and Anglican ministers, who went into exile were able to return.[34] As in New York and Philadelphia, merchants possessed abilities needed to reinvigorate the economy, and those with friends among the patriots also found reintegration relatively easy. Maas attributed the tolerance of former loyalists in Massachusetts to what he has called "honest graft"—the systematic plunder of loyalist property by patriot politicians, creditors, and court officials during the War for Independence which substantially depleted the value of the estates returning loyalists might have hoped to reclaim.[35] "Maryland's Samuel Chase . . . was an early advocate of leniency toward Loyalists," Norman K. Risjord notes in a similar instance, "even while he busily bought and sold their property."[36]

The most weighty contingency favoring loyalist reintegration was the belief that strict compliance with Articles IV through VI of the Treaty of Paris was an essential precondition to establishment of a national reputation for justice and civility. The earliest and most complete linkage between the treatment of the loyalists and the formation of a reputable national state appeared in Alexander Hamilton's defense of Joshua Waddington in a trespass action arising from a dispute over the rental of a brewery held by British merchants in New York City during the war. Hamilton's brief to the New York court in 1784 and his *Phocion* letters made justice and moderation toward the loyalists and scrupulous observance of Articles IV to VI a unique opportunity to inculcate the right kind of civic habits. He set forth a theory of federalism that made state law clearly inferior to national law and treaty-making, and he lodged in the judiciary power to set aside state laws that contradicted national law or treaties. Other publicists followed Hamilton's lead. The need to attract capital to restimulate the economy, the useful entrepreneurial skills of many departed loyalist merchants, the danger that persecuted loyalists would provide Britain with a pretext for hostile intervention, and the conviction that a country "formed for commerce" had to open its marketplace to British creditors and loyalist merchants lest "Private Resentment...distract the Tranquility of Government, Trade forsake our Shores, and Contempt and Reproach...of consequence take [its] place" all appeared as themes in a well-orchestrated campaign. If Hamilton was the legal theorist of loyalist reintegration, Benjamin Rush was its social interpreter. The Pennsylvania Test Acts of 1777–1779, Rush declared, were tyrannical measures reflecting the insecurity of the constitutionalist regime because they denied nonjurors the right to grant or withhold assent to taxes imposed on them, offended conscientious pacifism, and damaged the prosperity of the community by excluding productive members of society from full citizenship.[37]

If the political reintegration of the loyalists was a nationalist imperative, reconciliation of loyalists, patriots, and neutralists within American churches was a necessary first step in the adjustment of the churches to a republican polity and culture. Each of the European religious traditions transplanted to the colonies in large or concentrated enough numbers to become a nascent denomination had members on both sides of the Revolutionary struggle—and some outside of it as well. One of the catalysts for the formation of Protestant denominations in the 1780s was the need to heal divisions arising from the Revolution within and between sects and confessional traditions.

No church had such a deep stake in legitimizing its place in American culture following the Revolution as the Anglicans. Anglicans in the South and around Philadelphia who had been predominantly patriots, or like the Rev. William Smith very passive loyalists, were willing to accept lay participation in church governance and forego for the time being strict adherence to episcopal ordination. High Church traditionalists in Connecticut, led by Samuel Seabury, many of them staunch opponents of the Revolution, moved vigorously to secure sanction from the new state government as a necessary prerequisite to consecration in England of a bishop. The Church of England shrank from any such intrusion into American civic life, though Seabury thereupon secured consecration as bishop of Connecticut from the Scottish Episcopal Church in 1783. Over the next six years, the two Anglican factions finally coalesced to form the Protestant Episcopal Church. What is not generally recognized in this familiar story is that Episcopalians, like other Protestant churches, opted for denominational polity as a way of

Part III: Practice

resolving internal ecclesiastical problems and also establishing for themselves a stable position in the culture of the new republic.[38]

Quaker history contains another suggestive case of the origins of denominationalism. Torn like the Anglicans between English-based orthodoxy and acculturation in the new republic, the Revolution forced the Society of Friends to admit that it was not the True Church to which all believers would some day repair but rather a distinct kind of Protestant church. This movement toward a conventional definition of their sect was a positive reflection of American religious pluralism and a negative response to the hostility engendered by Quaker pacifism during the War for Independence. Similarly, the taint of toryism among Methodists arose not only from John Wesley's harsh attacks on the Revolution or because the earliest preachers were apolitical Englishmen but also because Methodists disregarded social norms, shunned politicization, and alienated patriot elites. The potency of that impulse in a democratic society and the suitability of circuit-riding organization in an extensive, rural setting made what had been social liabilities before 1783 into cultural assets in the years which followed. A reputation for political intolerance may well have prompted Presbyterians to present a more moderate and congenial face to their fellow citizens as they sought to heal Old and New Side divisions and to identify national prosperity with the operation of divine providence.[39]

Scholarship on the Revolution has produced a fragmented but richly varied portrayal of loyalist reintegration as a social and political process, but historians have been far less successful in recreating the interior experiences that underlay that process. There are isolated exceptions; of the serious biographies of loyalists,[40] two of the best deal with men successfully integrated into the life of the new republic: Tench Coxe of Pennsylvania and William Samuel Johnson of Connecticut. Coxe sided with the British in 1776 and traded actively in Philadelphia during the British occupation. Johnson operated at the highest levels of the whiggish provincial government in pre-Revolutionary Connecticut but temperamentally could not support independence and was jailed briefly in 1779 when his attempts to mediate between a British raiding force and frightened neighbors in Stratford were deemed "treasonous" by patriot officials. Both men had distinguished post-Revolutionary careers—Coxe as merchant, Treasury official under Hamilton, Jeffersonian publicist and journalist, and far-sighted advocate of industrialization; Johnson as influential delegate to the Constitutional Convention who was instrumental in the Great Compromise of July 1787, United States senator, and president of Columbia College.

Their parallel experiences were illuminating. Both were Anglicans, Johnson actively and Coxe inactively, but neither was doctrinaire in religion. Both secured political rehabilitation in 1779, well ahead of the charged and

Reintegration of the Loyalists

confusing atmosphere of 1783. Both had professional talents that were widely respected and not in overabundant supply in the new nation. Both had powerful friends within Revolutionary society and each handled himself with considerable discipline and sophistication at the crucial moment. "The Propriety, Modest, and Prudence of your Conduct will probably in a little Time wholly remove the Impressions which have been made and fully restore you to your Friends and Country," Joseph Reed wrote to Coxe in early 1779, in a statement alluding to the delicacy of the task of winning forgiveness and understanding from moderate Pennsylvania patriots.[41] When Johnson came before the Connecticut Council of Safety on July 28, 1779, he saw only four familiar faces from his pre-Revolutionary days and nine newcomers to political power with whom he had never dealt. After three years of painful isolation, he took only two weeks to accept the Council's terms that he swear an oath of allegiance.[42] Opportunity, ability, and luck rank high in American success stories.

Conclusion: Causal and Contextual History

A long tradition of loyalist historiography has presented the loyalists as a self-contained category of historical experience: victims of a popular seizure of power, exponents of a coherent philosophy of subordination and obedience, a military force willing to risk life itself in service of the Crown, and exiles who paid in concrete terms part of the human price for success of the Revolution.[43] A study of loyalist reintegration, based on these assumptions, ought to be written. Conceptual insights favoring such an approach can be found in the novels of James Fenimore Cooper, William Gilmore Simms, Harold Frederic, and Kenneth Roberts, through which the loyalists entered the literary consciousness of the United States;[44] in the gilded age historians' appreciation of the loyalists, which Bernard Bailyn has brought to light;[45] and in Canadian nationalism, which has preserved the memory of loyalist political philosophy carried to Nova Scotia and New Brunswick in the 1780s and 1790s.[46]

This chapter, in contrast, regards the loyalists as fragments of historical experience within the larger context of the Revolution. The distinction between loyalism as a subspecialty of scholarship and as a topic inextricably linked to the whole of the Revolution resembles the choice between what Ronald G. Walters calls "causal" and "contextual" history. Causal history identifies the participants in a historical event and studies what they did; contextual history asks what that event and those actions meant to affected individuals and to the people and culture surrounding them. "Contextual history," Walters explains, "is a history of commonality and structure rather than of distinctiveness and movement."[47] The scholarship examined in this

Part III: Practice

chapter illuminates the shared social space inhabited by patriots and loyalists and the common dilemmas they encountered. But neither a causal nor a contextual interpretation of loyalist reintegration can be completely satisfactory, and historians need to devise a way of integrating the two approaches into a single, coherent vision of the subject.

The five interpretive insights employed here as organizing devices indicate both the utility and intrinsic limitation of a contextual treatment of loyalist reintegration. The committee infrastructure in 1774–1775, the work of moral arbiters of republicanism in 1776–1777, the legal and political evolution of volitional allegiance in 1778–1779, the increasing military triangularity of the conflict in 1780–1781, and the cosmopolitan-localist dispute over treatment of the loyalists in 1782–1785 emphasize that the social logic of the Revolution was unplanned and unanticipated and was shaped first by ideas and visions and next by social needs. In that sense, the treatment of the loyalists served to reinforce and protect an initially fragile republican polity constructed from grassroots politics, moralistic revolutionary norms, philosophical and legal dilemmas, violence, and partisanship.

This formulation cannot contain all the complexities and paradoxes of the situation. The best town studies show many local leaders just as anxious as their cosmopolitan counterparts to ease the rehabilitation of the loyalists.[48] Volitional allegiance was so egalitarian and libertarian in its implications that during the early nineteenth century the law of allegiance sharply curtailed free blacks, Indians, and women from the enjoyment of citizenship. Linda K. Kerber has shown that courts in New York and Massachusetts refused to hold wives of male loyalists accountable for their behavior on the ground that republican society had a transcendent interest in upholding the authority of husbands and preserving wives in a state of political innocence and impotence.[49] Runaway slaves and native American supporters of the Crown—and ultimately all blacks and Indians—faced a post-Revolutionary regime that was much more monolithic in its assertions of racial hegemony than pre-Revolutionary British-Americans had thought of being.[50] The unexpected removal of large numbers of British, French, and Spanish operatives from the lower Mississippi Valley and Great Lakes regions during the Napoleonic wars deprived some former loyalists of a potentially historic role in thwarting manifest destiny.[51] Finally, the return of large numbers of the Canadian descendants of loyalist exiles to the United States during the nineteenth century indicates that reintegration was a century-long rather than a decade-long process.

---

1. Merrill Jensen, ed., *American Colonial Documents to 1776* (London, 1955), 815.
2. David Ammerman, *In the Common Cause: American Response to the Coercive Acts of 1774* (Charlottesville, Va., 1974), 109.

3. Peter Shaw, *American Patriots and the Rituals of Revolution* (Cambridge, Mass., 1981, 2.

4. Quoted in Robert M. Calhoon, *The Loyalists in Revolutionary America, 1760–1781* New York, 1973), 304.

5. Ibid., 305. Congress apparently distinguished between committees of inspection created in consequence of the Continental Association and the existing network of committees of correspondence that had existed in New England since early 1773.

6. *Virginia Gazette* (Pinckney), Feb. 9, 1775, in Robert L. Scribner, ed., *Revolutionary Virginia: The Road to Independence*, vol. 2, *The Committees and the Second Convention, 1773–1775: A Documentary Record* (Charlottesville, Va., 1975), 179–80.

7. Rhys Isaac, "Dramatizing the Ideology of Revolution: Popular Mobilization in Virginia, 1774 to 1776," *William and Mary Quarterly*, 3rd ser., 33 (1976), 357–85.

8. Timothy M. Barnes and Robert M. Calhoon, "John Witherspoon and Loyalist Recantation," see above, chapter 10.

9. For a listing of scholarship on the British garrison towns, see Robert M. Calhoon, *Revolutionary America: An Interpretive Overview* (New York, 1976), 158–59; see also Janice Potter and Robert M. Calhoon, "The Character and Coherence of the Loyalist Press," in Bernard Bailyn and John B. Hench, eds., *The Press and the American Revolution* (Worcester, Mass., 1980), 262–72; Robert Ernst, "Andrew Eliot, Forgotten Loyalist," *New York History*, 57 (1976), 284–320; Milton M. Klein. "An Experiment that Failed: General James Robertson and Civil Government in British New York, 1779–1783," *New York History*, 61 (1980), 228–54; Milton M. Klein and Ronald W. Howard, eds., *The Twilight of British Rule in Revolutionary America: The New York Letterbook of General James Robertson, 1780–1783* (Cooperstown, N.Y., 1985); Elaine F. Crane, *A Dependent People: Newport, Rhode Island, in the Revolutionary Era,* (New York, 1985); and Barnes and Calhoon, "John Witherspoon and Loyalist Recantation."

10. James H. Kettner, *The Development of American Citizenship, 1608–1870* (Chapel Hill, N.C., 1978), chap. 7.

11. Ibid., 188–189.

12. Ibid., 195–96. See also G.S. Rowe, *Thomas McKean: The Shaping of an American Republicanism* (Boulder, Colo., 1978), 138–40; Henry J. Young, "Treason and Its Punishment in Revolutionary Pennsylvania," *Pennsylvania Magazine of History and Biography*, 90 (1966), 278.

13. Peter Brock, *Pacifism in the United States from the Colonial Era to the First World War* (Princeton, 1968), chap. 4; Henry J. Young, "The Treatment of the Loyalists in Pennsylvania," (Ph.D. diss., Johns Hopkins University, 1955), 267–71.

14. Eugene R. Fingerhut, *Survivor: Cadwallader Colden II in Revolutionary America* (Port Washington, N.Y., 1983), 58, 84–85. See also my review in *American Historical Review*, 89 (1984), 1388–89. For a similarly complex dilemma of a leading garrison town loyalist leader, see Sheila L. Skemp, "William Franklin's Fight for Equality," paper read at the Southeastern American Society for Eighteenth-Century Studies, Columbia, S.C., February 28, 1985.

15. Joseph S. Tiedemann, "Communities in the Midst of the American Revolution: Queens County, New York," *Journal of Social History*, 18 (1984), 58–87.

16. Jonathan Clark, "The Problem of Allegiance in Revolutionary Poughkeepsie," in David D. Hall, John M. Murrin, and Thad W. Tate, eds., *Saints and Revolutionaries: Essays on Early American History* (New York, 1984), 285–317.

17. Jack P. Greene, Richard L. Bushman, and Michael Kammen, *Society, Freedom, and Conscience*, Richard M. Jellison, ed. (New York, 1976), 135, 139.

18. Gordon S. Wood, *The Creation of the American Republic, 1776–1787* (Chapel Hill, N.C., 1969), 606.

19. John Shy, "The American Revolution: The Military Conflict Considered as a Revolutionary War," in Stephen G. Kurtz and James H. Hutson, eds., *Essays on the American Revolution* (Chapel Hill, N.C., 1973), 126. This essay is conveniently available in John Shy, *A People Numerous and Armed: Reflections on the Military Struggle for American Independence* (New York, 1976), a book that contains several essays amplifying his views on the social configuration of the War for Independence; see chaps. I–II, VI–IX.

20. Samuel McCorkle, "The Curse and Crime of Plundering: A Sermon," McCorkle Papers, Duke University Library. Rob Skorski and Thomas T. Taylor are preparing an edition of McCorkle's Revolutionary War sermons. See in general my review of Jeffrey J. Crow and Larry E. Tise, eds., *The Southern Experience in the American Revolution* and Don Higginbotham, ed., *Reconsiderations of the Revolutionary War: Selected Essays,* in *Journal of Interdisciplinary History,* 10 (1979), 367–70.

21. Ronald Hoffman, *A Spirit of Dissension: Economics, Politics, and the Revolution in Maryland* (Baltimore, 1973), 183–95, 223–41.

22. Harold B. Hancock, *The Loyalists of Revolutionary Delaware* (Newark, De., 1977), 37, 82, 96 and Keith Mason, "Localism, Evangelicalism, and Loyalism: Popular Opposition to Elite Authority on the Eastern Shore of Maryland during the American Revolution," Conference on The Colonial Experience: The Eighteenth-Century Chesapeake, George Peabody Library, Baltimore, Maryland, Sept. 14, 1984.

23. Hoffman, *Spirit of Dissension,* 227–30; Hancock, *Loyalists of Delaware,* 80–86; Mason, "Localism, Evangelicalism, and Loyalism," 20–23, 33–35; see also William Henry Williams, *The Garden of American Methodism: The Delmarva Peninsula, 1769–1820* (Wilmington, Del., 1984).

24. David H. Villers, "King Mob and the Rule of Law: Revolutionary Justice and the Supression of Loyalism in Connecticut, 1774–1783," unpublished paper based on Villers, "Loyalism in Connecticut, 1763–1787," (Ph.D. diss., University of Connecticut, 1976.)

25. Jeffrey J. Crow, "Liberty Men and Loyalists: Disorder and Disaffection in the North Carolina Backcountry," in Ronald Hoffman, Peter J. Albert, and Thad W. Tate, eds., *An Uncivil War: The Southern Backcountry during the American Revolution* (Charlottesville, Va., 1985), 129, 138, 140, 143–48, 161–62, 167–74. See also Paul D. Escott and Jeffrey J. Crow, "The Social Order and Violent Disorder: An analysis of North Carolina in the Revolution and the Civil War," *Journal of Southern History,* 52 (1986), 373–402; Jeffrey J. Crow, "Tory Plots and Anglican Loyalty: The Llewelyn Conspiracy of 1777" and "What Price Loyalism? The Case of John Cruden, Commissioner of Sequestered Estates," *North Carolina Historical Review,* 55 (1978), 1–17 and 58 (1981), 215–33; and Clyde R. Ferguson, "Functions of the Partisan-Militia in the South during the American Revolution: An Interpretation," in W. Robert Higgins, ed., *The Revolutionary War in the South: Power, Conflict, and Leadership* (Durham, N.C., 1979), 239–58.

26. John S. Watterson III, "The Ordeal of Governor Burke," *North Carolina Historical Review,* 48 (1971), 95–102; Lindley S. Butler, ed., *The Narrative of Col. David Fanning* (Charleston, S.C. and Davidson, N.C., 1981), 6–10; Robert M. Calhoon, "Civil, Revolutionary, or Partisan: The Loyalists and the Nature of the War for Independence," *Military History of the American Revolution* (Washington, D.C., 1976), 93–108; Harry Eckstein, "On the Etiology of Internal Wars," *History and Theory,* 4 (1964), 133–163.

Reintegration of the Loyalists

27. Robert M. Weir, " 'The Violent Spirit,' the Reestablishment of Order, and the Continuity of Leadership in Post-Revolutionary South Carolina," in Hoffman et al., eds., *An Uncivil War,* 76, 77, 85. Robert S. Lambert, *The South Carolina Loyalists* (Columbia, S.C., 1987), devotes a detailed chapter to Loyalist rehabilitation. See also the Loyalist recantations in the *Journals of the House of Representatives, 1783–1784,* Theodora J. Thompson and Rosa Lumpkin, eds., (Columbia, S.C., 1977), 39, 46, 127, 178–79; George C. Rogers, "Aedanus Burke, Nathanael Greene, Anthony Wayne and the British Merchants of Charleston," *South Carolina Historical Magazine,* 67 (1966), 76–83; and Jerome J. Nadelhaft, *The Disorders of War: The Revolution in South Carolina* (Orono, Me., 1981), chap. 4. Rebecca K. Starr, in "Loyalism on Daufuskie Island, South Carolina, 1775–1783," unpublished paper, explains the postwar reintegration of loyalists who sought refuge on one of the sea islands as an extension of wartime "cultural memory, investing peace-keeping in authorized groups" among conflicting loyalist and patriot communities in the islands. Cf. article by Joseph S. Tiedemann, note 30 below.

28. Peter J. Onuf, *The Origins of the Federal Republic: Jurisdictional Controversies in the United States, 1775–1787* (Philadelphia, 1983), chap. 6. For a discussion of earlier scholarship on the Vermont Loyalists, see Calhoon, *The Loyalists,* 330–34 and "The Floridas, the Western Frontier, and Vermont: Thoughts on the Hinterland Loyalists," in Samuel Proctor, ed., *Eighteenth-Century Florida: Life on the Frontier* (Gainesville, Fla., 1976), 1–15. A similar set of circumstances in Georgia produced the same narrow line between patriots and loyalists. See Albert H. Tillson, Jr., "The Localist Roots of Upper Valley Loyalism: An Examination of Popular Political Culture," *Journal of Southern History,* forthcoming; George R. Lamplugh, "Up from the Depths: The Career of Thomas Gibbons, 1783–1789," *Atlanta Historical Journal,* 25 (1981), 37–44 and *Politics on the Periphery: Factions and Parties in Georgia, 1776–1806* (Newark, De., 1986); C. Ashley Ellefson, "Loyalists and Patriots in Georgia during the American Revolution," *The Historian,* 24 (1962), 347–56; Robert S. Lambert, "The Confiscation of Loyalist Property in Georgia, 1782–1786," *William and Mary Quarterly,* 20 (1963), 80–94; and James A. Henretta, "Southern Social Structure and the American War for Independence," in *The American Revolution: The Home Front, West Georgia College Studies in the Social Sciences,* 15 (1976), 1–14.

29. Paul H. Smith, "Sir Guy Carleton, Peace Negotiations, and the Evacuation of New York," *Canadian Historical Review,* 50 (1969), 245–64. See also Eldon Jones, "The British Withdrawal from the South, 1781–1785," in Higgins, ed., *Revolutionary War in the South,* 259–85.

30. Joseph S. Tiedemann, "Loyalism, Conflict Resolution, and New York Politics in the Critical Period, 1783–1787," *New York History,* 68 (1987), 27–43. Tiedemann's model applies closely to the dealings between patriot officials and native-born Virginia loyalists studied in Adele Hast, *Loyalism in Revolutionary Virginia: The Norfolk Area and the Eastern Shore* (Ann Arbor, 1979), 140–188.

31. Jackson Turner Main, *Political Parties before the Constitution* (Chapel Hill, N.C., 1973), 32, 44–47, 348–53. Sigmund Diamond, in a prepared comment on a paper by Main read at the Southern Historical Association in Memphis, Nov. 10, 1966, suggested the application of the cosmopolitan-localist concept to Confederation-period partisanship.

32. Roberta Tansman Jacobs, "The Treaty and the Tories: The Ideological Reaction to the Return of the Loyalists, 1783–1787," (Ph.D. diss., Cornell University, 1974), chapters III–VI. See the seminal and quite durable articles by Oscar Zeichner, "The Loyalist Problem in New York after the Revolution," *New York*

Part III: Practice

History, 21 (1940), 284–302 and "The Rehabilitation of the Loyalists in Connecticut," *New England Quarterly,* 11 (1938), 324–29; and a fascinating case study, John M. Sheftall, "The Sheftalls of Savannah: Colonial Leaders and Founding Fathers of Georgia Judiasm," in Samuel Proctor and Louis Schmier, eds., *Jews in the South* (Macon, Ga., 1984), 73–75.

33. David E. Maas, *Divided Hearts: Massachusetts Loyalists, 1765-1790, A Biographical Directory* (Boston, 1980), xvi–xxvi.

34. David E. Maas, "The Massachusetts Loyalists and the Problem of Amnesty, 1775-1790," paper read at the American HIstorical Association, December 1975, Atlanta, tables 1 and 5. Another notorious loyalist physician who secured quick readmission from American officials was Dr. John Pyle of North Carolina. See Carole Watterson Troxler, *The Loyalist Experience in North Carolina* (Raleigh, N.C., 1976), 28–29.

35. David E. Maas, "Honest Graft in Revolutionary Massachusetts," *Boston Bar Journal,* 23 (1979), 7–15.

36. Norman K. Risjord, *Chesapeake Politics, 1781-1800* (New York, 1978), 193, and R. Don Higginbotham, "James Iredell and the Revolutionary Politics of North Carolina," in Higgins, ed., *Revolutionary War in the South,* 79–97.

37. Jacobs, "The Treaty and the Tories," 117–121. See also Robert Michael Dructor, "The New York Commercial Community: the Revolutionary Experience," (Ph.D. diss., University of Pittsburgh, 1975), and Philip Ranlet, *The New York Loyalists,* (Knoxville, Tenn., 1986), and Hendrik Hartog, *Public Property and Private Power: The Corporation of the City of New York in American Law, 1730-1870* (Chapel Hill, N.C., 1983), 82–86, 103–105.

38. Bruce E. Steiner, "New England Anglicanism: A Genteel Faith?" *William and Mary Quarterly,* 27 (1970), 133–35 and *Samuel Seabury, 1729-1796: A Study in the High Church Tradition* (Athens, Ohio, 1971) chap. 6. For an excellent analysis of the subject, and a valuable discussion of scholarship on post-Revolutionary Anglicanism, see David L. Holmes, "The Episcopal Church and the American Revolution," *Historical Magazine of the Protestant Episcopal Church,* 47 (1978), 283–88.

39. Sydney V. James, "The Impact of the American Revolution on Quakers' Ideas about Their Sect," *William and Mary Quarterly,* 19 (1962), 360–82; Donald G. Mathews, *Religion in the Old South* (Chicago, 1977), 29–37; Rhys Isaac, *The Transformation of Virginia, 1740-1790* (Chapel Hill, N.C., 1982), 260–64; Jonathan Powell, "Presbyterian Loyalists: A 'Chain of Interest' in Philadelphia," *Journal of Presbyterian History,* 57 (1979), 135–60; and Young, "Treatment of Loyalists in Pennsylvania," 294–304.

40. Bernard Bailyn, *The Ordeal of Thomas Hutchinson* (Cambridge, Mass., 1974); Carol Berkin, *Jonathan Sewall: Odyssey of an American Loyalist* (New York, 1976); Don R. Byrnes, "The Pre-Revolutionary Career of Provost William Smith, 1751-1778," (Ph.D. diss., Tulane University, 1969); John E. Ferling, *The Loyalist Mind: Joseph Galloway and the American Revolution* (University Park, Pa., 1977); Lawrence Henry Gipson, *American Loyalist: Fared Ingersoll* (New Haven, 1971); Leroy Hewlett, "James Rivington, Loyalist Printer, Publisher, and Bookseller of the American Revolution: A Biographical and Bibliographical Study, 1763-1783," (Ph.D. diss., University of Michigan, 1958); Albert Lawrence Lorenz, *Hugh Gaine: A Colonial Printer-Editor's Odyssey to Loyalism* (Carbondale, Ill., 1972); Alice M. Keys, *Cadwallader Colden* (New York, 1906); Eugene R. Fingerhut, *Survivor: Cadwallader Colden II in Revolutionary America;* Lawrence Shaw Mayo, *John Wentworth* (Cambridge, Mass., 1921); Bruce E. Steiner, *Samuel Seabury;* :L. S. F.

Upton, *The Loyal Whig: William Smith of New York and Auebec* (Toronto, 1969); and Anne Y. Zimmer, *Jonathan Boucher: Loyalist in Exile* (Detroit, 1978). As their titles suggest, not all of these books are biographies in a strict sense of the term, but all employ a biographical framework and define the genre of loyalist biography against which the books by Cooke and McCaughey, below are judged.

41. Jacob E. Cooke, *Tench Coxe and the Early Republic* (Chapel Hill, N.C., 1978), 45.

42. Elizabeth P. McCaughey, *From Loyalist to Founding Father: The Political Odyssey of William Samuel Johnson* (New York, 1980), 189.

43. For a discussion of this tradition, see Robert M. Calhoon, "Loyalist Studies at the Advent of the Loyalist Papers Project," *New England Quarterly,* 46 (1973), 284–85.

44. Donald G. Darnell, " 'Visions of Hereditary Rank': The Loyalist in the Fiction of Hawthorne, Cooper, and Frederic," *South Atlantic Bulletin,* 42 (1977), 45–54; Michael Kammen, *A Season of Youth: The American Revolution and the Historical Imagination* (New York, 1978), 24–26, 52, 154–56.

45. Bailyn, *Ordeal of Thomas Hutchinson,* 394–98.

46. Jane Errington and George Rawlyk, "The Loyalist-Federalist Alliance of Upper Canada," *American Review of Canadian Studies,* 14 (1984), 157–176 and Janice Potter, " 'Is This the Liberty We Seek?': Loyalist Ideology in Colonial New York and Massachusetts," (Ph.D. diss., Queen's University, 1977), 353–96.

47. Ronald G. Walters, *The Anti-Slavery Appeal: American Abolitionism after 1830* (Baltimore, 1976), 147.

48. Clark, "Problem of Allegiance in Poughkeepsie"; Fingerhut, *Survivor,* chap. 9; John J. Waters. *The Otis Family in Provincial and Revolutionary Massachusetts* (Chapel Hill, N.C., 1968), chap. 9; Calhoon, *Loyalists,* 292–94, 340–49; Francis T. Bowles, "The Loyalty of Barnstable in the Revolution," *Publications of the Colonial Society of Massachusetts,* 25 (1922–1924), 265–345; Nathaniel Freeman Papers, 1775–1785, William E. Clements Library, Ann Arbor, Mich.; and Robert J. Wilson, III, *The Benevolent Piety of Ebenezer Gay and the Rise of Rational Religion in New England, 1696–1787* (Philadelphia, 1984), 225–29.

49. Linda K. Kerber, *Women of the Republic: Intellect and Ideology in Revolutionary America* (Chapel Hill, N.C., 1980), 130–36.

50. Peter Marshall, "First Americans and Last Loyalists: An Indian Dilemma in War and Peace," in Esmond Wright, ed., *Red, White, and True Blue: The Loyalists in the Revolution* (New York, 1976), 33–53.

51. J. Leitch Wright, *Anglo-Spanish Rivalry in North America* (Athens, Ga., 1971); *Britain and the American Frontier* (Athens, Ga., 1975); and *William Augustus Bowles: Director General of the Creek Nation* (Athens, Ga., 1967). I am also indebted to Paul Perry, "They Did Not Wish Us Well: European Intrigues in America, 1782–1798," unpublished research paper, University of North Carolina at Greensboro, 1979.

BIBLIOGRAPHICAL ESSAY

The best introduction to the loyalists remains William H. Nelson, *The American Tory* (1961), which anticipated the interest of the next quarter century of scholarship in both pre-Revolutionary motivation and war-time victimization of the loyalists. Also valuable are Claude H. Van Tyne, *The Loyalists in the American Revolution* (1902) and Moses Coit Tyler, *The Literary History of the American Revolution* (1897), chapters 13–17 and 27–29, which respectively charted the legal and intellectual history of the loyalists with a vigor and acuteness that is still instructive. Lorenzo Sabine, *Biographical Sketches of Loyalists of the American Revolution* (1864), considerably expanded and expertly updated by Greg Palmer, *Biographical Sketches of Loyalists of the American Revolution* (1984), provide a vivid picture of the sufferings and experiences of more than twelve thousand individuals. Clifford K. Shipton, *Sibley's Harvard Graduates,* volumes 7 to 17 (1951–1975) presents, through biographical sketches, a portrait of a whole generation of New England leadership. Shipton was sympathetic to the loyalists; they constituted about 15 percent of Harvard graduates alive during the 1770s. See also David E. Maas, *Divided Hearts: Massachusetts Loyalists, 1765–1790, A Biographical Directory* (1980). Wallace Brown, *The Good Americans: The Loyalists in the American Revolution* (1969), is knowledgeable and also sympathetic to its subject; North Callahan, *Royal Raiders* (1963) and *Flight from the Republic* (1967), are fast-paced episodic accounts; Robert M. Calhoon, *The Loyalists in Revolutionary America, 1760–1781* (1973), relates the loyalists to a wide range of interpretive questions about the ideological, social, political, and military nature of the Revolution; Esmond Wright, ed., *A Tug of Loyalties* (1975) and *Red, White,*

216

and True Blue: The Loyalists in the Revolution (1976), are wide-ranging collections of original essays; Mary Beth Norton, *The British-Americans: The Loyalist Exiles in England, 1774–1789* (1972), utilizes the exile experience in England as a perspective from which to reinterpret the entire loyalist experience. Catherine S. Crary, ed., *The Price of Loyalty: Tory Writings from the Revolution* (1973), is an excellent anthology of primary sources.

After these kinds of comprehensive studies, readers should next turn to biographical writings. Edmund S. and Helen M. Morgan, *The Stamp Act Crisis: Prologue to Revolution* (1953), and W. W. Abbott, *The Royal Governors of Georgia, 1754–1775* (1953), contain some of the finest chapters ever written on individual Crown officials and supporters, several of whom were colonists who became loyalists. William A. Benton, *Whig Loyalism: An Aspect of the Political Ideology of the American Revolutionary Era* (1969), describes the experience of nine pre-Revolutionary whigs who became loyalists after 1775 or 1776, unfortunately omitting John Jacob Zubly, the most whiggish and defiantly loyal of all those who supported resistance but opposed independence. In addition to these biographical chapters, a growing body of full-scale biographies includes Bernard Bailyn, *The Ordeal of Thomas Hutchinson* (1974); Carol Berkin, *Jonathan Sewall: Odyssey of an American Loyalist* (1976); Jacob E. Cooke, *Tench Coxe and the Early Republic* (1978); Brian C. Cutherbertson, *Loyalist Governor: Biography of John Wentworth* (1983); John E. Ferling, *The Loyalist Mind: Joseph Galloway and the American Revolution* (1977); Eugene R. Fingerhut, *Survivor: Cadwallader Colden II in Revolutionary America* (1983); James T. Flexner, *States Dyckman: American Loyalist* (1980); Lawrence Henry Gipson, *American Loyalist: Jared Ingersoll* (1971); Albert Lawrence Lorenz, *Hugh Gaine: A Colonial Printer-Editor's Odyssey to Loyalism* (1972); Alice M. Keys, *Cadwallader Colden* (1906); Elizabeth P. McCaughey, *From Loyalist to Founding Father: The Political Odyssey of William Samuel Johnson* (1980); Lawrence Shaw Mayo, *John Wentworth* (1921); Bruce E. Steiner, *Samuel Seabury* (1971); Earle Thomas, *Sir John Johnson: Loyalist Baronet* (1986); L. S. F. Upton, *The Loyal Whig: William Smith of New York and Quebec* (1969); and Anne Y. Zimmer, *Jonathan Boucher: Loyalist in Exile* (1978). In addition Edward J. Cashin's forthcoming biography of Thomas Brown and Shiela Skemp's of William Franklin promise to illuminate a great deal of the now murky history of loyalist support for, and efforts to shape, the British military and political struggle against the rebellious Americans. The latter book will supplant Willard S. Randall, *A Little Revenge: Benjamin Franklin and His Son* (1984), which argues that William was the admirable and inept son of an adept, opportunistic father—a plausible distortion of both men. Francis Kinloch Bull's forthcoming study of William Bull II will likewise be an important addition to loyalist biography.

After general introductory volumes and biographical studies, still curious readers should examine various attempts by historians to distinguish loyalists from patriots along broad lines of ideology, social standing, economic interest, and psychology. Of these the most inventive—in the best sense of that word—is Edwin G. Burrows and Michael Wallace, "The American Revolution: The Ideology and Psychology of National Liberation," *Perspectives in American History* (1972), which argues that "the prospect of living without a system of external supports and control filled... the loyalists... with anxiety" and determined their choice of allegiance. Kenneth S. Lynn, *A Divided People* (1977), makes the same case, stressing that loyalists in his sample had a pattern of unsatisfactory relationships with their fathers while patriots tended to imbibe the more liberating influence of restrained parental authority. N. E. H. Hull, Peter C. Hoffer, and Steven L. Allen find a pattern of traits—need for order, intolerance of dissonance and ambiguity, submissiveness, esteem for the powerful, aggressive hostility toward dissenters, fondness for harmony, peer group acceptance, and stereotypic thinking about outsiders—among New York loyalists in "Choosing Sides: A quantitative study of the Personality Determinants of Loyalist and Revolutionary Political Affiliation in New York," *Journal of American History* (1978).

A different kind of diagnostic study of loyalists as qualitatively different from patriots combines a variety of ideological, social, and cultural considerations. William Pencak, *War, Politics, & Revolution in Provincial Massachusetts* (1981), finds that "loyalists tended to be inductive thinkers, materialists and individualists" while patriots "thought deductively and acted idealistically and communally." Just the opposite pattern appears in Thomas S. Martin, *Minds and Hearts: The American Revolution as a Philosophical Crisis* (1984), which depicts the patriots as "individualistic or self-assertive" and the loyalists as "integrative or corporatist." John A. Schutz, "Those Who Became Tories: Town Loyalty and Revolution in New England," *New England Historical and Genealogical Register* (1975), finds the patriots both self-assertive *and* integrative in the context of most New England towns and loyalists there to have been marginal and random figures.

L. F. S. Upton, "The Dilemma of the Loyalist Pamphleteers," *Studies of Burke and His Time* (1977) and Jeffrey M. Nelson, "Ideology in Search of a Context: Eighteenth Century British Political Thought and the Loyalists of the American Revolution," *Historical Journal* (1977), both connect the loyalists to English conservatism of the late seventeenth century and Augustan political conservatism of the early eighteenth century.

Heading the list of specialized works which attribute loyalism to a coherent conservative English ideology are Janice Potter, *The Liberty We Seek: Loyalist Ideology in Colonial New York and Massachusetts* (1983) and William Pencak, *America's Burke: The Mind of Thomas Hutchinson* (1982), as well as Jonathan M. Atkins, "Novanglus and Massachusettensis: Different Conceptions of a Crisis," *Historical Magazine of Massachusetts* (1985), Robert J. Chaffin, "Whig vs. Tory: The Ideological Response to the Townshend Acts of 1767," *North Dakota Quarterly* (1977), John Ferling, "The American Revolution and American Security: Whig and Loyalist Views," *Historian* (1978), Leopold Launitz-Shurer, "A Loyalist Clergyman's Response to the Imperial Crisis in the American Colonies: A Note on Samuel Seabury's Letters of a Westchester Farmer," *Historical Magazine of the Protestant Episcopal Church* (1975), Thomas S. Martin, "The Long and the Short of It: A Newspaper Exchange on the Massachusetts Charters, 1772," *William and Mary Quarterly* (1986), James E. McGoldrick, "1776: A Christian Loyalist View," *Fides et Historia* (1977), Rodney K. Miller, "The Political Ideology of the Anglican Clergy," *Historical Magazine of the Protestant Episcopal Church* (1976), and James C. Spaudling, "Loyalist as Royalist, Patriot as Puritan: The American Revolution as a Repetition of the English Civil Wars," *Church History* (1976). Among the best published primary sources on loyalist ideology are Douglass Adair and John A. Schutz, eds., *Peter Oliver's Origin and Progress of the American Rebellion: A Tory View* (1961), Jonathan Bouchier, ed., *Reminiscences of an American Loyalist, 1738–1789* (1925) and "Letters of Jonathan Boucher," *Maryland Historical Magazine* (1912–1913), Bernard Bailyn, ed., "A Dialogue between an American and a European Englishman (1768) by Thomas Hutchinson," *Perspective in American History* (1975), Thomas Hutchinson, *History of Massachusetts Bay* (1936), and Catherine B. Mayo, ed., "Additions to Thomas Hutchinson's *History of Massachusetts Bay,*" *Proceedings of the American Antiquarian Society* (1949). Also useful is Wallace Brown, ed., "An Englishman Views the American Revolution: The Letters of Henry Hulton, 1769–1776," *Huntington Library Quarterly* (1972–73).

A somewhat different approach to the cleavages between loyalists and patriots examines fault lines in the social and political structure along which Americans divided during the Revolution. Christopher S. Carson, "The Oliver Family in Peace and War, 1632–1860," *New England Historical and Genealogical Register* (1976) and Peter C. Hoffer and N. E. H. Hull, *Impeachment in America, 1635–1805* (1984), are the best treatments of Peter Oliver and his family and associates who, as a social group, were driven from power in Massachusetts in 1776. John H. Cary, " 'The Juditious are Intirely Neglected': The Fate of a Tory," *New England Historical and Genealogical Register* (1980), Robert C. Coughlin, "Jonathan Ashley: Tory Minister," *Historical Journal of Western Massachusetts* (1979), Eduard M. Mark, "The Reverend Samuel Peters and Patriot Mobs in Connecticut," *Bulletin of the Connecticut Historical Society* (1975), Glen Weaver, "Anglican-Dissenter Tension in Pre-Revolutionary Connecticut," *Historical Magazine of the Protestant Episcopal Church* (1957), and Joel A. Cohen, "Rhode Island Loyalism and the American Revolution," *Rhode Island History* (1958) are other New England studies of loyalist social cleavage. One of the finest primary sources on the actual

Bibliographical Essay

event of community-fracturing along whig-tory lines is Albert Mathews, ed., "Documents Relating to the Last Meetings of the Massachusetts Royal Council, 1774–1776," *Colonial Society of Massachusetts Publications* (1937), which contain vivid eye-witness accounts of patriot demonstrations in front of the homes of Massachusetts Crown sympathizers.

For the same process in the middle colonies, see Carl Becker, "John Jay and Peter Van Schaack," in *Everyman His Own Historian* (1935), Rick J. Ashton, "The Loyalist Congressmen of New York," *New York Historical Society Quarterly* (1976), L. S. Lauritz-Schurer, "The Loyalist Response to the American Revolution: Whig Loyalism in Colonial New York," *Australian National University Historical Journal* (1971), and Dorothy Colburn, "No More Passive Obedience and Non-Resistance," *Historical Magazine of the Protestant Episcopal Church* (1977). Two Maryland studies are Anne Alden Allen, "Patriots and Loyalists: The Choice of Political Allegiances by Members of Maryland's Proprietary Elite," *Journal of Southern History* (1972) and John R. Wennersten, "The Travail of a Tory Parson: Reverend Philip Huges and Maryland Colonial Politics, 1767–1777," *Historical Magazine of the Protestant Episcopal Church* (1975).

For loyalist-patriot division in Virginia, see Patrick Henderson, "Smallpox and Patriotism: The Norfolk Riots, 1768–1769," *Virginia Magazine of History and Biography* (1965), J. H. Soltow, "Scottish Traders in Virginia, 1750–1775," *Economic History Review* (1959), Cortlandt Canby, ed., "Robert Munford's *The Patriots*," *William and Mary Quarterly* (1949), Benjamin Quarles, "Lord Dunmore as Liberator," *William and Mary Quarterly* (1958), George M. Curtis III, "The Goodrich Family and the Revolution in Virginia, 1774–1776," *Virginia Magazine of History and Biography* (1976), and Larry Bowman, "The Virginia County Committees of Safety, 1774–1776," *Virginia Magazine of History and Biography* (1971). For North Carolina, see Charles G. Sellers, "Making a Revolution: The North Carolina Whigs, 1765–1775," in J. C. Sitterson, ed., *Studies in Southern History* (1957) and Laura Page Frech, "The Wilmington Committee of Safety and the Loyalist Rising of February, 1776," *North Carolina Historical Review* (1964). For South Carolina, see David H. Villers, "The Smythe Horse Affair and the Association," *South Carolina Historical Magazine* (1969), B. D. Bargar, ed., "Charleston Loyalism in 1775: The Secret Reports of Alexander Innes," *South Carolina Historical Magazine* (1963), George C. Rogers, "The Conscience of a Huguenot," *Transactions of the Huguenot Society of South Carolina* (1962), Edmund and Dorothy Berkeley, *Dr. Alexander Garden of Charlestown* (1969), Gary D. Olson, "Loyalists and the American Revolution: Thomas Brown and the South Carolina Backcountry, 1775–1776," *South Carolina Historical Magazine* (1967–1968), James H. O'Donnell, ed., "A Loyalist View of the Drayton-Tennent-Hart Mission to the Upcountry," *South Carolina Historical Magazine*

(1966), Marvin L. Cann, "Prelude to War: The First Battle of Ninety Six, November 19–21, 1775," *South Carolina Historical Magazine* (1975), Robert Stansbury Lambert, *The South Carolina Loyalists in the American Revolution* (1987). Finally on Georgia, see Edward J. Cashin, "Sowing the Wind: Governor Wright and the Georgia Backcountry on the Eve of the Revolution," in Harvey H. Jackson and Phinizy Spaulding, eds., *Forty Years of Diversity: Essays on Colonial Georgia* (1984), Kenneth Coleman, *The American Revolution in Georgia, 1763–1789* (1958), Robert G. Mitchell, ed., "Sir James Wright Looks at the American Revolution," *Georgia Historical Quarterly* (1969), and Randall M. Miller, ed., *"A Warm & Zealous Spirit": John J. Zubly and the American Revolution, A Selection of His Writings* (1982). For a loyalist perspective on the Revolution, stressing the extreme localism existing just beneath the surface of American life and jeopardizing the unity of the patriots, see Mary Beth Norton, ed., "John Randolph's 'Plan of Accommodations,' " *William and Mary Quarterly* (1971).

Loyalist activity during the Revolution was, to be sure, not entirely reactive and defensive. Some viable loyalist communities maintained a precarious, if short-lived, existence outside of the reach of rebel administration. Stephen P. McGrath, "Connecticut's Tory Towns: The Loyalty Struggle in Newtown, Redding, and Ridgefield," *Connecticut Historical Society Bulletin* (1979) and Catherine Crary, "Guerilla Activities of James Delancey's Cowboys in Westchester County: Conventional Warfare of Self-Interested Freebooting?" in Robert A. East and Jacob Judd, eds., *The Loyalist Americans: A Focus on Greater New York* (1975) depict such communities in region adjoining New York City. See also Jean F. Hankins, "A Different Kind of Loyalty: The Sandamanians of New England during the Revolutionary War," *New England Quarterly* (1987). A similar situation on the Delmarva Peninsula of southern Delaware and Eastern Shore Maryland and Virginia has attracted several historians: Edward C. Papenfuse, "Economic Analysis and Loyalist Strategy during the American Revolution: Robert Alexander's Remarks on the Economy of the Peninsula or Eastern Shore of Maryland," *Maryland Historical Magazine* (1973), Ronald Hoffman, *A Spirit of Dissension: Economics, Politics, and the Revolution in Maryland* (1973), Harld B. Hancock, *The Loyaliss of Revolutionary Delaware* (1977), Keith Mason, "Localism, Evangelicalism, and Loyalism: Popular Opposition to Elite Authority on the Eastern Shore of Maryland during the American Revolution," *Journal of Southern History* (forthcoming), William Henry Williams, *The Garden of American Methodism: The Delmarva Peninsula, 1769–1820* (1984), and Adele Hast, *Loyalism in Revolutionary Virginia: The Norfolk Areas and the Eastern Shore* (1979). A loyalist populace coalesced early in New Jersey, see Adrian C. Leiby, *The Revolutionary War in the Hackensack Valley: The Jersey Dutch and the Neutral Ground* (1962) and Paul H. Smith, "The New Jersey Loyalists and the British 'Provincial'

Bibliographical Essay

Corps in the War for Independence," *New Jersey History* (1969). Almost evenly split between loyalist and patriot factions, Barnstable, Massachusetts began the War tilting to the British side and later shifted to the rebel cause, see John J. Waters, *The Otis Family in Provincial and Revolutionary Massachusetts* (1968) and Francis T. Bowles, "The Loyalty of Barnstable in the Revolution," *Colonial Society of Massachusetts Publications* (1924). Similar stories are told in John M. Bumstead, "Orthodoxy in Massachusetts: The Ecclesiastical History of Freetown, 1683–1776," *New England Quarterly* (1979), in Bruce C. Merrit, "Loyalism and Social Conflict in Revolutionary Deerfield," *Journal of American History* (1970), and in Jonathan Clark, "The Problem of Allegiance in Revolutionary Poughkeepsie," in David D. Hall, John M. Murrin, and Thad W. Tate, eds., *Saits & Revolutionaries: Essays on Early American History* (1984). A particularly cohesive ethnic loyalist community existed among the Albany, New York Dutch, see Alice P. Kenney, "The Albany Dutch: Loyalists and Patriots," *New York History* (1961). Vermont was a mosaic of loyalist and patriot communities which sometimes struggled for supremacy with each other and more often cooperated in defense of Vermont separatism, a story told in Gwilyn R. Roberts, "An Unknown Vermonter: Sylvanus Ewarts, Governor Chittenden's Tory Brother-in-Law," *Vermont History* (1961), Hamilton V. Bail, "Zadock Wright: That 'Devilish' Tory of Hartland," *Vermont History* (1968), and Sarah V. Kalinoski, "Sequestration, Confiscation, and the 'Tory' in the Vermont Revolution," *Vermont History* (1977).

More often, Revolutionary efforts at community building simply overwhelmed fragments of loyalist communities, but the process was never easy. In New York, Staughton Lynd found sharp class conflict at the core of this struggle in "Who Should Rule at Home? Dutchess County, New York, in the American Revolution" and in "The Tenant rising at Livingston Manor, 1777" in *Class Conflict, Slavery, and the United States Constitution: Ten Essays* (1967); Michael Kammen found an acute moral crisis in "The American Revolution as a *Crise de Conscience:* The Case of New York," in Richard Jellison, ed., *Society, Freedom, and Conscience* (1976), and Philip Ranlet found only weak, episodic loyalist opposition to the Revolution in *The New York Loyalists* (1966), a view supported by Joseph S. Tiedemann, "Communities in the Midst of the American Revolution: Queens County, New York," *Journal of Social History* (1984). For variants on these themes, see William F. Willingham, "The Strange Case of Eleazer Fitch: Connecticut Tory," *Connecticut Historical Society Bulletin* (1975), Richard C. Haskett, "Prosecuting the Revolution," *American Historical Review* (1954), Thomas R. Meehan, "Courts, Cases, and Counselors in Revolutionary and Post-Revolutionary Pennsylvania," *Pennsylvania Magazine of History and Biography* (1967), Henry J. Young, "Treason and Its Punishment in Revolutionary Pennsylvania,"

Bibliographical Essay

Pennsylvania Magazine of History and Biography (1966), Anne M. Ousterhout, *A State Divided: Opposition in Pennsylvania to the American Revolution* (1987), James O. Lehman, "The Mennonites of Maryland during the Revolutionary War," *Mennonite Quarterly Review* (1976), Richard A. Overfield, "A Patriot Dilemma: The Treatment of Passive Loyalists and Neutrals in Revolutionary Maryland," *Maryland Historical Magazine* (1973), Peter G. Yackel, "Criminal Justice and Loyalists in Maryland: Maryland vs. Caspar Frietsche, 1781," *Maryland Historical Magazine* (1978), Emory G. Evans, "Trouble in the Backcountry: Disaffection in Southwest Virginia during the American Revolution," in Ronald Hoffman, Thad W. Tate, and Peter J. Albert, eds., *An Uncivil War: The Southern Backcountry during the American Revolution* (1985), Jeffrey J. Crow, "Liberty Men and Loyalists: Disorder and Disaffection in the North Carolina Backcountry," in Hoffman, Tate, and Albert, eds., *An Uncivil Civil War,* Jeffrey J. Crow, "Tory Plots and Anglican Loyalty: The Llewelyn Conspiracy of 1777," *North Carolina Historical Review* (1978), Robert M. Weir, " 'The Violent Spirit,' the Reestablishment of Order, and the Continuity of Leadership in Post-Revolutionary South Carolina," in Hoffman, Tate, and Albert, eds., *An Uncivil Civil War,* and Edward J. Cashin, " 'But Brothers, It Is Our Land We Are Talking About': Winners and Losers in the Georgia Backcountry," in Hoffman, Tate, and Albert, eds., *An Uncivil Civil War,* and Paul V. Lutz, "The Damnation of the Disaffected," *Manuscripts* (1979) and "The Oath of Absolution," *Manuscripts* (1976). For a study of women which illuminates the entire process of redefining community in Revolutionary America, see Mary Beth Norton, "Eighteenth Century American Women in Peace and War: The case of the Loyalists," *William and Mary Quarterly* (1976), as do individual examples in Wallace Brown, *The King's Friends: The Composition and Motives of the American Loyalist Claimants* (1966).

For the loyalists' treatment by and contribution to American law, see J. Willard Hurst, *The Law of Treason in the United States* (1971), Bradley Chapin, *The American Law of Treason: Revolutionary Origins* (1964), Linda K. Kerber, *Women of the Republic: Intellect and Ideology in Revolutionary America* (1980), and James H. Kettner, *The Development of American Citizenship, 1608–1870* (1978).

Communities of loyalists in British garrison towns—many of them exiles from patriot-held areas—are a fascinating and insufficiently understood feature of the loyalist experience. For the British occupation of Boston from the imposition of the Coercive Acts in July 1774 through British evacuation in March 1776, see John Richard Alden, *General Gage in America* (1948) and Allen French, *The First Year of the American Revolution* (1934). There is no adequate study of the British occupation of Newport, Rhode Island, from 1776 to 1779 but see Elaine F. Crane, *A Dependent People: Newport, Rhode Island in the Revolutionary Era* (1985) and Ralph Adams Brown, "The *Newport Gazette:* A

Tory News Sheet," *Rhode Island History* (1954–1955). For the major British garrison town, New York, held from 1776 until 1783, there is an abundant literature: Oscar T. Barck, *New York City during the War for Independence with Special Reference to the Period of the British Occupation* (1931), Thomas Jefferson Wertenbaker, *Father Knickerbocker Rebels: New York City during the Revolution* (1948), Robert Ernst, "Andrew Eliot, Forgotten Loyalist," *New York History* (1976), Milton M. Klein, "An Experiment that Failed: General James Robertson and Civil Government in British New York, 1779–1783," *New York History* (1980), Milton M. Klein and Ronald W. Howard, eds., *The Twilight of British Rule in Revolutionary America: The New York Letterbook, of General James Robertson, 1780–1783* (1985), William B. Willcox, *Portrait of a General* (1962), William A. Polf, *Garrison Town: The British Occupation of New York City, 1776–1783* (1976), and Robert Ernst, "A Tory-eye View of the Evacuation of New York," *New York History* (1983). For the occupation of Philadelphia in 1777–1778, see John M. Coleman, "Joseph Galloway and the British Occupation of Philadelphia," *Pennsylvania History* (1963), Jacob E. Cooke, "Tench Coxe: Tory Merchant," *Pennsylvania Magazine of History and Biography* (1972), and Ira D. Gruber, *The Howe Brothers and the American Revolution* (1972).

John S. Watterson III, "The Ordeal of Governor Burke," *North Carolina Historical Review* (1971), is useful on the brief British occupation of Wilmington, North Carolina, in 1781. George Smith McGowan, *The British Occupation of Charleston, 1780–1782* (1972) and Patrick J. Furlong, "Civilian-Military Conflict and the Restoration of the Royal Province of Georgia, 1778–1782," *Journal of Southern History* (1972) are respectively the standard works of the British garrison towns in Charleston, South Carolina, and Savannah, Georgia. Otto Lohrenz, "The Discord of Political and Personal Loyalties: The Experiences of the Reverend William Andrews of Revolutionary Virginia," *Southern Studies* (1985), deals with the brief British occupation of Portsmouth, Virginia, in 1781.

Songs and poetry emanating from garrison town presses were important expressions of loyalist anger and allegiance, see Margaret H. Hazen, "Songs of Revolutionary America," *New England Historical and Genealogical Register* (1976), Bruce Granger, "The Hudibrastic Poetry of Jacob Bailey," *Early American Literature* (1982), Thomas B. Vincent, "Keeping the Faith: The Poetic Development of Jacob Bailey, Loyalist," *Early American Literature* (1979), and Cynthia Dubin Edelberg, *Jonathan Odell: Loyalist Poet of the American Revolution* (1987).

The history of the loyalists in the War for Independence rests on the solid foundation laid in Paul H. Smith, *Loyalists and Redcoats: A Study in British Revolutionary Policy* (1964) and in John Shy, "The American Revolution: The Military Conflict Considered as a Revolutionary War," in Stephen G. Kurtz and James H. Hutson, eds., *Essays on the American Revolution* (1973). Shy re-

Bibliographical Essay

printed that essay—which presented the War as a triangular struggle between the patriots, the British and their loyalist allies, and an apolitical mass of the population subject to coercion and cajolery by both sides—in *A People Numerous and Armed: Reflections on the Military Struggle for American Independence* (1976). That volume contained important essays on Thomas Gage, on Charles Lee, and on "Armed Loyalism: The Case of the Lower Hudson Valley" which amplify the triangularity thesis as applied to the loyalists. He developed it further in "British Strategy for Pacifying the Southern Colonies, 1778–1781," in Jeffrey J. Crow and Larry E. Tise, eds., *The Southern Experience in the American Revolution* (1978) and in "American Society and Its War for Independence," in Don Higginbotham, ed., *Reconsiderations on the Revolutionary War: Selected Essays* (1978).

For more accounts and studies of the loyalists and the War for Independence, see John S. Pancake, *1777: The Year of the Hangman* (1977), Paul H. Smith, "The American Loyalists: Notes on their Organization and Numerical Strength," *William and Mary Quarterly* (1968), Philip Katcher, "The Provincial Corps of the British Army, 1775–1783," *Journal of the Society for Army Historical Research* (1976), Rene Chartrand, "Sergeant Vrooman, Butler's Rangers," *Military Collector and History* (1982), David L. Mann, "Bennington: A Clash between Patriot and Loyalist," *Historical New Hampshire* (1977), Wyman W. Parker, "Recruiting the Prince of Wales Loyalist Regiment from Middletown, Connecticut," *Connecticut Historical Society Bulletin* (1982), David H. Villers, "The British Army and the Connecticut Loyalists during the War for Independence, 1775–1783," *Connecticut Historical Society Bulletin* (1978), Barbara Graymont, *The Iroquois in the American Revolution* (1972), Philip Klingle, "Soldiers of Kings," *Journal of Long Island History* (1976), Philip Katcher, "Loyalist Militia in the War for Independence," *Journal of the Society for Army Historical Research* (1976), Carole W. Troxler, *The Loyalist Experience in North Carolina* (1976), Lindley S. Butler, ed., *The Narrative of Col. David Fanning* (1981), Clyde R. Ferguson, "Functions of the Partisan-Militia in the South during the American Revolution: An Interpretation," in W. Robert Higgins, ed., *The Revolutionary War in the South: Power, Conflict, and Leadership* (1979), Robert D. Bass, "The South Carolina Rangers: A Forgotten Loyalist Regiment," *Proceedings of the South Carolina Historical Association* (1977), Randall L. Miller, "A Backcountry Plan to Retake Georgia and the Carolinas, 1778," *South Carolina Historical Magazine* (1974), Louis D. F. Frasche, "Problems of Command: Cornwallis, Partisans, and Militia, 1780," *Military Review* (1977), Martha C. Searcy, *The Georgia-Florida Contest in the American Revolution, 1776–1778* (1985), Gary D. Olson, "Thomas Brown, Loyalist Partisan, and the Revolutionary War in Georgia, 1777–1782," *Georgia Historical Quarterly* (1970), James H. O'Donnell, *Southern Indians in the American Revolution* (1973), and W. Calvin Smith, "Mermaids Riding Alliga-

Bibliographical Essay

tors: Divided Command on the Southern Frontier, 1776–1778," *Florida Historical Quarterly* (1976).

The failure of the British to secure control of any of the thirteen rebelling colonies and reward supporters with security, prosperity, and a bright future contrasts vividly with the North American colonies where that scenario became reality, British East and West Florida. In a forthcoming article in the *Journal of Southern History,* Carole W. Troxler will analyze the kinds of people who migrated from the Carolinas and Georgia to East Florida prior to the Revolution and established a flourishing culture. See also J. Leitch Wright, *Florida in the American Revolution* (1975), J. Barton Starr, *Tories, Dons, & Rebels: The American Revolution in British West Florida* (1976), Robin Fabel, *Bombast and Broadsides: The Lives of George Johnstone* (1987) and *The Economy of British West Florida, 1763–1783* (1988), Robert R. Rae, " 'Graveyard for Britons': West Florida, 1763–1781," *Florida Historical Quarterly* (1969) and his many other articles conveniently listed in Starr, *Tories, Dons, & Rebels, p. 260.*

For additional bibliography on the loyalists and American society, see the notes to chapter 11, above. The loyalists' contribution to the post-Revolutionary peace settlement is described and explained in Mary Beth Norton, *The British-Americans,* Wallace Brown, *The King's Friends,* Richard B. Morris, *The Peacemakers: The Great Powers and American Independence* (1965), and Charles R. Ritcheson, *Aftermath of Revolution: British Policy Toward the United States, 1783–1795* (1969) and "British Policy and the Loyalists," *Journal of Eighteenth Century Studies* (1973).

For loyalists' thrust to the periphery of United States territory during and after the Revolution and their efforts to establish pro-British or pro-Spanish enclaves along the frontier, see J. Leitch Wright, *Britain and the American Frontier* (1975), Madel Jacobs Morgan, "Sarah Truly, A Mississippi Tory," *Journal of Mississippi History* (1975), and Robert W. Sloan, "New Ireland: Men in Pursuit of a Forlorn Hope, 1779–1784," *Maine Historical Society Quarterly* (1979).

Far and away the most important accomplishment of the loyalists was their role in creating new British colonies in the future country of Canada. For this story see David G. Bell, *Early Loyalist St. John: The Origins of New Brunswick Politics, 1783–1786* (1983), Phyllis R. Blakeley, *Eleven Exiles: Accounts of Loyalists in the American Revolution* (1982), Ann Gorman Condon, *The Envy of the American States: The Loyalist Dream for New Brunswick* (1984), E. T. Crowson, "John Saunders: An Exiled Virginia Loyalist and a Founder of New Brunswick," *Virginia Cavalcade* (1977), Jane Errington and George Rawlyk, "The Loyalist-Federalist Alliance of Upper Canada," *American Review of Canadian Studies* (1984), Doris W. Jones-Baker, "The Huguenot Factor in American Loyalism, 1775–1785," *Proceedings of the Huguenot Society of London* (1985), John G. Leefe, " 'And They Shall Devour Israel,' " *Nova Sco-*

Bibliographical Essay

tia Historical Review (1981), Neil MacKinnon, *This Unfriendly Soil: The Loyalist Experience in Nova Scotia, 1783–1791* (1986), W. S. MacNutt, "The Loyalists: A Sympathetic View," *Acadiensis* (1976), Christopher Moore, *The Loyalists: Revolution, Exile, Settlement* (1984), H. V. Nelles, "Loyalism and Local Power: The District of Niagara, 1792–1837," *Ontario History* (1966), Larry Turner, *Voyage of a Different Kind: The Associated Loyalists of Kingston and Adolphustown* (1984), Mason Wade, "Odyssey of a Loyalist Rector," *Vermont History* (1980), and David Mills, *The Idea of Loyalty in Upper Canada, 1784–1850* (1988).

For the black loyalists who sought a new homeland first in Nova Scotia and finally in Sierra Leone, see Mary Beth Norton, "The Fate of Some Black Loyalists of the American Revolution," *Journal of Negro History* (1973), James W. St. G. Walker, *The Black Loyalists: The Search for a Promised Land in Nova Scotia and Sierra Leone, 1783–1870* (1976), and Ellen Gibson Wilson, *The Loyal Blacks* (1976).

The *Oxford English Dictionary* entries for "Whig" and "Tory" respectively trace these terms to "country bumpkin" and "Irish outlaw" in the seventeenth century before they became labels for the opponents and supporters of James, Duke of York, during the Exclusion Controversy in England, 1679–1683. Sidney Forman, letter to the editor, *William and Mary Quarterly* (October 1987) discusses the meanings of the terms "loyalist" and "tory." John Adams allegedly estimated that the American populace consisted of equal thirds of loyalists, patriots, and neutralists; for the controversy over this point, see Robert M. Calhoon, review of Crow and Tise, *The Southern Experience in the American Revolution* and Higginbotham, *Reconsiderations of the Revolutionary War* in the *Journal of Interdisciplinary History* (1979), p. 368, note 4.

For earlier bibliographical essays on the loyalists, see Wallace Brown, "The View at Two Hundred Years: the Loyalists of the American Revolution," *Proceedings of the American Antiquarian Society* (1970), George Athan Billias, "The First Un-Americans: the Loyalists in American Historiography," in G. A. Billias and Alden T. Vaughan, eds., *Perspectives on Early American History: Essays in Honor of Richard B. Morris* (1973), and Bernard Bailyn, "The Losers: Notes on the Historiography of Loyalism," in *The Ordeal of Thomas Hutchinson* (Appendix).

INDEX

Index

Index

Index

Index